Poli
the Sunflower
State

Policing Sex in the Sunflower State

The Story of the Kansas State Industrial Farm for Women

NICOLE PERRY

UNIVERSITY PRESS OF KANSAS

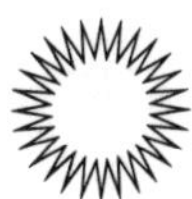

Published by the University Press of Kansas (Lawrence, Kansas 66045), which was organized by the Kansas Board of Regents and is operated and funded by Emporia State University, Fort Hays State University, Kansas State University, Pittsburg State University, the University of Kansas, and Wichita State University.

Library of Congress Cataloging-in-Publication Data
Names: Perry, Nicole, author.
Title: Policing sex in the Sunflower State : the story of the Kansas State Industrial Farm for Women / Nicole Perry.
Description: Lawrence : University Press of Kansas, 2021 | Includes bibliographical references and index.
Identifiers: LCCN 2020040364
ISBN 9780700631872 (cloth)
ISBN 9780700631889 (paperback)
ISBN 9780700631896 (epub)
Subjects: LCSH: Kansas State Industrial Farm for Women. | Reformatories for women—Kansas—History—20th century. | Women prisoners—Kansas—History—20th century. | Sexually transmitted diseases—Government policy—Kansas—History—20th century. | Women—Sexual behavior—Kansas—History—20th century. | Sex discrimination against women—Kansas—History—20th century. | Sex—Kansas—History—20th century.
Classification: LCC HV9306.L362 K3674 2021 | DDC 365/.978138–dc23
LC record available at https://lccn.loc.gov/2020040364.

British Library Cataloguing-in-Publication Data is available.

Printed in the United States of America

10 9 8 7 6 5 4 3 2 1

The paper used in this publication is acid free and meets the minimum requirements of the American National Standard for Permanence of Paper for Printed Library Materials Z39.48-1992.

This book is dedicated to the women imprisoned
under Chapter 205 in Kansas.
May we hear your stories now, and do better.

CONTENTS

PREFACE

As I work on the final edits of this book in the spring of 2020, the world has been gripped by the COVID-19 pandemic. The death toll ticks higher as government leaders struggle to stem the spread of this highly contagious virus. Countries across the world are in lockdown, millions are unable to work, and entire industries face economic collapse.

Perennial questions in public health about the balance between the public good and individual freedoms have been put to the test on an unprecedented scale as states across the country have closed schools and businesses and issued stay-at-home orders. While the majority of Americans support these measures, these restrictions have also met with resistance. Protestors are lobbying state governments to open back up, while public health experts warn of potential resurgences of the virus without adequate testing and a targeted approach to reopening.

Resistance to public health measures aimed at reducing the spread of disease are not new. During the 1918 flu epidemic, which some have argued should have been called the "Kansas Flu" due to its possible origin in the state, some people were impatient to emerge from isolation orders and resistant to wearing masks in public. Eager to celebrate the end of World War I, Americans ignored mass-gathering restrictions. Resurgences of the flu took off across the country, leading to a death toll of some 675,000 Americans by the end of the pandemic. Public health measures to prevent the spread of disease need the voluntary compliance of a critical mass of the population, requiring public health officials to understand not just the science behind diseases' spread but also the whims of human behavior.[1]

The COVID-19 pandemic is amplifying and exacerbating stereotypes, inequalities, and social divisions in the United States. The blame for disease outbreaks has a long history of coming down on stigmatized groups, including associations between African Americans and cholera, the gay community and HIV/AIDS, and immigrants and the poor in the case of syphilis and gonorrhea in the 1910s and 1920s. Asian Americans are reporting increased incidents of racial harassment as a result of the COVID-19 outbreak, which originated in China. As people search for a scapegoat, deep-seated stereotypes rear their ugly heads. The virus is also exposing gaps in health-care infrastructure, the social safety net, and existing health disparities, leaving behind higher mortality rates for racial minority groups. Kansas, the place central to this book, has one of the highest rates of racial disparities in infection and death rates from COVID-19, with Black Kansans amounting to nearly a third of the state's deaths from the virus, yet accounting for only 5.6 percent of the state's population. Prisons, which were used in the time of this book as a place to contain the spread of syphilis and gonorrhea, are emerging as epicenters of coronavirus outbreaks. This pandemic, like many throughout history, has exposed and amplified the fault lines in society for all to see.[2]

Kansas has not been immune from the effects of COVID-19. While confirmed infections are currently lower here than they are in many other parts of the country, the death toll, social consequences, and economic impact have been devastating, especially for those who are most vulnerable. The idea of quarantine, something that has seemed like an abstract idea to me as I have worked on this research over the past several years, is now a part of the daily reality for many Kansans, as it is for people across the globe. In Kansas the set of laws that provide the legal basis for public health restrictions have their roots in the events detailed in this book. A little-known statute called Chapter 205, first passed in 1917 and used to detain women who had syphilis and gonorrhea in the interwar period, is still on the books today in amended form, giving state authorities broad powers to address the coronavirus outbreak. The Kansas legislature passed further guidelines for quarantine and county-level health officers in 2005, adding more clarity to the procedures to be followed and providing recourse for individuals to challenge quarantine orders in court. Legal challenges to forced quarantine orders are few and far between, given how rarely states have ordered them on a wide scale. However, among those legal precedents that support the state's power to quarantine its citizens in Kansas are cases dating back to the 1920s and 1930s, when men and women filed suit to challenge their confinement under Chapter 205 for venereal diseases.[3]

The impact and historical legacy of the COVID-19 pandemic remain to be written. As you read this book to hear the story of another time, another cast of characters, another public health crisis, and, unfortunately, a very similar set of social inequities, my hope is that we can use the lessons learned from Chapter 205 to navigate and move forward from our current situation. The social systems in which the story of Chapter 205 played out—the prison system and the health-care system—are structuring the evolution of the COVID-19 outbreak as I write, and they will be at a crossroads as we look to define what postpandemic life looks like in the United States. While pandemics expose our social fractures, they also provide an opening to confront them and reenvision how our society is structured and whom it serves.

ACKNOWLEDGMENTS

I would like to thank the many people who helped shape this book and supported me personally while I worked on it. First, this project would not have been possible without the continued guidance and support from Brian Donovan, who saw some glimmer of hope in those first awful papers I turned in during graduate school and has read countless iterations of the chapters contained in this book. Everyone should be so lucky to have such an outstanding mentor and friend. I would also like to thank Bill Staples and Katie Batza, whose feedback and advice through the initial stages of this research and the publishing process have been critical to keeping the project on track. The outstanding staff and editors with the University Press of Kansas, including Kim Hogeland and David Congdon, as well as the reviewers for this manuscript, provided excellent feedback that improved this book tremendously. Early versions of this research also benefited from the insights of Aislinn Addington, Christy Craig, Jane Webb, and Gabriella Smith. I would like to thank the many archivists and librarians who assisted with this project, including the staff at the Kansas State Historical Society and the Spencer Research Library at the University of Kansas. The Midwest Sociological Society and several offices at the University of Kansas, including the Department of Sociology, the Hall Center for the Humanities, and the Office of Graduate Studies, provided critical financial support to early stages of this research. I am grateful for the opportunity that these grants afforded me to move forward with this research.

I could not have completed this work without the support of my friends and family. To Holly: thank you for serving as my unofficial medical consultant on this project and being genuinely excited when I asked about advanced-stage syphilis. To all the other people in my life who have supported me, offered encouraging words, and just generally helped life be enjoyable: know that you are appreciated, even if I cannot name you all individually. A special thanks goes to my parents: your belief in me as I have tackled this project (as well as many other things in life) has helped me have faith in myself. To Max and Oliver: thank you for providing the comic relief and sense of perspective needed in life. And, finally, for Zack: you have supported me through this whole process with a sense of humor, a supportive attitude, and a willingness to make sacrifices even when you did not have much left to give. Thank you—this book would not have been possible without you.

ABBREVIATIONS

ASHA	American Social Hygiene Association
CTCA	Commission on Training Camp Activities
KGFWC	Kansas chapter of the General Federation of Women's Clubs
KSHS	Kansas State Historical Society
KSIFW	Kansas State Industrial Farm for Women
KWCTU	Kansas Woman's Christian Temperance Union
PIRA	Prison Industries Reorganization Administration
TCF	Topeka Correctional Facility
WCTU	Woman's Christian Temperance Union
YMCA	Young Men's Christian Association

Policing Sex in the Sunflower State

INTRODUCTION

In August 1925 eighteen-year-old Hattie Campbell was admitted as inmate number 2568 at the Kansas State Industrial Farm for Women (KSIFW) in Lansing, Kansas. She was a waitress at the Sunflower Lunch Café in Arkansas City, Kansas, earning four dollars per week. Hattie had no close family relations; her father had died the previous year, and she described a distant relationship with her mother, saying, "Have not felt right toward my mother, she never took the right interest in me." The prison documents for Hattie do not list any offenses that we typically think of as a crime. Instead, they simply state "Violation Chapter 205" next to a spot on the form that reads "Physician's Report: Gonorrhea." Hattie was sentenced to the Farm under Chapter 205, a Kansas state law that allowed for the quarantine of those diagnosed with a venereal disease. Since it was a quarantine measure and not a criminal charge, Hattie received no trial before being sent to the Farm for an indefinite sentence. At the time she was incarcerated, Hattie was four and a half months pregnant. Though she stated that she did "not know who father of child" was, Hattie planned to keep her baby. Hattie was just one of the 5,331 women that the state of Kansas detained at the KSIFW under Chapter 205 between the years of 1918 and 1942. The law was part of a wave of legislation passed during the Progressive Era that expanded the role of government in defining proper sexual behavior. However, this government intrusion into the sex lives of everyday Americans was not indiscriminate. The father of Hattie's baby was not likely to receive the same fate. With a handful of exceptions, Chapter 205 was only applied against women.[1]

The KSIFW was founded as a regular women's reformatory in 1917, yet it was quickly inundated with women arrested under the state quarantine law as part of the nationwide response to the problem of venereal

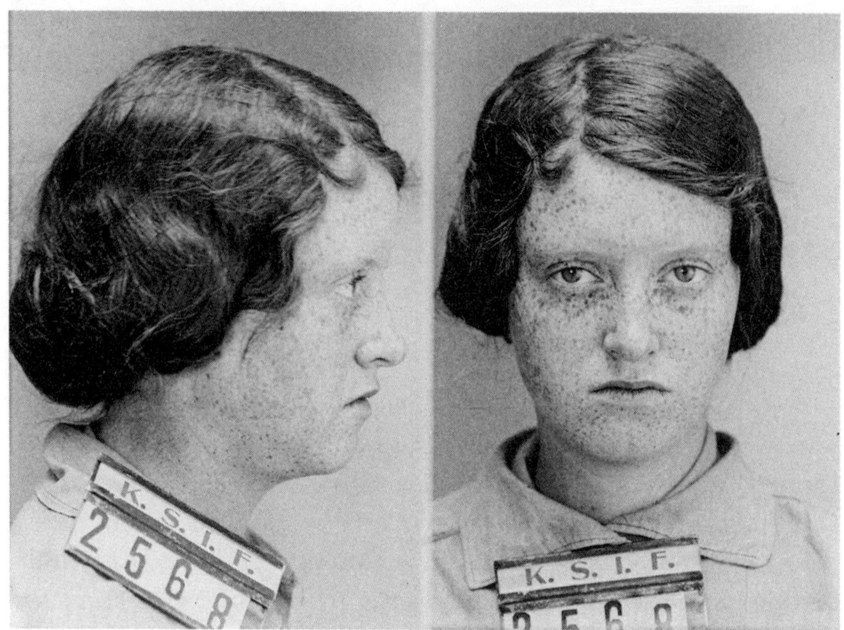

Mugshot of Hattie Campbell when she arrived at the KSIFW in 1925. Photo has been cropped. KSHS, "Prisoners 2568 and 2578, Kansas State Industrial Farm," https://www.kansasmemory.org/item/444284.

disease in the armed forces during World War I. Military officials considered several options to control syphilis and gonorrhea in the population of soldiers, including maintaining a regulated system of prostitution and providing condoms to soldiers, yet they settled on a two-part plan: provide moral training for the soldiers and imprison women suspected of spreading venereal disease. Nationally, more than eighteen thousand women were quarantined for venereal diseases in federally funded facilities during the war.[2] The Kansas legislature passed Chapter 205 in 1917 in response to these national developments, receiving federal political and financial backing.[3] Though Chapter 205 was officially gender-neutral, it was primarily enforced against women. By March 1919 the state had detained 410 women at the KSIFW under Chapter 205, but only forty-four men at the state penitentiary.[4] This gendered enforcement became even more dramatic as Chapter 205 transitioned from a wartime emergency measure to a peacetime public health strategy. Women were quarantined alongside regular female prisoners at the KSIFW throughout the 1920s and 1930s. Women detained under Chapter 205 constituted 71 percent of the total inmate population between 1918 and 1942.[5] Their confinement at the KSIFW was indefinite, with doctors and superintendents deciding when they were physically and morally cured enough to reenter society; in practice, women detained under Chapter 205 spent an average of four months at the Farm. While at the KSIFW, inmates received treatment for their diseases and were subjected to a plan of moral reform focusing on the value of hard work and the inculcation of middle-class norms for proper feminine behavior. Though the number of women imprisoned under Chapter 205 declined in the 1940s, women were quarantined under the law as late as 1955.[6]

Despite the number of women detained, the story of the gendered enforcement of Chapter 205 in Kansas is largely untold. Chapter 205 is mentioned in a few sources, yet the number of women detained, the fact that the practice of detaining women extended far past the end of World War I, and the different groups of people who were involved with enforcing the policy have yet to be fully explored. Some sources accept the premise of official state documents from the time that the women at the Farm were mostly prostitutes.[7] However, as this book will show, the story of the women imprisoned at the KSIFW was much more complicated, and far-reaching, than simply a government-led effort to crack down on prostitution. While some of the inmates were prostitutes, many others came to have a disease through other means.[8] There were wives who contracted a disease from unfaithful husbands. There were teenagers exploring the new youth culture of the Roaring Twenties and getting caught up in the unfortunate intersection of looser sexual morals and lackluster sexual education. There were victims of rape or sexual abuse, forced to go to a prison to get treatment while their attackers often went free. Regardless of their background or how they contracted a disease, these women entered the KSIFW as inmates.

Kansas was not alone in detaining women such as Hattie Campbell during this period in history. States across the country sought ways to regulate and define proper sexual behavior, especially among young women. With the growth of large urban centers, the emergence of youth popular culture, and the fervor of the Progressive movement, the first few decades of the twentieth century witnessed dramatic changes in sexual behaviors among youth and a growing government presence in regulating these behaviors. Though historical accounts of policies like Chapter 205 often stop with the end of World War I, quarantine laws stayed on the books across the country. and many state officials continued to enforce them during the interwar years. These quarantine laws came to be known as the American Plan, a term first used in a 1919 American Social Hygiene Association (ASHA) publication to differentiate this approach from European plans to control the spread of disease through such actions as inspecting prostitutes.[9] While quarantine laws were often the legal mechanism to detain young women suspected of promiscuous sexual behavior, states also used such loosely defined charges as "vagrancy" or "lascivious conduct" to detain women in new reformatories that were popping up across the country. Much of the research on sexuality during this period focuses on large cities on the East or West Coast, yet what happened to Hattie Campbell in Kansas was not all that different from what happened to her peers in other states.[10]

These efforts to control women's sexuality came not only from male government officials but also from other women. In Kansas women from higher social positions had a vested interest in what was happening at the Farm. Seeking to build on women's newfound political power after winning state suffrage in 1912, a group of activist-oriented women orchestrated a campaign to establish the Kansas State Industrial Farm for Women in 1917. These white, well-connected women used their social prestige to advocate for a humane women's prison in the state, finding a social cause that fit with perceptions of proper femininity in the process. Another group of women benefited from the opportunity that the KSIFW afforded: the professional staff that were employed at the Farm. Building on the momentum of the emerging field of social work, the women who ran the KSIFW found steady employment and positions of authority as they sought to morally reform the women imprisoned under Chapter 205. The series of events and decisions that led to the incarceration of more than five thousand women for nothing else than having a disease were thus made not just by men in power but also by women in different social positions. As it turns out, women were complicit in the enforcement of Chapter 205 as well.

Chapter 205 is a clear example of institutionalized gender discrimination and state enforcement of the sexual double standard. However, it did not affect all women equally. Just as social privileges positioned activist and professional women to benefit from their involvement with the Farm, social hierarchies of race and class positioned some women to be more at risk of being seen as a public health menace and subject to quarantine.

This is a story not just of gender discrimination in a particular moment of Kansas history but also of the relationship between our larger social systems, social hierarchies of race, class, and gender, and the individual actors who make up these structural and cultural forces.

Boundary Work and Respectability in Kansas

The incarceration of women under Chapter 205 unfolded at the intersection of the health-care and penal systems. The social problem of venereal disease could have been treated as a matter of public health, yet it came to be understood as a criminal issue in Kansas, with young women as the chief perpetrators. Scholars have pointed to parallel examples of social issues at the intersection of health and deviance that have ultimately fallen under the ever-expanding scope of the penal system in the twentieth century. The deinstitutionalization of mental hospitals and shifting of resources from the health-care to the penal system were part of a larger reconceptualization of the social issue of mental illness.[11] Similarly, drug addiction is a social issue that could be understood as either a public health or a criminal problem, yet people with addiction, particularly those who are Black, have found themselves behind bars.[12] The expansive growth of the penal system in the United States in the second half of the twentieth century has meant that an ever-increasing number of social problems have come to fall under the umbrella of the prison system, leading many scholars to refer to the system of government in the United States as a "carceral state," or one in which incarceration is a central facet of governing.[13] The social problem of venereal disease in Kansas coming under the jurisdiction of the prison system was a precursor of things to come.[14]

Much of the research on our modern era of mass incarceration focuses on the prison system itself, or its relationship to other structural forces like the economy or the health-care system. However, one key to understanding how social problems come to be defined as being under the jurisdiction of the penal system, both in our current moment and in the time of Hattie Campbell, is to take a close look at the larger cultural stereotypes that are created through discussions of the groups most commonly imprisoned. Social control involves a continuum of actors, from prison guards to bystanders who call the police to the regulations we impose on ourselves.[15] These actors construct narratives about the justice of imprisonment that create and reinforce conceptions of the "other" and justify inequities. Rather than patterns of imprisonment simply reflecting larger social inequalities, the uneven enforcement of laws along lines of social division creates and reinforces wider cultural stereotypes about certain groups.[16] Today, the hyperpolicing of Black communities generates stereotypes of "Black thugs." In the era of the KSIFW, the state of Kansas imprisoning young women for venereal disease drove stereotypes of working-class culture as being sexually out of control, and "loose women" as being at fault for the moral failures of the country.

This book draws on academic research about social boundaries to further explicate this connection between incarceration and the stereotypes that are created and reinforced as a result of imprisonment. This research asks the question: how do ideas about certain groups of people get created and reinforced in the first place? The literature on boundaries takes as its premise that social identities—such as those centered around social class, race, gender, or sexuality—are relational, meaning that a large part of how we identify who "we" are is by defining ourselves against "them." Boundaries provide solidarity within a group and justify treating those outside a group in certain ways. Boundary work consists of the actions that people take in order to distinguish themselves from others; it is the process by which social actors determine who is part of their group and who is not. Michèle Lamont and Virág Molnar identify two types of boundaries: (1) symbolic boundaries, "the conceptual distinctions made by social actors to categorize objects, people, practices, and even time and space," and (2) social boundaries, the "objectified forms of social differences manifested in unequal access to and unequal distribution of resources (material and nonmaterial) and social opportunities."[17] In the case of Chapter 205, state authorities created symbolic boundaries when they portrayed poor women as being sexually immoral; they created social boundaries when they used those symbolic distinctions to detain women based on their actual or perceived sexual history. The study of boundaries thus brings together cultural and structural approaches to studying inequality.[18]

The primary way that activist and professional women associated with the KSIFW drew symbolic and social boundaries was through discussions of respectability—both their own respectability and that of the women detained under Chapter 205. In everyday use, respectability is a term that can mean different things in different situations, though ideas of proper sexual behavior are often an important component of the definition.[19]

Respectability is a versatile tool in drawing moral distinctions between groups precisely because it is so vague. Someone can reference a person's class status, racial identity, and gender performance all in one simple reference to the person's respectability. Though flexible, respectability has particular meanings for people at different social intersections. Having sex outside of marriage has different implications for a poor woman's respectability than it does for a wealthy woman's, just as it has different implications for men versus women. The flexibility of the concept of respectability makes it well suited to intersectional studies that do not simply seek to "add in" other social hierarchies to the analysis but instead wish to consider the complex ways that different social hierarchies interact with each other and the conditions under which certain facets of identity become more salient than others.[20] While respectability often entails issues of class, gender, sexuality, and race, the conditions under which each of these elements becomes more important than others will vary. The concept of respectability also gives scholars a simple term that references multiple social hierarchies at once.[21] The term "respectability" can become a shorthand for multiple social hierarchies, enabling scholars to move forward in the work of unpacking how these different hierarchies function together rather than getting bogged down in linguistically awkward descriptions. Studying the conditions under which different facets of identity become salient to the perception of respectability has the potential to develop intersectional theory and the literature on boundary work in productive ways.[22]

Respectability thus indexes multiple facets of identity while serving as an anchor around which symbolic and social boundaries can be formed. Though people in different social positions may seek to be seen as "respectable," their ability to achieve respectability varies.[23] The connection between respectability and social boundaries is fundamentally about power—who has the ability to define what "respectable" means, who has the cultural and financial resources to achieve that ideal, and who is in a position to translate symbolic distinctions around respectability into concrete social boundaries. Individuals can use symbolic and social boundaries that pivot on respectability in several ways. Respectability can be used to reinforce existing social boundaries, such as when female-dominated professions are paid less than more "respectable" male-dominated occupations.[24] Respectability can also be used to contest existing social boundaries, such as when Black Americans or South Africans make claims to respectability in a culture that regularly denies them that status.[25] Thus, the notion of respectability has the potential to reinforce or challenge social hierarchies, depending on how it is employed by social actors.

The connection between respectability and boundary work helps us understand the motivations and consequences of different groups of women's involvement with Chapter 205. What boundaries were created or reinforced when an activist woman lobbied for a women's prison, or when the superintendent of the Farm lamented inmates' lack of feminine manners? Looking at the KSIFW through this lens, one can see that the boundary work that went into constructing the inmates as sexually out of control accomplished much more than merely justifying a narrowly defined public health policy. Discussions of women like Hattie Campbell reinforced the importance of sexual chastity for women's role in society, bolstered stereotypes that associated the poor with immorality and the middle class with self-control, and cemented associations between whiteness and moral authority. In Kansas these perceptions of respectability moved beyond individual thoughts and cultural discourses and became embedded in institutional practices.[26] From the initial assessment by health officers of whether a woman could be trusted to get treatment to prison officials' judgment about when she was morally "cured" enough to reenter society, guidelines about enforcing Chapter 205 incorporated perceptions of respectability into official state policy. This institutionalization of respectability was key to the durability of Chapter 205 in Kansas: once notions about respectability and stereotypes about working-class women became embedded in state policies and practices, the discriminatory enforcement of Chapter 205 gained the inertia needed to carry on imprisoning thousands of innocent young women and girls for over two decades. The three groups of women central to this book—the women who fought to create the Farm, the women who ran it, and the women imprisoned there—navigated and shaped this institutional context as they tried to stake a claim to respectability. Though each group's position differed, they all found that their respectability was in question.

The white female activists involved with creating the KSIFW came from a reform tradition that involved both elite clubwomen and middle-class reformers. They argued that society could benefit from the maternal instincts of women. Though they were meddling in the public affairs of men, their focus on domestic and moral issues lent them authority based on their status as morally superior "ladies."[27] However, moral influence did not necessarily equate to social power: female reformers often ran into roadblocks in implementing their reforms. Clubwomen and female reformers gained some public recognition and authority from the late 1800s through the Progressive Era, but by the 1920s many of these women were regarded as meddling and sentimental old women from a bygone era. Much of these women's initial activism surrounding issues of sexuality was rooted in a critique of the sexual double standard. Yet criticisms of unrestrained male sexuality faded as professional social workers, medical doctors, and government bureaucrats took over activist women's causes in the 1910s and 1920s, leaving a system of regulation for women's sexuality and little serious challenge to male sexual privilege. Thus, female activists faced a crisis in respectability: their charitable work was no longer recognized as being socially valuable, the version of benevolent femininity from which they drew their public authority was dated, and their causes had been co-opted by authorities that did not share their moral vision for society.[28]

The professionally trained social workers who took over many of these charities from female reformers also faced a crisis in respectability. Female social workers like those running the KSIFW were often critical of the sentimental benevolence of the older reformers and sought to gain legitimacy by projecting a rational, professional identity for the emerging field of social work. However, as continues to be the case today, feminized professions such as social work received lower pay and less esteem than male-dominated professions.[29] Additionally, women who worked outside the home faced scrutiny in a time when femininity was so closely associated with domesticity, particularly as the Great Depression set in and government policies and public sentiment criticized working women for taking jobs away from men. While some social workers conceptualized their work as maternal in order to claim this feminine identity, this conflicted with the desire to portray social work as a respected profession. These professional women faced conflicts as they attempted to both establish a respectable professional identity and fulfill the expectations of femininity.[30]

Working-class women also entered into these public negotiations over sexuality and gender with their respectability at stake. The state's intervention into their sex lives made these women's struggles for respectability the most public and the most consequential for their everyday lives. As the power of the state to regulate sexuality grew with the interventions justified by the prevalence of venereal disease during World War I, young working-class women's behavior in public came under heightened scrutiny. New laws broadened the definitions of public disorder and led to many women being arrested for merely the suspicion of illicit sexual activity. Throughout the Progressive Era, the state began to take on a more active role in regulating the nation's sexual life, and working-class women faced the brunt of this intervention. As their lives became wrapped up in the criminal justice system, their own and their families' reputations came under attack.[31]

While the inmates' respectability was most publicly and consequentially challenged, all three groups of women were attempting to claim a respectable status in the midst of cultural currents that questioned the role of women in public. The relationship between each group of women and social norms of respectability offers a rich site for investigating how symbolic and social boundaries are formed and institutionalized. Understood in this way, the story of Chapter 205 becomes not just an isolated case of injustice but also a window into how social inequities inform public policy and shape cultural ideas about groups of people.

About This Book

Chapter 1 provides an overview of the major trends and events important for understanding the development of the KSIFW and Chapter 205 leading up to and during World War I. Several social patterns informed the creation of Chapter 205 in Kansas: broad changes in sexual culture, the development of the social hygiene movement, and the venereal disease crisis made apparent as the United States entered World War I. Widespread concern about sexual morals combined with more openness to government intervention into sexuality to make Chapter 205 seem like a feasible solution to address the problem of soldiers contracting venereal disease in Kansas.

The transition of Chapter 205 from a wartime emergency measure to a peacetime public health policy is detailed in chapter 2. Operating primarily under the Kansas State Board of Administration that governed penal institutions, but also loosely connected with the Kansas State Board of Health, the KSIFW straddled the line between a penal institution and a medical facility. However, guidelines for enforcing the law made clear that the women detained were viewed as in need of moral reform: they were prisoners first, patients second. Withstanding legal challenges and treatment options that offered, at best, mediocre results, Chapter 205 continued to be enforced in Kansas during the 1920s and 1930s. A look at the demographic information of the inmates gives a glimpse of the women who were overrepresented among this population: the young, the poor, and Black women. Chapter 205 was informed by cultural ideas of race, class, and gender, from its initial conception to how it was implemented. Together, these details provide the context needed to delve into the rest of the book.

The activist women who lobbied to create the KSIFW in the 1910s are the focus of chapter 3. The campaign to create the women's prison came at a key political juncture. After a hard-fought campaign, Kansas women earned the right to vote in 1912. Under an umbrella organization called the Kansas Council of Women, activist women set creating a separate women's prison as one of the first legislative priorities to test women's newfound voting powers in the state. This begs the question: why did these women choose to focus on women's prison reform at such a key political moment? How did their involvement with the KSIFW reflect and reinforce their positions along hierarchies of gender, race, and class? To answer these questions, chapter 3 explores the issue of the KSIFW in the larger context of women's activism in Kansas and these women's social positions. Through the fight for women's suffrage, the campaign to establish the KSIFW, and efforts to promote social hygiene work in the state, Kansas activist women utilized their political experience and social capital to try to make changes in the state. While activist women's involvement with the KSIFW was brief (they were not intimately involved with the Farm after the original push for the creation of the institution), lobbying for this issue was in line with their overall legislative efforts and social position as elite white women. Women's activism surrounding suffrage, the KSIFW, and social hygiene had some common threads that coalesced around issues of citizenship, eugenics, and respectability. The women who lobbied to create the KSIFW benefited from their involvement with this issue; they were able to carve out a respectable place for white women's public activism while simultaneously positioning themselves as the models of white femininity and modern civilization.

Chapter 4 gives an account of the professional women who ran the KSIFW and describes daily life at the Farm. Similar to the activist women who lobbied to create the Farm, the professional women who worked there were able to use their association with the institution to bolster their own respectability and their contested roles as female professionals. The KSIFW embodied the ideals of the women's reformatory movement during this period, with a physical layout and philosophy geared toward reforming wayward young girls. Chapter 4 explores the competing demands that were put on the KSIFW, its limited funding, and the lack of respect given to female professionals. Indeed, women such as Julia Perry, who served as superintendent of the Farm from its inception in 1917 until her death in 1932, found themselves in a challenging position as they sought to balance the sometimes conflicting missions of the Farm. Women had limited social power within the state bureaucracy, but their involvement with the KSIFW allowed them to carve out a respectable public role for themselves. Through insisting that women must staff the prison, implementing a plan of moral reform on the inmates, and holding themselves up as the models of respectable femininity, the professional women who worked at the Farm were able to highlight their social privileges in ways that helped them stand apart from the inmates that they worked with every day.

Drawing from a set of over two thousand intake interviews from women who were quarantined at the Farm between 1923 and 1933, chapter 5 gives the inmates' accounts of how they came to be detained under Chapter 205. Whether it was through state agents directly arresting women, someone turning them in to authorities as venereal disease suspects, or women volunteering to go to the Farm in order to access health care, the variety of paths that inmates took to get to the Farm complicate the simplistic narrative coming from state documents that they were all prostitutes in dire need of moral reform. Their stories expose the ways that race, class, and gender informed the implementation of Chapter 205. They also reveal the complete failure of Chapter 205 to address the actual social problem at hand: the spread of venereal diseases.

Chapter 6 dives into these same inmate interviews in order to understand how women talked about their sexual pasts. Inmates found themselves in a highly charged situation when they were interviewed: they were detained under an indefinite sentence and asked probing questions about their sexual histories. Through their answers, the inmates tried to stake a claim to respectability by talking about their sexual pasts in a way that minimized their perceived moral failures. Two narratives emerge from the interviews. First, inmates claimed that they had not broken any moral norms surrounding sexuality. Whether inmates claimed that they contracted a disease through philandering husbands, nonsexual contact with an infected person, parents who passed on a disease, or rape or sexual abuse, these women distanced their disease from their own sexual choices. Second, the inmates claimed that they were not fully responsible for their actions because they were negatively influenced by others. Describing the influence of "bad company," dances, and car rides, these inmates acknowledged that their sexual choices may have led to their having a disease while also diverting some of the blame onto others. Similar to accounts of how they were arrested, the way that the inmates described contracting a venereal disease complicates any simplistic generalizations about their sexual pasts or moral character. Some women reported the type of casual attitude toward sex that was of deep concern to moral reformers at the time. Others reported that they were the victims of men's sexual vices and aggressions. Regardless of the success of their claims to respectability, though, these women had ended up at the Farm as inmates.

Finally, the conclusion recounts the declining enforcement of Chapter 205 following the discovery of penicillin during World War II and explores the larger implications of Chapter 205. The story of venereal disease control in Kansas during the 1920s and 1930s informs our understanding of this particular period in history, as well as our current moment. As a public health policy, imprisoning only women under Chapter 205 made little sense. Public health officials in Kansas chose not to pursue measures that would have reduced transmission of venereal diseases, such as handing out condoms or providing free testing and treatment. Instead, the state imprisoned thousands of women at the KSIFW under Chapter 205. This policy failed to address pressing public health problems while wasting resources and contributing to social inequities. This book argues that perceptions of respectability, which are informed by larger social currents of race, class, sexuality, and gender, are a key mechanism by which social boundaries are created and reinforced. These widespread cultural assumptions about groups of people allow systematic injustices to happen, from the story of the women incarcerated under Chapter 205 to modern debates about the prison system. The social issues that led to Hattie Campbell being detained at the KSIFW in 1925 are still very much with us today.

CHAPTER 1

WORLD WAR I, SEXUALITY, AND VENEREAL DISEASE CONTROL IN KANSAS

On April 18, 1918, Private Joseph Coleman wrote a letter to Kansas governor Arthur Capper. Joseph was stationed at Camp Funston, a major military base built in Kansas to train troops preparing to head to the battlefields of World War I. Joseph was desperate. The day before he was set to be married, his fiancée, Zoe Barnes, was arrested. Joseph reported that Zoe "was forested to take the Culture test and symptions showed slightly and now she is under way to PRISON [*sic*]." The soldier pleaded with the governor: "I appeal to you as one with sympathy and feeling upon Miss [Barnes's] part and mine and I do beg that lady be given a fair chance." Governor Capper took Joseph's plea seriously, writing to the mayor of Manhattan and the warden of the state prison to inquire into Zoe's case. These inquiries did little to change Zoe's fate: both men replied to the governor that Zoe had gonorrhea and was lawfully being detained under Chapter 205 in order to protect troops like Joseph from the menace of venereal disease.[1]

Zoe and Joseph were caught in the competing social currents of their moment in history: anxiety about changing sexual mores, the demands of a nation gearing up for war, and a public health crisis that precipitated a set of laws that punished young women for their sexual behaviors. This chapter traces the origins of these social currents, the development of laws like Chapter 205 (known as the American Plan) across the country, and the way that Chapter 205 was first implemented in Kansas during the war. The privileging of Joseph's physical health over Zoe's freedom was not unique to Kansas; across the country, government officials enforced laws like Chapter 205 to quarantine women suspected of having venereal disease. A system of laws and enforcement practices emerged during the war that gave official government sanction to the sexual double standard, imprisoning women across the country for their sexual behaviors.

Origins of the Social Hygiene Movement

Chapter 205 arose in Kansas amid drastic changes in sexual culture that were brought into public focus by the events of World War I. Though the image of the sexually liberated flapper is often associated with the 1920s, the cultural shifts in sexual behavior that the flapper embodied had their roots in the changing social and moral conditions between 1900 and World War I. Women's growing participation in the paid work force led to greater economic independence and social autonomy for young working-class women, particularly in urban areas. As they gained greater entry into the public world of paid labor, many young women began to demand independence in their personal lives, resisting familial control of their sexuality. Causing much concern on the part of parents, progressive reformers, and journalists, these young, working-class women frequented the thriving commercial amusements in urban areas in search of adventure and fun, which sometimes involved sexual activity. Together with young women's increased independence, this shift in courting from neighborhood or family settings to commercial spaces facilitated sexual experimentation among youth. These new norms around sexual activity in working-class communities developed in contrast to and alongside older middle-class Victorian attitudes that emphasized self-control and limited sexual expression.[2]

The shift toward more open attitudes surrounding premarital sex overall, as well as differences between social groups, can be seen in survey data from the period between 1900 and World War I. Historical demographer Daniel Scott Smith looked at national survey data from the period, finding that 13.5 percent of young white women reported having sex before marriage in the years between 1900 and 1910. This number nearly doubled to 26 percent during the 1910s, and it doubled again to around 50 percent in the 1920s.[3] Working-class women were more likely to report premarital sexual experiences than middle- or upper-class women. However, these higher rates of premarital sex do not necessarily indicate an acceptance of promiscuous sexuality. Most of the women reported having sex with their fiancés; this reflects a common practice in many working-class families that engaged couples would have sex before marriage, provided that the couple would marry if a pregnancy occurred. As familial control over youth diminished and large urban areas provided less community control, this pressure to marry became difficult to enforce in the first two decades of the twentieth century. Thus, the trend toward having sex before marriage was part of a longer transformation in sexual behaviors that led to the changed sexual culture of the 1920s.[4]

These changes in sexual culture did not enter mainstream society without controversy. Progressive reformers from a variety of backgrounds viewed these changes in sexual culture and behaviors with grave concern. Whether they focused on anti-prostitution, dance halls, or the prevalence of venereal disease, progressive reformers viewed the combination of old vices like prostitution with new sexual mores that permitted sexual experimentation among youth as a dangerous mix.

One such reform mission was the social hygiene movement, which brought together different groups to combat the public health threat posed by venereal disease. Beginning with the activism of New York physician Prince Morrow in the early 1900s, the movement gained momentum with the formation of the American Social Hygiene Association (ASHA) in 1913. With generous funding from John D. Rockefeller Jr., ASHA sought to take a modern, scientific approach to the problem of venereal disease through scientific study and planned social actions. Two different groups of advocates united in this organization: the female moral purity reformers who denounced the sexual double standard and prostitution, and the male public health professionals who worried about the spread of venereal disease. For the female reformers, challenging the sexual double standard was a key step in the fight to gain equality between the sexes. For the male medical professionals, controlling prostitution was the most efficient means of reducing rates of venereal disease. Though their motives differed, in the 1910s these two groups agreed on the strategy of aggressively fighting prostitution and advocating for sex education.[5]

ASHA faced steep resistance to public discussions of sexuality and venereal disease. When the *Ladies' Home Journal* published a series on venereal disease in 1906, they lost 75,000 outraged subscribers.[6] Venereal disease was a taboo topic for many in society, including those in the medical profession. Many doctors and hospitals refused to treat people with venereal disease, and some even hid the diagnosis from patients in an effort to protect their reputation. On the eve of World War I, many people viewed venereal disease as a just punishment for sexual indiscretions and questioned the legitimacy and moral implications of even treating the diseases. Contracting venereal disease was a natural consequence of sin, and as such was not something that was a proper matter in which reformers should be trying to intervene. Despite this public resistance, the social hygiene movement had some successes in the 1910s. ASHA was successful in making public discussions of sexuality and venereal disease more common, as evidenced by a 1922 US Bureau of Education study that found that 46.6 percent of secondary schools offered some type of sex education program. However, this increasingly public presence of sex had mixed results in terms of the sexual morality imagined by social hygienists.[7]

Though the social hygiene movement pushed for more awareness and treatment of venereal disease, they were in many ways ahead of the science in the area. Particularly because of the stigma associated with researching venereal disease pathology and treatments, medical understanding of venereal disease was still in its rudimentary phases in the first two decades of the twentieth century. To start with, gonorrhea and syphilis were difficult to diagnose given the medical understanding and lab techniques of the period. While German scientists discovered new diagnostic tests for syphilis and gonorrhea between 1905 and 1910, few doctors had access to the types of laboratory facilities that could make good use of these tests. In the absence of reliable, accessible testing, doctors often relied on "social factors," such as whether the woman engaged in prostitution, in their diagnoses as well. In other words, if a woman's tests came back positive, she was assumed to have venereal disease, but if they came back negative and her lifestyle was not fitting with middle-class notions of respectability, she also might be diagnosed with venereal disease. The subjective nature of venereal disease diagnosis created a challenge for public health officials and social hygiene reformers who sought to raise alarm about the dangers of syphilis and gonorrhea by citing the prevalence of the diseases. This inconsistency led to wildly varying figures about rates of venereal disease infection, with Prince Morrow claiming that 80 percent of New York City men had at some point had gonorrhea in 1901 and the army reporting that 20 percent of new admissions had a venereal disease in 1909. While some of the claims were purposely exaggerated for the point of publicity, they also reflect the fact that there were no clear-cut ways of diagnosing who did and did not have a venereal disease.[8]

It is within this context of changing sexual behaviors and social hygiene activism that Chapter 205 emerged as official state policy in Kansas. As the circumstances of war brought private sexual behaviors into the public eye, the nation began to come to grips with how dramatically sexual values and behaviors had changed in the United States. Concern about the threat that venereal disease posed to the boys in uniform fueled changes nationwide that brought women's sexual behaviors under increasing government control.

World War I and the Fight against Venereal Disease

The United States' entrance into World War I catapulted venereal disease into a national, high-stakes issue. No longer just about sexual morality or the sexual double standard, the topic of venereal disease took on the status of a factor in the victory or failure of the American war machine. Even before the United States officially declared war in April 1917, military officials and civilian activists worried about the impact of venereal disease on the fighting power of the American military. In the first few decades of the twentieth century, fully one-third of lost manpower days in the US military resulted from soldiers being treated for venereal disease. Somewhere between a quarter and a third of all troops came to the military during World War I already infected, reflecting high rates of venereal disease among the civilian population. Other soldiers contracted a disease while serving in the armed forces. Regardless of the source of the disease, military officials faced the challenge of how to treat soldiers and prevent further infection.[9]

To further complicate this already daunting medical situation, the military had to address the venereal disease crisis while navigating hotly contested public debates about sexual morality. Actions that might have mitigated the spread of disease, such as the French system of regularly inspecting prostitutes around military bases for disease, drew ire from American reformers who did not want the government to be explicitly condoning the sexual double standard. The military refused to hand out condoms to soldiers on a large scale to prevent contraction of disease due to fears about promoting sexual immorality. In fact, when the American Expeditionary Force eventually provided chemical treatments to try to prevent venereal disease transmission to soldiers after they had unprotected sex, there was a public outcry that the military was enforcing a system of regulated prostitution. Activist Edith Houghton Hooker railed against this apparent endorsement of the sexual double standard, arguing that "prophylaxis concedes the necessity of a continual sacrifice of fresh girls to the moloch of men's lust."[10] For many reformers and government officials, advocating for complete chastity outside of marriage was the only solution that met both the medical and moral needs of the country.[11]

Concerns about the moral conditions of the troops emerged in Kansas as the state geared up for war. Effie Gellow, a member of the Women's Council of Defense from Hamilton, Nebraska, wrote to Kansas governor Arthur Capper to report local rumors about immoral conditions, illegitimate births, and rampant venereal disease at Camp Funston, a major military base built in 1917 near Junction City, Kansas. Though she doubted the veracity of these reports, Gellow acknowledged the effect such rumors could have on morale: "Of course this is German propaganda—but the trouble is, it is circulated finally by Americans, who give it the ring of truth as they tell it."[12] As thousands of young men left their homes for military bases across the country, parents and social reformers voiced similar worries about the military's effect on the moral development of their "boys." A 1917 newspaper article out of Hays, Kansas, titled "To Protect Soldier Boys," noted that "the state is prepared to go to any length in removing and keeping out any women who might attempt to prey upon the soldiers."[13] Much of this concern was premised on soldiers' sexual innocence and susceptibility to negative influences, which largely ignored the high rates of venereal infection among inducted troops that indicated prior sexual experience. This anxiety about soldiers' morality can be seen in a letter sent by Governor Capper to President Woodrow Wilson in May 1917. Capper reported that civic and religious organizations throughout the state were demanding high moral conditions in military training camps and urged the president to do everything within his power to protect soldiers "from contaminating and debauching influences." Capper went on to say: "Hundreds of mothers are appealing to me by letter to intercede with you on behalf of their sons. These mothers have a right to be heard; these boys have a right to be protected." Amid these calls to protect Kansas's sons, it was less clear who would look out for the rights of Kansas's daughters.[14]

This anxiety about providing an upright moral atmosphere for soldiers informed the military's strategies to address the venereal disease crisis. The US military's official campaign against venereal disease kicked off when Secretary of War Newton Baker created the Commission on Training

Camp Activities (CTCA) on April 17, 1917. Designed to protect American doughboys from the dual threats of vice and venereal disease, the CTCA sought to create a wholesome experience for troops while training in the United States and prepare them to resist temptations, both at home and overseas. Secretary Baker appointed New York anti-vice reformer Raymond Fosdick to head up the CTCA, setting up the organization to take on a truly progressive tenor. Fosdick drew heavily from the ranks of the ASHA to staff the CTCA, giving reformers official government legitimacy and resources to ramp up their campaign against sexual immorality and venereal disease. Through a program that combined educational campaigns, wholesome distractions, and repressive measures, they hoped to keep rates of venereal disease low and dissuade soldiers from visiting prostitutes.[15]

Educational Measures to Control Venereal Disease during the War

The CTCA launched an educational campaign on military bases across the country to try to convince soldiers to abstain from sex. Through pamphlets, lectures, and films, the CTCA largely framed the problem of venereal disease as one of military efficiency and national security, not a question of morality. Part of a soldier's responsibility to his country was to keep his body clean and ready to engage in battle. The military produced a feature-length film titled *Fit to Fight* in which many of the characters contracted syphilis and gonorrhea and were forced to sit out the war. What was particularly groundbreaking about these educational campaigns was the degree to which they emphasized male sexual chastity. The syllabus used by lecturers in the navy emphasized that refraining from sex was the only surefire way to protect oneself against venereal disease and that, while sailors should expect to have a "clean girl" to marry once they returned from war, the same standard should apply to them as well.[16] However, these educational efforts also continued a long history of scapegoating women for the spread of venereal disease. Government officials often portrayed loose women as the enemy of the American military and warned soldiers of the dangers of prostitutes. A CTCA pamphlet cautioned soldiers: "WOMEN WHO SOLICIT SOLDIERS FOR IMMORAL PURPOSES ARE USUALLY DISEASE SPREADERS AND FRIENDS OF THE ENEMY."[17] Though the message coming from the CTCA focused more on military efficiency than morality, the omission of condoms from the government's strategies to prevent the spread of venereal disease belied the moral controversies the military had to navigate in addressing venereal disease in the armed forces.

Between Camp Funston, Fort Riley, and Fort Leavenworth, Kansas health officials had plenty of soldiers to educate about sexual morality and venereal disease. The Kansas State Board of Health worked with military officials and local organizations, such as the Young Men's Christian Association (YMCA), to deliver CTCA-approved educational materials and provide wholesome recreational outlets, such as movies and sports, for the soldiers. Recognizing that rates of venereal disease in surrounding communities impacted rates within the military, state officials also worked to educate the general public about venereal disease and the importance of maintaining high moral standards. The Committee on Social Hygiene of the State Council of Defense focused on promoting good moral conditions in the state, providing lectures and distributing educational pamphlets throughout Kansas. Governor Capper proclaimed April 28, 1918, Social Hygiene Sunday, urging pastors across the state to deliver sermons on social hygiene and initiate educational and recreational activities in their communities. Though careful not to actually use the words "syphilis" or "gonorrhea" in his proclamation, the governor highlighted the need for "the nation to face frankly the problem of social diseases."[18] In Kansas and across the country, educational campaigns focused not only on military bases but also on the civilian populations around them. Federal campaigns to educate workers in industry about venereal disease echoed the messages used with soldiers, urging chastity and the importance of keeping your body healthy to help the United States win the war.[19]

The military's educational efforts faced a new landscape as American troops began arriving on the European front. The American message of strict chastity contrasted with the approaches of European allies that often tolerated more sexual activity on the part of soldiers. The US government sought to create the same moral conditions in Europe as they had at the training camps at home, continuing the educational campaigns and imposing restrictions designed to limit soldiers' engagement with vice of all kinds. Worries about the moral conditions of life at training camps on the home front only escalated as Kansas soldiers went overseas. After reading a newspaper article about the commander of the American Expeditionary Forces, John J. Pershing, banning hard liquor for soldiers in Europe, Governor Capper wrote Pershing an appreciative letter on behalf of the people of Kansas. Capper noted that Kansans were "anxious that our Kansas boys who go to the front to fight for world freedom shall be made just as secure from the preying influences of liquor, vice and immorality after they land in France as they were in their home communities."[20]

Pershing was keenly aware of the need to continue educational efforts once soldiers landed in Europe, and one famous Kansan helped implement these educational campaigns in France. Best known as the inventor of basketball, Dr. James Naismith was a physical education instructor at the University of Kansas when the United States entered the war. Building on his previous experience as an army chaplain and an instructor of sex education, Naismith was well qualified to instruct soldiers on the importance of social hygiene and to orchestrate other recreational outlets for the soldiers to occupy their time. The YMCA sent Naismith to the European front in June 1917, and he eventually had a team of eight lecturers working underneath him to provide social hygiene instruction to soldiers at ports of entry and along the front. Naismith and his team employed similar methods as the CTCA had stateside to try to convince the soldiers to abstain from sex, including lectures, pamphlets, exhibits, posters, and films. His team used a bulletin titled "The Basis of Clean Living" to facilitate small group discussions. In a letter to his wife shortly after he arrived in Europe, Naismith acknowledged the challenges of trying to ensure a clean moral environment for the soldiers, "especially when it is among the old-fashioned type of soldier and in France where ideals are so different." Naismith spent nineteen months in France trying to create a clean moral atmosphere among the soldiers of the American Expeditionary Force. The rate of venereal disease cases on the European front was actually quite low, at 3.4 percent, compared to 12.7 percent of soldiers who were stationed stateside. While this lower rate may have been because the military administered chemical prophylaxis treatments after possible exposure to venereal disease, Naismith's educational campaigns could still claim some success.[21]

Overall, the impact of these educational campaigns did not always match government officials' expectations. The CTCA gave out over a million pamphlets during the war and delivered lectures to more than 775,000 soldiers, exposing a large number of young recruits to the ideals of sexual chastity in service to one's country. However, just because the government promoted this message does not mean that soldiers were receptive to the idea. High rates of venereal contraction among soldiers and an explosion of prostitution around military bases indicate that many soldiers failed to take the message to heart. The minimal success of educational efforts led to the CTCA's second major approach to tackling venereal disease: repression.[22]

Repressive Measures to Control Venereal Disease during the War

Though the CTCA began with the idea of preventing soldiers' contraction of venereal disease through education, they soon turned to shutting down red light districts surrounding military bases and incarcerating women suspected of carrying venereal disease. If they could not convince men to refrain from having sex with women, the next best option seemed to be to remove the women.

The military's most immediate concern was shutting down the many red light districts across the country that were within easy reach of military bases. Instrumental to the CTCA's efforts were new laws that broadened the legal definition of prostitution and made it easier to incarcerate women suspected of immoral behavior. ASHA pushed ten states to adopt their model law against prostitution word for word, and another thirty-two to adopt it in part. The model law defined prostitution as "the giving or receiving of the body, for hire, or the giving or receiving of the body for indiscriminate sexual intercourse, without hire." Under this very generous definition of prostitution, nearly any person suspected of indecent behavior could be charged, equipping local and federal authorities with unprecedented power to intervene in Americans' sex lives. The CTCA claimed to have closed 110 red light districts by the end of the war.[23]

In Kansas the man leading the state's efforts to control prostitution and venereal disease was Samuel J. Crumbine, who was charged by the army to head a six-state unit to control venereal disease in addition to his duties as secretary of the Kansas State Board of Health. Crumbine earned a medical degree from the University of Kansas in 1889 and worked as a pharmacist in Dodge City, Kansas, before starting work with the state board of health at the turn of the century. Known for employing creative marketing techniques in public health work, Crumbine pioneered a "swat the fly" campaign to try to prevent the spread of disease and convinced brickmakers to imprint "Don't spit on the sidewalk" on thousands of their products. As young men streamed into military bases from across the state, Crumbine would need this creativity to stem the spread of venereal disease.[24]

Kansas authorities realized that soldiers continued to contract venereal disease despite the clean conditions they were attempting to create on military bases. A medical officer at Camp Funston reported to Crumbine that "soldiers were making their dangerous contact in" Kansas City, Missouri. After finding that the police and courts were controlled by notoriously corrupt political boss Tom Pendergast, Crumbine visited "Boss Tom" directly and threatened to deny soldiers' leave to Kansas City unless the conditions were improved. According to Crumbine, Pendergast remedied the situation within a week: "Instead of spreading disease among our young men, gilded women, their paint removed, were now crowding the city hospital where they were receiving treatment for venereal infection." The state board of health repeated this strategy of threatening to prohibit soldiers from visiting cities and towns across the state if they did not comply with efforts to control prostitution and venereal disease.[25]

Military officials had hoped that by closing down the red light districts they could halt the spread of venereal disease, but they found that another class of women was having sex with soldiers: the charity girl. These young women blurred the lines between casual sex and prostitution, often engaging in "treating," the practice of having sex in exchange for an item of clothing or a night out on the town. Whether there was a commercial element to the interactions or not, charity girls' sexual behaviors factored into the spread of venereal disease. Seen as being driven by misguided patriotism and a sense of romance about the men in uniform, young women flocked to military bases in pursuit of soldiers. What government officials found particularly problematic about the "girl problem" was that it involved young women from respectable middle-class families. One CTCA social worker worried about the effect that the glamour of men in uniform was having on girls' moral compasses; one girl she had worked with "said she had never sold herself to a civilian but felt she was doing her bit when she had been with eight soldiers in a night."[26] Sometimes called "patriotic prostitutes," these women were difficult for military officials to categorize: they were not prostitutes, yet they willingly had sex with men outside of marriage. Their very existence complicated any simplistic dichotomy of women as either sinners or saints.[27]

Whether they understood the phenomena of the charity girl as a form of prostitution or a temporary abnormality caused by the emotions of wartime, the CTCA took the plight of these young women seriously and sought to prevent their moral downfall. In 1917 Fosdick created the Committee on Protective Work for Girls, enlisting social workers to convince young women to direct their patriotic urges in more productive directions.

Under the direction of reformer Maude Miner, this committee viewed wartime charity girls as a group of young women who were in need of protection from both their own lustful urgings and the misguided influence of a new, more sexually permissive youth culture. Unlike prostitutes, who were viewed as a menace to society, charity girls were basically "good" girls who were swept up in the moment. If they were to avoid the path to prostitution, they needed the government's help and guidance. However, social workers with the CTCA met with limited success in convincing young women of the value of chastity and the inherent danger of sexual relationships.[28]

Development of the American Plan

Recognizing that anti-prostitution laws alone would not prevent the spread of venereal diseases by charity girls, the federal government began pushing another legal mechanism that could be used to detain women who might spread disease to soldiers: quarantine laws. During World War I, states across the country began passing laws that built the legal basis for what came to be known as the American Plan. These state laws gave government officials the power to detain, test, and quarantine individuals for venereal diseases, usually with no due process or recourse for the person arrested.

As the Kansas legislative session began and the nation prepared for the official declaration of war in the spring of 1917, the Kansas legislature began debate on what would become one of the most consistently enforced American Plan laws in the country. Chapter 205 (Senate bill no. 135) was a regulation that allotted the board of health broad powers to make rules regarding health policies in the state, including the right to quarantine people considered at risk of spreading disease. On January 31, 1917, the Kansas Senate overwhelmingly passed a version of the bill sponsored by Sen. James Milligan that gave the board of health the authority to determine which diseases were eligible for quarantine, with thirty-five senators voting for the measure, zero opposing, and five not voting. The House first considered a different version of the bill in early February that contained a set list of diseases for which the board of health could quarantine people. Local newspapers reported that legislators "laugh[ed the] measure to death" and expressed concern about the effect of such a bill on personal liberties.[29] However, the Senate's version of the bill, which gave the board of health the power to designate which diseases might warrant quarantine, was again taken up in the House on February 20. The *Topeka Capitol* mockingly commented that the Senate legislation "gives to the board the power to do what the house a few weeks ago refused to do itself, largely because the members couldn't pronounce nor understand a long list of medical terms." The measure passed, though with considerably more resistance than it faced in the Senate. With sixty-eight votes for, forty-five against, and twelve not voting, the measure survived the "vociferous protests" of Rep. George Holland, "who declared his personal liberties were being trampled under foot."[30] The language of Chapter 205 was much broader than American Plan laws that would later pass in other states. Rather than focusing exclusively on venereal disease, Chapter 205 gave the Kansas State Board of Health the power to "designate such diseases as are infectious, contagious, or communicable" and authorized the board to make rules and procedures for quarantining people "as may be necessary to prevent the spread and dissemination of diseases dangerous to the public health."[31] The bill went to Governor Capper for his signature on February 27, 1917, all with little public mention of venereal disease or the impending public health crises of wartime. Chapter 205, the law that would have huge implications for venereal disease, sexuality, and social control in Kansas in the following decades, was in effect in the Sunflower State before most other states had even begun to formulate their own American Plan laws.[32]

Kansas was ripe for this type of government intervention into people's personal lives. Many reform-minded individuals had flocked to the state prior to the Civil War, eager to establish Kansas as a free state and bringing with them the linked values of promoting abolition, women's suffrage, and Prohibition. This reform tradition combined with strong populist and evangelical traditions in the state to position Kansas as a ready home for progressive ideals in the early 1900s. The Progressive movement called for increased government involvement in many details of economic and social life that had previously been considered outside the proper scope of government intervention. With a base in white, middle-class values, Progressives sought to influence the morality of the nation through education and more far-reaching government policies. The issue of Prohibition is one example of the eagerness of Kansans to embrace this call for government involvement in shaping the morality of its citizens. Kansas was one of the earliest states to adopt laws limiting the production and sale of alcohol, establishing Kansas as a model for effective implementation of

Prohibition before the national Prohibition amendment went into effect in 1920. In his 1918 letter to John J. Pershing, Governor Capper touted the positive effect of such proactive government policies in shaping the moral character of Kansas soldiers headed to the European front: "We believe no state has contributed, or will contribute, better men than have been reared in abstentious Kansas homes and educated in the clean environments of our schools and colleges. Many of them have rarely seen a drunken man and their conduct and the quality of their manhood is of the best and highest."[33] The confidence that Capper placed in the positive influence of Prohibition on the moral development of Kansas youth was typical of the possibilities that Progressives saw in shaping moral values through education and government action. Beginning in 1904, Kansas elected nine progressive governors, setting the stage for Kansas political science professor Charles E. Hill to state in 1910: "It would be hard to find a state with more progressive measures than Kansas."[34] The social hygiene movement was in many ways a quintessential progressive issue: through both educational measures and repressive government policies, the movement sought to change the moral conditions of the country in an effort to improve society. Kansas's progressive tradition made it receptive to the mission and strategies of the social hygiene movement and primed it to become a leader in the implementation of American Plan laws. Chapter 205 established the legal basis to move Kansas in this direction.[35]

Several months after the governor signed Chapter 205 into law in Kansas, the California State Board of Health adopted a set of American Plan regulations that would become a model for states across the country. The legislation, passed on September 1, 1917, called for aggressive measures to combat venereal disease, including the inspection of all "persons reasonably suspected" of having a venereal disease and their quarantine when it was in the best interest of public health. Unlike the Kansas law, these regulations were specifically focused on venereal disease. ASHA promoted the California model legislation across the country, and on March 29, 1918, the US Public Health Service released model legislation that drew heavily from the California example. US attorney general T. W. Gregory issued directives to provide the legal rationale to states for mandatory inspections and reporting of venereal disease, as well as the right to suspend habeas corpus while awaiting venereal disease test results. With the passage of the Chamberlain-Kahn Act on July 9, 1918, which authorized the detention of unaccompanied women surrounding military bases for compulsory physical examinations and provided funding for venereal disease control programs in civilian populations, this policy gained new legitimacy. A flurry of states passed their own American Plan laws during World War I: thirty-nine states adopted the federal government's model law by the end of the war, and every state in the country would eventually have a similar law on the books.[36]

Even before the legal basis for detaining women had fully solidified, Kansas and states across the country began detaining women suspected of spreading venereal disease. In June 1917 the Kansas State Board of Health issued regulations requiring all cases of venereal disease be reported to state authorities. In September they created special areas, called extra cantonment zones, around the military bases in the state to prevent the spread of communicable diseases. On November 2, 1917, the board of health issued orders that people found within these cantonment zones with venereal disease be quarantined. In March 1918 these quarantine orders were extended to the entire state.[37]

These actions by the Kansas State Board of Health mirrored what was happening in other states as the federal government gave directives and support to states to attempt to contain the venereal disease problem. In early 1918 the Law Enforcement Division of the CTCA adopted a policy of compulsory physical examination, testing, and quarantine of women suspected of having a venereal disease. To help implement this policy, the federal government sent staff support. Lt. Charles Shelton and Capt. Millard Knowlton of the US Public Health Service were assigned to Kansas to help Crumbine lead the Venereal Disease Division of the Kansas State Board of Health. This group's first priority was to ensure that the areas immediately surrounding military bases were free of disease. Crumbine later reported that he enlisted the help of police and county sheriffs to round up suspected women, "and if questioning left little or no doubt that a woman was vicious, she was obliged to submit to examination." If women tested positive for a disease, they were quarantined under the authority of Chapter 205. When released, women "were warned to keep away from soldiers' camps" or they would be arrested again.[38]

As indicated in Crumbine's comments, these newly passed quarantine regulations were not applied equally to men and women. During the war, men found to be infected with venereal disease in Kansas faced one of two outcomes: if they were in the military, they received treatment within military hospitals; if they were not in the military, they faced the possibility of internment at the Kansas State Penitentiary. Although the number of civilian men interned during the war under Chapter 205 was never as high as the number of women, the state board of health did quarantine men in Kansas during World War I. By March 1919 the state of Kansas had detained 410 women under Chapter 205, but only forty-four men.[39] Crumbine later described many of these quarantined men as pimps "who lived off the earnings of prostitutes," keeping their "hold on these women in part by threatening to expose them to the military authorities." While this assertion reveals one way that Chapter 205 may have operated to give men leverage over women, Chapter 205 could also be used to control men. Noting that pimps' abuse of the women who worked for them was not officially within his purview, Crumbine went on to note that pimps' health was within his jurisdiction: "When we caught these despicable racketeers, we had them examined. If they were infected, they were quarantined on the penitentiary grounds and treated."[40] Crumbine's comments show that, at least during the war, men were also vulnerable to the broad powers that Chapter 205 gave the state. Similar to how the law functioned for women, Chapter 205 could be used as a cover to arrest problematic men who were difficult to convict under other state laws.

Though American Plan laws across the country were gender neutral in many respects, they also contained language that belied the assumption that they would primarily be applied against women. In describing who might be considered "reasonably suspected" of having a venereal disease, the California board of health resolutions declared, "Owing to the prevalence of such diseases among prostitutes all such persons may be considered within the above class."[41] Crumbine described the implementation of Chapter 205 in Kansas as "the isolation and treatment of infected prostitutes," belying his assumption that the law was primarily applied against women, as well as the idea that all of the women were prostitutes.[42] In their implementation, American Plan laws were largely focused on women nationwide.

Establishment of Women's Prisons

With this federal push to incarcerate women suspected of prostitution or having venereal disease came the obvious quandary of what to do with them. Many states lacked separate facilities for female prisoners, and few had the resources to detain the estimated thirty thousand women who were arrested during the period that the United States was embroiled in

World War I. For women detained for venereal disease, the facility problem was even more acute, as only eight states had facilities that could house and properly care for women with venereal disease in 1918. Particularly for first-time offenders, this lack of facilities led to probation, but the approximately eighteen thousand women who were imprisoned posed a serious logistical challenge to state penal systems. Just as they had pushed states to enact these new laws, the federal government provided financial backing to states in order to establish and expand women's correctional facilities. Between April 1918 and July 1920, the federal government gave states a total of $427,089 for women's prisons, establishing twenty-seven new correctional facilities and reformatories and expanding on another sixteen.[43]

In Kansas a bill that passed during the same legislative session as Chapter 205 laid the groundwork to expand the women's correctional system in the state. On March 8, 1917, the final version of the bill creating the KSIFW passed the Kansas Senate following a lobbying campaign from the leading women's groups in the state (for more details, see chapter 3). Though the passage of the bill coincided with the United States' entrance into World War I, this was a bill for which the Kansas Council of Women had been lobbying for several years, and the initial motivations were far removed from the worries of war. Rather, these women lobbied for the prison as part of a national progressive reform movement to establish separate women's prison facilities. With the passage of the bill creating the KSIFW, Kansas became the seventh state in the country to have a separate women's prison. The KSIFW officially opened as a separate institution in the spring of 1917, just as the state was beginning their efforts to combat venereal disease.[44]

State facilities were soon flooded with women detained under Chapter 205. The number of men arrested in Kansas was limited, given the military's main priority of protecting the troops from contracting venereal disease through their associations with women. Those men who were quarantined under Chapter 205 were sent to the men's prison in Leavenworth. Due to their large number and the few facilities already in existence to house them, however, the high number of women detained by the state posed a much larger logistical issue. Lacking any facilities to house the large number of women they wanted to quarantine, the state board of health made arrangements with the board of administration to detain quarantined women at the newly created KSIFW. However, as of the spring of 1917, the KSIFW was not equipped to handle so many inmates, particularly a population in need of medical attention. The Farm was temporarily located in an old twelve-room farmhouse on 160 acres owned by the state penitentiary in Lansing until a permanent location could be found. However, federal authorities pressured Kansas officials to keep the Farm in this temporary location, arguing "that its proximity to the Penitentiary was itself a deterrent to these women."[45] Despite this desire to keep the Farm in Lansing, the original buildings were grossly inadequate to accommodate the large number of women quarantined there under Chapter 205. In a matter of a few weeks, the population of the Farm went from eighteen to more than two hundred women. To accommodate these new inmates, the board of administration employed male prison labor to throw up temporary tar-paper shacks constructed from lumber harvested on site. The federal government committed funds to the project as well, giving $22,750 for general expenses and another $3,000 to begin building a hospital in June 1918.[46] In just a few months, the KSIFW was thus transformed from a small farmhouse with fewer than twenty inmates to a full-fledged institution detaining hundreds of women at a time, primarily for the crime of having a sexually transmitted disease.[47]

Conclusion

The Kansas legislature passed Chapter 205 as the nation sat on the brink of war. Over the eighteen months that the nation was at war, Kansas ramped up its enforcement of Chapter 205 across the state, responding to federal pressure to contain disease and local worries about keeping their "boys" protected from immorality. A system to control the spread of venereal disease in Kansas emerged that centered on the protection of soldiers like Joseph Coleman. The state's role in regulating men's sexual behaviors was minimal, in part because the military provided health care and moral training to the soldiers under their charge. The regulation of women's sexual behaviors and health-care needs fell to state officials, local law enforcement, and county health officers. As the war ended and young men across the country found themselves returning to life outside the military, the systems that were set up to control women's sexual behaviors during the war remained in place. Chapter 205 was first implemented in Kansas to protect soldiers' health, but it continued to be enforced for women long after American soldiers returned home.

CHAPTER 2

PRISONERS FIRST, PATIENTS SECOND

THE TRANSITION TO A PEACETIME VENEREAL DISEASE CONTROL POLICY

National efforts to combat venereal disease came to a turning point when World War I officially ended on November 11, 1918. Like many other aspects of life, the war had dramatically changed the landscape of social hygiene work in the United States. At both the local and national levels, social hygienists and boards of health saw an unprecedented investment in venereal disease public health measures during the war. At the federal level, the momentum of the war years initially spilled over into peacetime. The activities of the CTCA were transferred over to the Interdepartmental Social Hygiene Board. ASHA remained active, and Rockefeller continued to provide financial backing to the social hygiene movement.[1]

The mood in Kansas about continuing efforts to combat venereal disease was mixed. In a 1920 report by the Kansas State Board of Health, Secretary Crumbine celebrated the campaign against venereal disease in Kansas as "one of the most important gains of the World War" and argued that its continued implementation was essential due to "the recognition that the widespread prevalence of venereal disease has attained such magnitude as to make it a race peril."[2] During the war and the years that followed, several Kansas towns and cities passed their own local ordinances calling for the quarantine of venereal disease patients in addition to the statewide Chapter 205.[3] A small-town newspaper, the *Baxter Spring News*, ran a story on January 10, 1919, expressing its continued enthusiasm for public health measures to combat syphilis and gonorrhea. The story was optimistic that wartime campaigns against venereal disease had "so revolutionized the attitude of the people" that "subjects heretofore not mentioned in the public are now being discussed freely and frankly in a manner undreamed of a few years ago."[4] However, this eagerness to continue the fight against venereal disease was not universal. In a report dated June 30, 1920, field agent C. A. Bantleon informed the Kansas State Board of Health that he had to work hard to convince local officials to do "their part in carrying on an effective and efficient program" to control venereal disease in the state. He lamented that by the summer of 1919, many city officials no longer saw venereal disease as an imminent threat and "seemed to be of the opinion that the same efforts in combating venereal disease were not necessary, as the war was at an end and most of the soldiers returned to their homes."[5] With this mix of enthusiasm and trepidation, states across the country had to decide whether they would continue to implement American Plan laws and other public health efforts against venereal disease after the war was over.

Some states and cities stopped enforcing their American Plan laws after the war, letting statutes lie dormant until they would again be resurrected to detain women during World War II. Other places continued to enforce quarantine measures for venereal disease after World War I, including the cities of Los Angeles and Chicago. When the US assistant surgeon general wrote to state health departments in 1925 to inquire whether they were still enforcing American Plan laws, many states responded that they were continuing to enforce quarantine laws for venereal disease patients, though some states faced lack of cooperation from local doctors. ASHA was active in promoting the continued enforcement of American Plan laws, sending undercover agents to investigate vice in states across the country and continuing to advocate for states and cities to adopt supportive legislation.[6]

In perhaps no other state did the enforcement of an American Plan law come to define its women's reformatory in the interwar years as much as Chapter 205 did in Kansas.[7] The location of the Farm in Lansing, which was initially supposed to be temporary, became permanent. The pattern of implementing Chapter 205 along gendered lines was only amplified after the war. State authorities stopped enforcing Chapter 205 against men as the 1920s got under way, and the board of administration discontinued the men's quarantine camp at Lansing in August 1921.[8] The state focused its quarantine efforts exclusively on women, detaining over five thousand women under Chapter 205 by 1942. The number of women detained under Chapter 205 at the KSIFW peaked immediately following World War I and slowly declined over the next two decades, as seen in figure 2.1. Though historian Scott Stern presents a compelling case that American Plan laws were consistently enforced across the country during

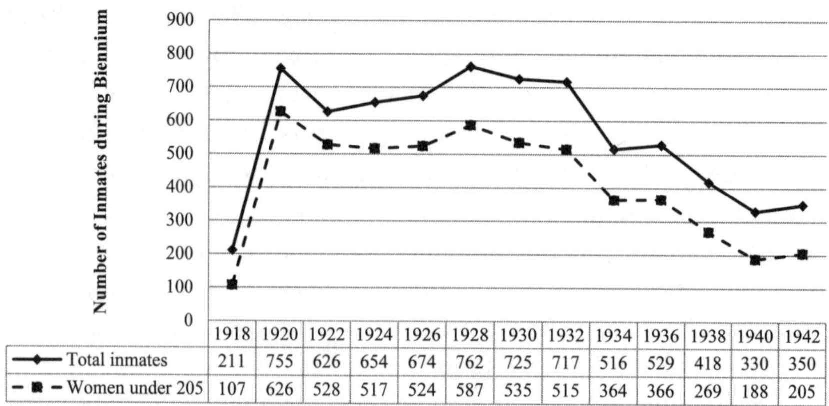

	1918	1920	1922	1924	1926	1928	1930	1932	1934	1936	1938	1940	1942
Total inmates	211	755	626	654	674	762	725	717	516	529	418	330	350
Women under 205	107	626	528	517	524	587	535	515	364	366	269	188	205

Figure 2.1: Total inmate numbers from the 1918 report are lower because they only include one year of the KSIFW's operation, whereas other reports reflect two years. KSIFW 1918 Report, *14;* KSIFW 1920 Report, *20;* KSIFW 1922 Report, *11;* KSIFW 1924 Report, *26;* KSIFW 1926 Report, *16;* KSIFW 1928 Report, *15;* KSIFW 1930 Report, *16;* KSIFW 1932 Report, *16;* KSIFW 1934 Report, *13;* KSIFW 1936 Report, *12;* KSIFW 1938 Report, *17;* KSIFW 1940 Report, *28;* KSIFW 1942 Report, *25.*

the interwar period, Kansas stood out by the sheer number of women detained and the fact that quarantined women became the defining population of its women's reformatory.[9] As a percentage of the total inmate population at the KSIFW, women detained under Chapter 205 made up between 51 percent (1918) and 84 percent (1922) of the inmates, with an average of 71 percent of the total inmate population between 1918 and 1942.[10] Women detained under Chapter 205 spent, on average, around four months at the KSIFW during this period. Though they intermingled with inmates who were detained for other charges, such as burglary, liquor violations, and even murder, women quarantined under Chapter 205 made up the majority of the population at the Farm.

This chapter outlines how Chapter 205 was enforced in the interwar years, from the KSIFW's position within the bureaucratic structure of the state to the medical treatment provided at the facility. As this chapter will show, enforcement of Chapter 205 in Kansas relied on much more than a medical diagnosis, and reinforced social boundaries that were beyond the narrow scope of a public health policy. As women's sexual behaviors came under the purview of government control, perceptions of their respectability played an important role. Respectability informed women's diagnoses as having a disease to begin with, as the unreliable nature of medical diagnostics at the time led many physicians to use social criteria, such as whether a woman was sexually active, in determining whether that person had a venereal disease. Once diagnosed, perceptions of respectability factored into a health officer's decision about whether a woman could be trusted to get treatment on an outpatient basis or needed to be imprisoned. This emphasis on respectability opened up avenues for racial and class biases to enter into the process. In Kansas and across the country, poor women and women of color were more likely to feel the brunt of this newfound enthusiasm for government intervention into the sex lives of everyday Americans. As government officials continued to enforce Chapter 205 between 1918 and 1942, the KSIFW emerged as one of the premier women's prisons in the country, with a population consisting mostly of women charged with no other crime than having a venereal disease.

Administration of Chapter 205

As Chapter 205 shifted from an emergency wartime measure to a standard practice within the state, Kansas officials solidified their approach of treating the quarantined women as prisoners rather than patients. Though Chapter 205 gave the state board of health the authority to quarantine women for having venereal disease, the KSIFW was administratively run under the state board of administration. This four-member board, consisting of the governor and three other people appointed by the governor, oversaw a wide range of government programs, including the state's hospitals, universities, and penal institutions. The board had the power to appoint the superintendents of the various state institutions under its control, as well as to decide the budgets for the individual institutions. However, the overall budget for the institutions was set by the legislature, so the board had to answer to them to justify their decisions.[11]

The board of administration treated the KSIFW as a penal institution, despite the fact that most of its inmates were there under a state quarantine law. Board of administration documents frequently listed the State Hospital for Epileptics and the State Sanatorium for Tuberculosis under "Charitable Institutions," while the KSIFW was listed under "Correctional Institutions." The 1920 board of administration biennial report called for longer sentences for women detained under Chapter 205, arguing that the state would do "little to combat the prevalence and deadly effect of social evil" without taking the time to morally reform inmates. The report went on to state that the "temporary cure of the physical ills, unless it also develops habits of decent thinking and living, merely provides a convenient and cheap way station for those who are bent on lives of shame." Though women quarantined under Chapter 205 were merely diagnosed with a disease, not convicted of any crime, the board claimed that they were "a grave menace to the moral and physical health of the community."[12] Both in how they categorized the KSIFW in their organizational charts and how they talked about the inmates of the institution, board of administration officials viewed women quarantined under Chapter 205 as guilty of moral crimes beyond their official quarantine sentence.

However, the administrative costs of incarcerating so many women was also a factor in the board of administration's support for the continued use of the KSIFW as a venue for quarantining women under Chapter 205. While the board of health paid for the medicine administered to patients in Lansing, and at times for the medical staff as well, the cost of detaining hundreds of women a year was absorbed through the board of administration. This fact may have led to other comments in board of administration documents that expressed reservations about the effectiveness of Chapter 205. The 1924 biennial report recommended discontinuing the practice of housing women detained under Chapter 205 at the KSIFW, arguing instead "that each city or county bear full expense of such regulation."[13] However, with so many institutions to oversee, the KSIFW was not a high priority for the board of administration, and little mention was made of this recommendation in future reports.

While the board of administration funded the KSIFW throughout the interwar years, the Kansas State Board of Health was in charge of enforcing Chapter 205. As guidelines were developed for implementing Chapter 205 during and immediately following World War I, a system of regulation emerged that placed women's respectability front and center. Individuals could be reported to the board of health through several means. Since the early 1910s, all doctors were required to report cases of venereal disease to the state board of health, although compliance with this directive was always an issue. However, doctors only had to report a patient number to the authorities; if the doctor was willing to assume responsibility for the patient's conduct, then he could withhold all personal information about the patient. On the other hand, if the doctor felt that the patient was "conducting or about to conduct himself or herself in such manner as to expose other persons to such infection," then he was obligated to report the patient's full information to the local health officer.[14] Individuals could also report suspected venereal disease cases directly to the health officer, who would then investigate the case as to its accuracy. Certain individuals, such as pharmacists, were required to report to the health officer any person who was purchasing supplies to treat venereal disease. If the health officer determined that a patient was not trustworthy enough to continue treatment and not spread the disease, then she would be sent to the KSIFW under the quarantine law.[15]

Local health officers exercised considerable discretion and autonomy during the implementation of Chapter 205. Once health officers were alerted to a potential venereal disease case, they were obligated to investigate. If reported by a doctor, the local health officer would confer with the doctor to "get all the information possible as to the character of such infected person and the likelihood that the patient's conduct may be such as might spread the disease to others." If the health officer questioned the patient's character, she would be sent to the KSIFW. The health officer also had the power to "make examinations of all persons reasonably suspected of having syphilis in communicable form, gonococcus infection or chancroid." Thus, the health officer exercised considerable discretion in determining who should be tested for venereal disease and who, if found infected, could be deemed trustworthy enough to get treatment before spreading the disease further. The board of health advised that health officers use restraint in sending women to Lansing in order to contain the high costs of quarantining patients at the KSIFW. However, sex workers were deemed automatically ineligible for treatment outside of Lansing, as it was "assumed that such persons cannot be trusted to protect others from exposure to infection." If the health officer determined that a patient needed to go to Lansing, then he would issue an arrest order that would then be carried out by local law enforcement officers.[16]

The patient's respectability was a central factor in all stages of this process, from the initial requirement that someone be tested for venereal disease, to the doctor's evaluation of whether the patient's name needed to be reported to the health officer, to the final decision by the health officer about whether the patient needed to be quarantined at the KSIFW. As a policy in practice, Chapter 205 was not merely a quarantine law to control venereal disease but a regulation that was selectively used to control the sexual behaviors of women who did not fulfill the requirements of respectability. Speaking of Chapter 205, one board of health report made this clear: "The purpose of the regulation is to require the reporting of persons who were irresponsible and could not be trusted to safeguard others from infection."[17] This sentiment was again expressed in a 1940 board of health report: "This regulation was, and is not, intended to provide a place for indiscriminate quarantine, but rather a place of quarantine for nonco-operative individuals, especially prostitutes or others who do not comply with local health authorities' directions."[18] Inherent in these descriptions of people who needed to be quarantined were the hallmarks of respectability: sexual propriety, social class, and gender norms.

Descriptions of the types of women who needed to be quarantined often directly mentioned social class. A 1920 board of health report commented: "Persons who are treated in clinics and institutions for venereal disease are drawn largely from the lower strata of society. Such people are, for the most part, in need of advice and counsel from someone with a broader point of view and a firmer grasp of the realities of life."[19] In her study of the initial influx of women quarantined at the KSIFW, social worker Alice Hill commented: "Although it is recognized that moral delinquency occurs irrespective of economic status, those girls who constitute a sufficient menace to the community to be placed under restraint usually come from families having small or insufficient incomes."[20] Social class thus entered into the decision-making process about who needed to be quarantined for venereal disease, not just because of economic reasons, but because of the implications of social class status for one's respectability. The group of women quarantined at the KSIFW was not simply in need of medical care; they needed instruction in respectable behavior. Or, as the board of health phrased it: "It is not generally appreciated that something more than drugs is required for the effective treatment of venereal diseases."[21]

This system of reporting venereal disease and then deciding who did and did not need to be quarantined at the KSIFW for treatment was subject to abuse, both on the part of individual citizens and government officials. The low bar for evidence and the general prevalence of venereal disease made Chapter 205 an easy mechanism to detain "problem girls" in the state. Social worker and researcher Alice Hill reported that government officials in Kansas first tried to deal with the young women that flocked to military bases during the war by committing them through the court system. This solution "did not cover the cases of girls whose delinquencies could not be proved in court, but who were sources of danger," leading to the use of Chapter 205 to detain women under a quarantine charge instead. The prevalence of venereal disease made this a viable solution since, in the words of Hill, the "girls committed through the courts, though arrested on various charges, were all infected with one or more venereal diseases." In Hill's account, Chapter 205 was intentionally used as a mechanism to imprison problematic women without the need for due process. Hill went on to comment that many of the women picked up around military bases "had been morally delinquent for years, though now committed for the first time chiefly because of the opportunity afforded the authorities by the new health regulations."[22] Chapter 205 opened up the opportunity for state officials to intervene in the sexual lives of young women who were not explicitly breaking any laws. A report from the Division of Venereal Diseases within the state board of health reported that, of the first 580 inmates at the KSIFW, 70 percent were there under Chapter 205, while 15 percent were there under a vagrancy charge. The report classified both of these categories as "a result of the campaign for the prevention of venereal disease," since vagrancy was "merely another procedure in dealing with this class of people."[23] State officials were looking for ways to detain women suspected of sexual activity in order to respond to federal pressures to control venereal disease among soldiers. Detaining women under a quarantine order rather than a criminal charge provided one avenue for avoiding the cumbersome demands of due process.

The relatively short sentence for quarantine patients made this solution less than ideal. Notes from a state board of health meeting on June 26, 1919, included the recommendation that health officers should try to get formerly quarantined patients who became "reinfected" to be "sent to Lansing under court sentence if the evidence will warrant such procedure, as the period of detention is apt to be longer under court sentence than under quarantine."[24] The underlying goal of this recommendation was that health officers and law enforcement should seek ways to detain women for the longest period of time possible, regardless of what their actual offense might have been. A 1933 independent evaluation of the KSIFW highlighted the problematic nature of this approach:

> There seems to be considerable feeling over the state as well as among certain officers of the prison that occasionally women are sent under the quarantine provisions of the laws simply as an easy way out of some police problem. The less pleasing term "railroading" is usually used in referring to this practice. It is impossible for us to give any statistics in this regard but the results of what investigation has been made justifies the assumption that it does occur. The charge "Hold for Interne" has been used by police powers to detain suspects of other crimes who otherwise might have secured release from jail. This practice, while undoubtedly rendering valuable aid to the police at certain times was scarcely the intent of the law.[25]

Rather than a criminal justice system built around offenses and corresponding punishments, recommendations about how to implement Chapter 205 encouraged state officials to use any legal mechanism available to detain women whom they deemed problematic.

Exacerbating Inequalities through Chapter 205

The discretion afforded to local health officers and the tendency to use Chapter 205 to detain women who failed to live up to standards of respectability allowed easy entry points for stereotypes about race and class to enter into decisions about who needed to be sent to the Farm. Kansas officials enforced Chapter 205 against poor and racial minority women at a higher rate, following a national pattern of American Plan laws having a disproportionate effect in minority communities.[26]

Officials implementing Chapter 205 in Kansas navigated a legacy of race relations that was full of contradictions. On the one hand, abolitionist settlers flocked to Kansas prior to the Civil War to fight for its entrance into the union as a free state. Nicodemus, a town in north-central Kansas, was at one point the largest all-Black settlement west of the Mississippi and a magnet for Black Exodusters fleeing the South after the end of Reconstruction. On the other hand, Kansas often failed to live up to its image as a haven for racial equality. These same abolitionist settlers displaced Native American tribes living in Kansas, and towns and cities across Kansas were often segregated by race. In an incident that prompted protests across the country, a Black soldier who was stationed at Camp Funston during World War I was denied admission to a local theater, leading to his commanding officer rebuking him and warning Black soldiers not to visit places where they were not wanted. Illustrating these contradictions around race in Kansas, the Ku Klux Klan had a following of some hundred thousand members in the state in the 1920s. Yet the state of Kansas banned the film *Birth of a Nation*, in part due to its racist depictions of Black people, and was the only state in the country to legally prohibit the KKK from operating in the state in 1927. While the idealism of the original abolitionist settlers was certainly alive in Kansas by the time the state began imprisoning women under Chapter 205, so too were strains of racism that worked their way into the implementation of the law.[27]

The population at the KSIFW reflected the overwhelmingly white racial makeup of the state, yet it also showed that minority women were more likely to be detained at the Farm than were their white counterparts. Census data from Kansas during this period paints a very white picture, with white people averaging 96.4 percent of the state's population, the Black population averaging 3.5 percent, and the "other" category making up less than 1 percent. Racial minority women were overrepresented at the KSIFW; between 1917 and 1942, white women averaged 78 percent of the population, Black women 19 percent, and Mexican or Indian women 1 percent. Immigration status did not seem to make as much of a difference as race, though this may have more to do with the way that immigration status was reported. Kansas census data from this period indicates that an average of 4.3 percent of the population were immigrants, while the average number of women listed as being from another country at the KSIFW during this same period was 1.7 percent.[28]

These overall numbers from the KSIFW biennial reports do not break down the category of "white," but an examination of the inmate interview sample to be discussed in later chapters reveals that a sizable number of Irish women were at the Farm. Of the 488 inmate interviews in the sample, 75 percent were white, 16 percent Black, 6 percent Native American, and 3 percent other.[29] Breaking down the category of white further, 55 percent of the total sample were women from a variety of northern European backgrounds, and a full 20 percent were women of Irish descent. Distinctions among groups of whites during this period were more prevalent than today, making some groups that would today be considered white, such as Irish, southern Europeans, or Jews, to be considered distinct racial groups. The fact that there was a relatively large population of women at the Farm who claimed Irish heritage suggests that social distinctions between categories of whiteness may have been at play in determining who would be sent to the KSIFW.[30]

Social class also factored into health officers' decisions about who needed to be sent to the Farm. One indicator of social class, occupation, suggests that the women imprisoned at the Farm were more likely to be from the working class.[31] Whether or not a woman was employed at this time was in itself an indicator of social class, as most families who could afford to have their wives and daughters forego paid work chose to do so. A comparison of the inmate population at the KSIFW with the general population of the state of Kansas reveals that the inmates were significantly more likely to participate in the paid labor force than their female peers outside the institution. In 1920, a year when only 15.3 percent of the female working-age population was in the paid labor force in Kansas, close to 85 percent of the women interned at the KSIFW reported some form of paid employment. While the young average age of the inmate population likely affected this number, since many women during this time period would work during their teen years before settling down in marriage, it nevertheless reveals that most of these women participated in the paid labor force.[32] The types of occupations listed for interned women also give some indication of their class status. The most common categories of female employment for inmates before coming to the Farm were common occupations for the working class: housework and waitressing. Though many of the inmates changed jobs frequently and might not have had an occupation per se, studies from the time suggested that many female inmates were domestic workers.[33] However, though in much lower numbers, there were some professionals interned at the Farm as well, primarily nurses, a few teachers, and a couple of doctors and chiropractors.

Other studies of the women at the Farm point to the conclusion that many of the women detained under Chapter 205 in Kansas were from lower socioeconomic backgrounds. In social worker Alice Hill's research about the backgrounds of the initial inmates of the Farm, she reported that of the sixty-three families on which they were able to get data, twenty-six had been the recipients of charity.[34] A 1933 report from the Public Welfare Commission examined the educational attainment of 29 girls at the Farm between the ages of 11 and 19. Of these 29, only 3 were at normal grade level, 10 were behind by one to two years, 12 were three to four years behind, and 4 were five to seven years behind where they should have been academically. This lower overall educational attainment could be an indicator of social class, as girls had to leave the school system to enter the paid labor force.[35] Another factor affecting the overall class makeup of the inmate population was the fact that some poor women actually volunteered to go to the KSIFW (see chapter 5 for more details). A combination of the high cost of venereal disease treatment and the lack of free clinics made this the only option for many women who sought treatment for their disease. The fact that women who could afford private treatment did not volunteer to be quarantined at the KSIFW meant that more working-class women were at the Farm compared to women with more economic resources. This mirrored national trends. Nationally, American Plan laws tended to have a larger impact on poor women. Research conducted under the US Interdepartmental Social Hygiene Board found that most of the women detained during World War I were working class and that 41 percent were unemployed at the time of arrest. The overrepresentation of poor women and women of color at the KSIFW was a result of the subjective nature of how Chapter 205 was implemented. The centrality of respectability in determining whether a woman should be detained or trusted to get treatment on her own created opportunities for biases related to race and class to enter into health officers' decisions.[36]

Broader Efforts to Control Venereal Disease

Incarcerating women suspected of having venereal disease was not the only part of the campaign against venereal disease that continued into peacetime. The Kansas State Board of Health emerged from World War I with plans to continue the educational and treatment options that had been part of the overall strategy to combat disease during the war. Administered through the Division of Venereal Diseases of the Kansas State Board of Health, which was created in June 1918 at the request of the federal government, Kansas officials sought a multifaceted approach to control syphilis and gonorrhea among Kansans in the first two or three years following World War I.

Part of these efforts through the Kansas State Board of Health involved providing free clinics to treat venereal disease throughout the state. Not everyone who was diagnosed with a venereal disease was sent to the KSIFW under Chapter 205. For those people who were deemed trustworthy and respectable enough to be treated as an outpatient, there were some treatment options available. Many doctors during the period refused to treat venereal disease due to its negative associations with illicit sexuality, yet many patients were able to obtain care through private doctors. A 1927 report prepared by Earle G. Brown, MD, of the board of health found that 42.04 percent of doctors in Kansas reported having cases of venereal disease under treatment, 47.5 percent reported no venereal disease cases under treatment, and 10.1 percent reported that they did not treat venereal disease.[37] Of course, given that the most effective treatment for syphilis at the time, Salvarsan, required weekly injections for up to a year, the high cost of treatment meant that this was a relatively small population of people who could actually have afforded to pay for private care. The cost of treatment for syphilis from a private physician in the early 1930s averaged from $305 to $380, but could be as high as $1,000. At these prices, some health economists at the time estimated that 80 percent of the US population would not be able to afford treatment.[38] For those who were not able to afford health care through private doctors, the Kansas State Board of Health offered some free clinics. The medical facilities at the KSIFW opened to the public several days a week to treat syphilis and gonorrhea on an outpatient basis. The number of free clinics in the state peaked in 1921, with eight clinics located throughout the state that could provide care for venereal diseases.

The Kansas State Board of Health also continued its educational campaign following World War I. Promoting the message that "the responsibility for moral training [should be placed] upon the parent and the home," the board of health sponsored speakers to address high school students and women's groups across the state about sex education and social hygiene.[39] The board of health also employed social workers to investigate the causes of vice in different communities and do follow-up work with venereal disease patients following initial treatments. Though repressive measures such as Chapter 205 were certainly a part of the board of health's approach to containing venereal disease following the war, it was only one of a number of ways in which the board sought to reduce the incidence of disease.[40]

However, as national interest and funding for venereal disease control dwindled in the 1920s, these broad efforts to control venereal disease were scaled back. Nationally, the pragmatic approach to alleviate the public health problems caused by venereal disease prompted by the war gave way to more moralistic understandings of the problem. The World War I military film *Fit to Fight* was deemed obscene in some states, and many worried that the government had gone too far in engaging in public discussions of sexuality. As public interest waned, so did funding. The US House did not renew funding for the Interdepartmental Social Hygiene Board in December 1920 after lobbying against it from the American Medical Association, which was wary of such a strong government role in health care. Kansas governor Henry Allen wrote to both Kansas senators to urge them to reintroduce funding for federal venereal disease control efforts, but this support was not enough. Congress did not renew funding for the Interdepartmental Social Hygiene Board. Yearly federal spending on venereal disease prevention dropped from $4 million per year in 1920 to $60,000 in 1926.[41]

As early as 1919, the Kansas State Board of Health began to feel the pinch of these dwindling federal and state budgets for venereal disease control. The biennial reports of the board of health of the early 1920s read like a laundry list of programs discontinued due to lack of funding: in 1919 the lab that processed venereal disease tests in Rosedale was closed for a month and a half due to a lack of funding; in 1920 the board of health reported that they lacked the funding to provide social workers to assist in tracking down venereal disease cases; and in 1921 they reported that the state had cut off all funds for local venereal disease control clinics and that the only way they were able to keep the state lab operating was through funding obtained through the Rockefeller Foundation. By the mid-1920s the board of health's plan to combat venereal disease consisted primarily of providing free medication to clinics and doctors to treat syphilis, including the health clinic at the KSIFW in Lansing. The 1932–1934 biennial report of the state board of health does not even mention syphilis.[42]

This decrease in services in the early 1930s coincided with the national economic depression that left fewer Americans able to pay for their own medical care. The number of clinics in Kansas that provided free care for venereal diseases had dropped to only four by 1930, including the clinic at the KSIFW in Lansing. At the same time, demand for public health services for venereal disease treatment nationally went up at least 20 percent between 1929 and 1933.[43] While free clinics would have provided needed medical services for patients when available, they also brought with them the threat of clinic medical staff reporting patients under Chapter 205 if they discontinued treatment. However unappealing it may have been, the option of going to a free clinic vanished for many Kansans as the number of free clinics in the state declined along with federal funding levels. Particularly in a rural state like Kansas, where a several hours' drive might stand between a patient and a clinic, the closing of clinics located throughout the state cut off one of the few options available to women in Kansas who wanted to get treatment for venereal disease. This situation led some women to go to the KSIFW in order to access health care. An evaluation of the KSIFW in 1933 critiqued this practice, observing that "women are frequently sent to the Industrial Farm for Women Clinic for no other reason than that they are unable to pay for private treatments in localities where no free clinics are in operation."[44] The combination of a poor public health infrastructure and poverty led some women to be sent to prison in order to get health care.

National public health efforts to combat venereal disease languished in the late 1920s and early 1930s but found a new champion when President Franklin D. Roosevelt promoted Thomas Parran to surgeon general in 1936. Parran launched a national campaign against syphilis, arguing that a rational, scientific approach, rather than a moralistic one, was necessary to combat this pressing national problem. In the spring of 1936 Parran published an article titled "The Next Great Plague to Go" in several national magazines outlining his plan to combat syphilis. Despite his critiques of moralistic approaches to venereal disease control, however, Parran's plan did not advocate the use of condoms to prevent the spread of venereal disease. Trying to avoid alienating Catholics through associations with birth control, Parran's campaign instead focused on educational efforts and free medical care. The public responded with great enthusiasm. By October Parran was on the cover of *Time* magazine, and Gallup polls were finding that 90 percent of Americans supported the federal government's efforts to combat venereal disease and the provision of free clinics for treatment. Riding this newfound enthusiasm for federal responsibility for public health problems, President Roosevelt signed the Venereal Disease Control Act into law on May 24, 1938, allocating significant federal dollars to states for venereal disease prevention programs for the first time since World War I. Though Parran himself did not make repression a central focus of his campaign, this renewed federal attention to venereal disease invigorated American Plan laws across the country. While Kansas had consistently enforced Chapter 205, other states had let their American Plan laws lie dormant and began to enforce them again as federal dollars became available.[45]

This increased federal investment led to an expansion in the Kansas State Board of Health's activities related to venereal disease control in the late 1930s and into the eve of World War II. For the fiscal year starting July 1, 1939, the state of Kansas designated $10,000 for venereal disease control, while the federal government allocated $58,425 of funds through the Venereal Disease Control Act. Most of this money went toward treatment and diagnostics, such as providing clinics, drugs, and laboratory facilities to identify and treat cases of venereal disease. However, some funding also went toward educational efforts: Dr. A. D. Gray toured rural areas of Kansas to educate doctors about the best practices for treating syphilis and to survey the availability of treatment in rural areas for the National Health Service.[46]

The reliance of state venereal disease control efforts on federal funding is illustrated in the fate of the Division of Venereal Diseases within the Kansas State Board of Health. After its start during World War I, the division saw decreases in staff and financial support. From 1923 to 1932, the division became one of the many responsibilities of the secretary of the board of health; it was run under the Division of Communicable Diseases from 1932 until 1936. In July 1936, as the federal government's renewed campaign against venereal disease gained steam and federal dollars were again allotted to venereal disease control, the Division of Venereal Disease became its own unit again, with a full-time staff member in charge.[47]

What is perhaps most striking about the records of the state board of health during this period is the nearly complete absence of any mention of the KSIFW. The biennial reports during World War I mention the KSIFW several times as part of the overall strategy of combating venereal disease. However, these references disappear entirely by the early 1920s. The incarceration of women under Chapter 205 became increasingly removed from the activities of the state board of health, to the point that it is not mentioned at all in the board's descriptions of their activities related to venereal disease control in the state other than an occasional reference to the health clinic at Lansing. By the time the board was again investing in venereal disease control in the late 1930s, the KSIFW was not even considered a component of their approach to controlling venereal disease. In 1938 the board congratulated itself on the "increased interest in the problem [of venereal disease] and the willingness of the public to consider it frankly" following its educational campaign, failing to even mention the fact that 269 women were incarcerated at the KSIFW under Chapter 205 in that same biennium.[48]

Legal Challenges

As states enacted American Plan laws across the country, detained men and women filed legal suits to challenge their imprisonment. Prior to World War I, American courts had frequently overturned laws to detain and test people for venereal disease, arguing that it violated an individual's right to due process. This changed in 1919 as a series of court cases affirmed the right of the state to test and quarantine people for venereal disease. An early and widely cited case was that of J. S. McBride in Seattle, Washington. The case centered on the question of who had the legal authority to decide who was diseased and needed to be quarantined. The Washington Supreme Court ruled that the legal authority to determine who was diseased belonged to the health officer, not the court. By saying that a venereal disease diagnosis was not subject to judicial review, this ruling had the effect of cutting off the possibility of legal action for people claiming not to be diseased. The McBride case was cited in court cases across the country as precedent for the authority of local health officers to enact American Plan laws.[49]

Another influential early case came out of the state of Kansas in 1919. In *Ex parte McGee*, three men who were sentenced to the State Quarantine Camp for Men for a gonorrhea diagnosis filed suit against the state, claiming that they were denied due process. The Kansas Supreme Court denied their request, arguing that the state's interest in protecting public health outweighed the individual rights that were limited by Chapter 205. The court argued that venereal disease "affects the public health so intimately and so insidiously, that considerations of delicacy and privacy may not be permitted to thwart measures necessary to avert the public peril."[50] Like McBride, the McGee case was cited in cases across the country as part of an increasingly strong court record of supporting the legal validity of American Plan laws.[51]

Nationally, court cases tended to affirm the state's power to detain and test people for venereal disease. There were, however, instances where individuals were successful in appealing their cases, and these cases often resulted in states or municipalities ceasing to enforce their American Plan laws. Both New York and Chicago briefly stopped enforcing their

American Plan laws in the early 1930s after successful legal challenges. Many cases hinged on the language in American Plan laws that health officers could detain and test anyone that they "reasonably suspected" of having a venereal disease. Given that "reasonably suspected" was an imprecise term, there was plenty of room for legal interpretation, and several people won their claims against American Plan laws by asserting that the health officer did not have enough reason to suspect them of having a venereal disease to test them to begin with. However, the court record was clear about one group of people who could always be considered "reasonably suspected" of having a venereal disease: prostitutes. Since prostitution was, by definition, a female crime in most states, this legal ambiguity about the meaning of "reasonably suspected" led to a more solid legal case for enforcing American Plan laws against women than against men.[52]

Another element of American Plan laws, indeterminate sentences, also gained a stronger legal footing for women than for men during this period. By 1920 the legal basis for separate punishments for men and women was solidifying, particularly due to a 1919 Kansas case, *State v. Heitman*. Building on earlier court cases, such as the 1908 US Supreme Court decision in *Muller v. Oregon*, that established the legal precedent that women and men were fundamentally different, the Kansas court endorsed the idea that the state could assign separate sentencing policies for men and women. Mrs. Heitman had appealed her indeterminate minimum sentence for a liquor violation, claiming that the separate sentencing guidelines for women violated her Fourteenth Amendment rights. The court rejected her claims, arguing that "woman enters spheres of sensation, perception, emotion, desire, knowledge, and experience, of an intensity and of a kind which man cannot know." This "radically different" feminine type demanded "special consideration in the study and treatment of nonconformity to law."[53] Under this ruling, the court endorsed the idea that women required different treatment under the law than men. Given their distinct personalities, women required longer periods of incarceration in more benevolent reformatories or work farms than did men, for whom shorter terms in local jails might suffice. This legal precedent for extended incarceration of female prisoners provided a stronger legal basis for quarantining women under American Plan laws than it did men.[54]

This solidifying of the legal precedent to detain women "reasonably suspected" of having a venereal disease and imprison them for indeterminate sentences amplified the gender differences in enforcing American

Plan laws that had started during the war, with fewer and fewer men being detained as time went on. This gendered enforcement of American Plan laws was, in the words of historian Barbara Meil Hobson, "one of the most blatant examples of sex discrimination in the history of American justice."[55] The expanded legal regulation of sexuality that was brought about during World War I fell primarily on women.

Support and Critiques of Chapter 205

The court of public opinion had mixed responses to the incarceration of women in Kansas under Chapter 205. Some newspapers, as shown by this quote from the *Hays Free Press* in 1918, reported on the imprisonment of women under Chapter 205 in a neutral way without much commentary: "More than 100 women now are at the Industrial Farm for Women on the prison grounds at Lansing, and more are arriving every week. . . . They are sent there on orders from the state and city health departments."[56] Other newspapers were more favorable in their reporting. Journalist Mildred Reed visited the KSIFW for several days just after World War I. She was thoroughly impressed with the wholesome meals and atmosphere created at the Farm through events like baseball games and dances. Reed also praised the ability of the superintendent to create a homelike atmosphere for both the sentenced criminals and the "social disease prisoner[s]" detained under Chapter 205.[57] In a 1919 editorial titled "Printers' Ink-Prophylactic," the *Emporia Gazette* promoted frank public discussion of venereal diseases and urged the community to support the US Public Health Service in their efforts to shut down houses of prostitution and enforce laws to quarantine patients. Though it did not mention Chapter 205 or what was happening in Kansas specifically, the editorial praised states that were "treating venereal diseases quite as openly and frankly as an epidemic of small pox."[58] Many newspapers in the state reported on the campaign against venereal disease in Kansas in neutral or positive ways.

On the other hand, many governmental committees and researchers who took a close look at the KSIFW during this period took issue with the injustices and inefficiencies of incarceration as a means of addressing the venereal disease problem in Kansas. Most critiques of Chapter 205 blended comments about the fairness of the situation and the more practical matter of whether this was the most effective way of combating venereal disease. These two sentiments can be seen in comments from a 1920 report from researchers who investigated the social backgrounds of the inmates of the KSIFW and published their results in the nationally distributed publication of the US Public Health Service. The researchers cited an example of two inmates at the KSIFW who were imprisoned under Chapter 205 while the man who gave both of them a disease went free. They argued that the "man's responsibility for contributing to a girl's delinquency and for the spread of venereal disease should be better recognized, and the man should be punished as well as the girl or woman."[59] The article went on to point out that men were seldom prosecuted under age of consent laws in connection with cases at the KSIFW, even though many of the women sent to the Farm were under eighteen. Dutch scholar Eugenia Lekkerkerker made a similar gender critique in her 1931 study of women's reformatories in the United States, commenting not only that the situation was unfair to women but also that "these one-sided methods, affecting only a negligible percentage of all persons affected with venereal diseases, are not effective means for venereal disease control."[60] Lekkerkerker pointed out that the system of imprisoning only women for venereal disease cases was both unfair and ineffective.

These critiques of the injustice of the situation often hinged on the respectability of the group of women in question. Social worker Darlene Doubleday Newby described the types of women being sent to the Farm during the initial influx of inmates in 1918: "Giddy young war brides who lingered around camp too long after their husbands went overseas, stupid prostitutes who were not clever enough to stay in hiding, [and] scores of wayward girls whose delinquencies could not be proved in court." Newby explained, "It was over the quarantining of this latter class of so-class 'innocent young girls' that so much furor was raised, and is still being raised."[61] This attempt to distinguish between respectable and disreputable young women was consistent with national trends, as federal officials were perplexed about what to do with otherwise respectable middle-class girls whom they characterized as getting caught up in "khaki fever" during the war. For these critics, the injustice of Chapter 205 hinged not on the fact that the state was officially endorsing the sexual double standard but on the respectability of the women in question.

Criticism from fellow prison administrators and government officials focused on whether Chapter 205 was the best method for addressing the venereal disease problem in the state. A 1938 government report reviewing prison facilities in Kansas was critical of the dual nature of the Farm as a prison and a medical facility, saying that the institution was "a sad confusion of a campaign to wipe out venereal disease with incarceration for crime." This report highlighted the confused mission of the KSIFW, particularly emphasizing how the practice of imprisoning women under Chapter 205 failed in the goal of reforming wayward girls. It went on to say: "Certainly the practice of dumping these problem girls into a state institution for short periods . . . is no solution of their problem."[62] A similar critique came from the 1929 edition of the *American Handbook of Prisons and Reformatories,* which commented about the KSIFW, "There is no question that these women should have hospital treatment but it seems equally clear that it might better be done in connection with some state hospital rather than with a correctional institution."[63] Overall, these critiques brought attention to the injustices created by the practice of imprisoning women under Chapter 205, but the major focus was on whether medical treatment was a legitimate part of the mission of a penal institution.

The presence of young girls at the Farm was one of the more controversial aspects of the institution. As a whole, the age of the women imprisoned at the KSIFW in Lansing was relatively young, as seen in figure 2.2. As this figure shows, most of the women confined at the KSIFW during this period were between the ages of thirteen and twenty-four. This was fitting with the general philosophy of women's reformatories: they were originally designed to reform young women before they could take the path of a hardened criminal. The demographics of the inmate population changed over time, however. As the general population of the Farm declined in the 1930s, so did the prevalence of younger women.

The presence of children at the Farm caused concern for many outside the institution. The population of children (under twelve years) remained low at the KSIFW throughout the interwar years, with the high being twenty-three during the two-year period ending in 1936. Female prisoners with children under the age of three could keep their children with them, according to the laws setting up the institution. Older children were often sent to the Farm for treatment of venereal disease, as regular juvenile offenders would have been sent to the Beloit Industrial School for Girls instead of the women's prison. A 1933 independent evaluation of the Farm recommended that Beloit develop the capacity to treat diseases to avoid needing to send girls to the Farm in Lansing. Concerned about the mixing of juvenile and adult offenders and the lack of proper educational

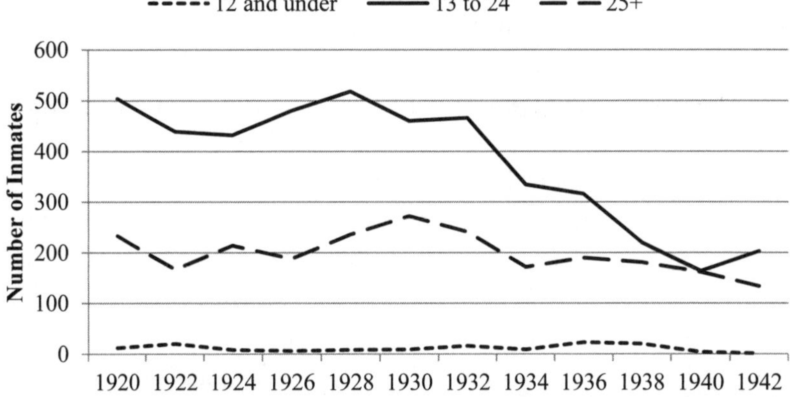

Figure 2.2: Age data for 1918 is not included because it was reported in a different format; that year's report listed the average age as twenty-four, with a minimum of fifteen and a maximum of forty-seven. For the 1936 data, the 13–24 age group is actually 13–25, due to how the report recorded the numbers. KSIFW 1918 Report, *12;* KSIFW 1920 Report, *21;* KSIFW 1922 Report, *13;* KSIFW 1924 Report, *27;* KSIFW 1926 Report, *17;* KSIFW 1928 Report, *16;* KSIFW 1930 Report, *17;* KSIFW 1932 Report, *17;* KSIFW 1934 Report, *14;* KSIFW 1936 Report, *13;* KSIFW 1938 Report, *18;* KSIFW 1940 Report, *29;* KSIFW 1942 Report, *26.*

programs at the Farm, the report noted: "There is a rather general belief among the professionally trained social workers in the state that the practice of sending young girls infected with venereal disease to the women's prison is fraught with social danger."[64] Although the numbers of girls at the Farm was always relatively low, this remained one of the more common points of critique of the institution.

Medical Treatment

Despite the criticisms mounted against it, the state of Kansas continued to enforce Chapter 205 throughout the 1920s and 1930s. Joining other American Plan laws across the country, Chapter 205 quarantined women under the authority of a medical diagnosis and subjected them to treatment from medical professionals. Foundational to the American Plan was faith in medical science. In the 1919 *Ex parte McGee* case, the Kansas Supreme Court rejected the plaintiffs' claim that they were not actually diseased, arguing, "The question is one of fact, determinable by practically infallible scientific methods."[65] Despite these "practically infallible scientific methods," both the diagnosis and treatment of venereal disease during this period were anything but reliable and safe.

Though scientific understandings of venereal diseases advanced greatly during the 1920s and 1930s, a clear laboratory diagnosis for gonorrhea or syphilis was far from a certainty during this period. Gonorrhea received far less public attention than did syphilis during the 1920s and 1930s, in part because it was hard to diagnose and in part because there were few effective treatment options available. The difficulty of diagnosing gonorrhea was problematic for state officials in Kansas charged with implementing Chapter 205 and providing care for the women quarantined under the law. For the health officer charged with deciding who should be sent to the KSIFW to begin with, this inaccuracy of diagnosis meant that social criteria, such as whether a woman was a prostitute, were often used in diagnosing venereal disease. For the physicians charged with treating venereal disease once the women were quarantined at the Farm, the lack of reliable diagnostic tests for gonorrhea posed another set of challenges. In 1920 the KSIFW physician lamented that it was "impossible to say what per cent of the women are infected with gonorrhea when received."[66] Since they could not reliably tell who had gonorrhea and who did not, the physicians at the Farm routinely treated all inmates (whether they were sentenced under Chapter 205 or another offense) for gonorrhea well into the 1930s. The 1942 biennial report stated: "Within the last three months we have instituted the use of the culture in the diagnosing our gonorrhea cases," indicating that this was a new practice.[67] This inability to accurately diagnose gonorrhea introduced another level of subjectivity into the process of implementing Chapter 205: not only was a woman's respectability an important factor in determining whether she needed to be sent to Lansing for treatment, but it was a factor in whether she was officially diagnosed with gonorrhea to begin with.[68]

While testing for syphilis was more reliable than testing for gonorrhea, a positive test result was still no guarantee that a woman was diseased. The most common method used to diagnose syphilis during this period was the Wasserman blood test. At the time, researchers were concerned about the rate of false positives with this test, projecting that between 2 and 14 percent of the results were inaccurate. Modern researchers have since concluded that Wasserman tests were so overly sensitive that as many as 25 percent of the results were false positives. In Kansas this meant that many women were likely sent to the KSIFW under Chapter 205 who did not in fact have a venereal disease. While board of health regulations permitted people to request to have a second test performed, this would have been at the expense of the patient.[69]

Together, the inaccuracy of diagnostic procedures for gonorrhea and syphilis led to the regular use of social criteria in determining who did and did not have venereal disease. This allowed state officials to use a law that was initially related to a specific disease as a broader ordinance to imprison women who violated the codes of female respectability within the state. There are several indications that women were sentenced under Chapter 205 who did not in fact have syphilis or gonorrhea. The KSIFW did not perform standard intake screenings for gonorrhea (all inmates were assumed infected and treated), but they did administer the Wasserman test to all inmates when they arrived at the Farm. Wasserman results from the 1920 biennial report were given for just the women sentenced under Chapter 205, revealing that 63 percent of the interned women tested positive for syphilis. For the reports from 1922 through 1942, results of Wasserman tests are only reported for the total inmate population (not just the quarantined women). These reveal that an average of 44 percent of the total inmate population at the Farm tested positive for syphilis at the time of their arrival, with a high of 62 percent in the 1924 report and a low of 25 percent in the 1940 report.[70] While interned women may have been sent to the Farm under a gonorrhea diagnosis, these numbers give reason to suspect that many of these women did not have a venereal disease when they were sentenced to Lansing under Chapter 205.[71] A 1933 independent evaluation of the KSIFW supports this conclusion, stating that "certain members of the prison and clinical staff state that occasionally women are admitted who have negative tests for the disease."[72] The doctor who took over as medical supervisor at the KSIFW in the mid-1930s noted: "During my short term as medical supervisor I have noted that several girls committed for treatment have been proved free of any venereal disease. The zealous social worker should make sure of the diagnosis by state laboratory tests before burdening the state with needless expense."[73] Far from the infallible scientific fact referenced by the Kansas Supreme Court's 1919 decision, there was considerable room for error in diagnosing venereal disease during this period in history.

Similar to the scientific uncertainty surrounding diagnosis, the exact dosage and treatment regime for gonorrhea and syphilis were unclear during the interwar period. Gonorrhea was a particularly challenging disease. While physicians sometimes prescribed oral medications or topical rubs containing silver compounds to try to alleviate gonorrhea infections, these were generally ineffective. A more effective treatment would not become available until the late 1930s, when researchers discovered that newly developed sulfa drugs were 90 percent effective in treating gonorrhea.[74]

Treatment for syphilis during the interwar period was also generally ineffective and in many cases caused more harm than good. At the turn of the twentieth century, the most common treatment for syphilis was mercury, a treatment that was not particularly effective and could cause fatal liver and kidney damage. In 1909 the first effective treatment for syphilis was discovered. Called Salvarsan, "606," or arsphenamine, the arsenic-based drug was not without its complications. Salvarsan was the first modern chemotherapeutic drug. Its high toxicity frequently led to nausea, vomiting, headaches, and open sores around the area of injection; the medical literature recorded a total of 109 deaths attributed to Salvarsan by 1914. It was also difficult to administer, requiring special handling to prevent the medicine from being ruined and a physician to give intravenous injections to the patient over a period of a year. Due to the painful, expensive, and lengthy treatment process, many patients stopped receiving treatments once their physical symptoms were relieved, even though they were still capable of transmitting the disease to others. By the 1920s the standard of care for syphilis was weekly injections of arsenic-based drugs (Salvarsan) rotated with mercury or bismuth compounds. Doctors and researchers continued to adjust the doses and timing of treatment during the 1920s and 1930s, but arsenic-based drugs remained the most effective method of treating syphilis until World War II.[75]

Whatever scientific consensus existed about how to treat venereal diseases was not necessarily reflected in everyday medical practice. The stigma associated with venereal disease often prevented this knowledge from reaching doctors, and thereby their patients. Medical schools spent minimal amounts of time teaching about treatments for venereal disease, and many doctors showed little interest in learning about a disease, let alone specializing in it, with such a strong social stigma. Actual patient care was thus far removed from medical knowledge. Although Salvarsan was a fairly effective treatment for syphilis if administered at the right time and for the right duration, only one in ten cases received treatment in the early stages of syphilis, when it could have been cured. Instead, many patients relied on quack remedies and homemade cures for venereal diseases and stopped medical treatments after immediate symptoms were relieved, even though they were still contagious.[76]

The treatment given at the KSIFW followed this general pattern of actual practice lagging behind the best scientific understandings of the time. Doctors at the KSIFW gave patients Salvarsan, but they also routinely gave them mercury, either intravenously or as a topical rub, into the early 1930s. Doctors treated all women imprisoned at the KSIFW for gonorrhea, administering local treatments to women several times per week. Given the generally ineffective nature of gonorrhea treatment during this time, however, many patients were never fully cured of the infection. In these cases, doctors at the KSIFW would cauterize their cervix, a procedure that may have gotten rid of infected tissue but would have also made the potential for future complications during childbirth more likely. These surgeries were more common in the 1920s, with a high of 137 reported in the 1928 biennial report.[77]

The treatment women received at Lansing was comparable to what they would have received outside of the institution. Indeed, given the high cost of treatment at this time, it was more than many of these women could have afforded. The KSIFW sought to provide the best possible care, providing, for example, dental services to all inmates starting in 1934, yet the primary limiting factor to effective treatment for a disease like syphilis was the short amount of time that women were interned in Lansing. Board of health regulations stated that women were to be released from quarantine once they were deemed noninfectious. For gonorrhea, this was usually defined as having three negative smears in a row. For syphilis, being noninfectious was defined as not having any open lesions or once the patient had received a specified number of treatments. Given that neither of these diseases had a cure at this time, the exact period of detention was somewhat arbitrary and depended on definitions of "noninfectious." In practice, women detained under Chapter 205 served sentences that averaged around four months (see figure 2.3).[78]

Throughout the interwar period, and particularly in the 1920s, the medical staff expressed dissatisfaction with the resulting level of "cure" for both gonorrhea and syphilis patients. The doctor in charge at the KSIFW clinic in 1924, Sherman Axford, commented: "The treatment of gonorrhea in women is necessarily both tedious and unsatisfactory. The

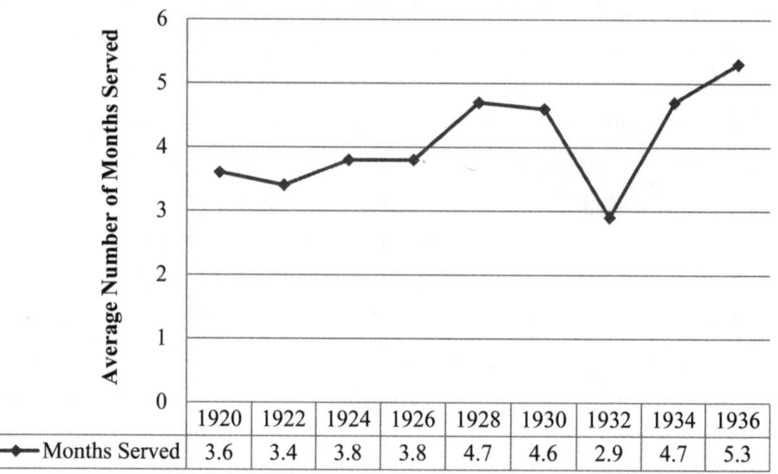

	1920	1922	1924	1926	1928	1930	1932	1934	1936
Months Served	3.6	3.4	3.8	3.8	4.7	4.6	2.9	4.7	5.3

Figure 2.3: Internment time for Chapter 205 inmates is not reported for 1918 or after the 1936 biennial report. KSIFW 1920 Report, *24;* KSIFW 1922 Report, *15;* KSIFW 1924 Report, *30;* KSIFW 1926 Report, *20;* KSIFW 1928 Report, *18;* KSIFW 1930 Report, *20;* KSIFW 1932 Report, *19;* KSIFW 1934 Report, *17;* KSIFW 1936 Report, *15.*

treatment of syphilis, while more scientific, is equally wrought with difficulties." Given that women were supposed to be quarantined at the Farm until "cured," Axford noted the gap between medical treatments available and official state policy: "The fact that it is well-nigh impossible to say when either disease is cured makes the quarantine officer's position an unenviable one."[79] The medical staff recognized the incomplete nature of the treatment given, viewing the care that women received as, ideally, a first step in the treatment process. The physician in charge of medical care in 1938 wrote that inmates should receive continued medical care in their home communities after they were released from the Farm, noting that it was "a physical impossibility to keep all the girls with syphilis at [the Farm] until they are cured. It would be a matter of months until [the] budget would be completely out of balance."[80] Thus, while the treatment offered at the KSIFW was fairly current with contemporary medical practices, it was still generally ineffective, in the case of gonorrhea, or for too short a duration to actually cure the disease, in the case of syphilis.

Another limitation to the effectiveness of the medical treatment at the KSIFW was inadequate resources, both in terms of facilities and staffing.

A 1938 governmental report revealed that "the equipment in the hospital [was] hopelessly inadequate and dangerous," noting that there was only room for fourteen of the fifty-eight venereal disease cases in the hospital as of February of that year.[81] The primary medical providers at the hospital were a physician, who worked seven hours per week, and a nurse, who was on call twenty-four hours a day and lived at the Farm. The reliance on one nurse to be the primary health-care provider to the number of patients going through the KSIFW was a cause for alarm for some outside evaluations of the institution, prompting the 1938 report to state that having only one nurse was not satisfactory and a separate 1933 report to comment, "Due to the seriousness of these cases the treatment of venereal diseases should never be in the hands of any other than a trained physician."[82] While there was a doctor in charge at the clinic, the bulk of the care was provided by an overworked nurse.

In Kansas and across the country, the legal infrastructure to quarantine women built through American Plan laws was far ahead of leading scientific knowledge about how to diagnose and treat venereal diseases. While American Plan laws were premised on the assumption that medical tests for syphilis and gonorrhea were accurate and that effective treatment for venereal diseases was possible, the reality was not nearly this straightforward. In many cases, women were detained who did not actually have a disease or underwent treatment that did more harm than good.

Conclusion

The state of Kansas first began enforcing Chapter 205 amid the crisis of wartime and a national outcry to keep soldiers safe from the ravages of venereal disease. As the policy carried through into the 1920s, the gendered pattern of implementation that began during the war continued, and guidelines about who should be detained placed women's respectability front and center. Chapter 205 took on an inertia that allowed it to survive dwindling federal funds to combat venereal disease and the departure of many of the individuals who had been instrumental to its original implementation. Samuel Crumbine, the secretary of the state board of health who had led the charge to fight venereal disease in Kansas during the war, left the state in 1923 to take a job in New York.[83] His leadership was no longer needed. The American Plan was in full force in the Sunflower State.

Though the practice of incarcerating women under Chapter 205 continued throughout the 1920s and 1930s, it became disconnected from any larger efforts to control venereal disease in Kansas. Instead of one component of a larger campaign to combat venereal disease, Chapter 205 continued as a mechanism for imprisoning women who violated norms for sexual behavior. Inaccurate medical testing led to social criteria being used in the diagnosis of syphilis and gonorrhea, centering the importance of a woman's respectability and opening up avenues for biases of race and class to enter into the implementation of Chapter 205. The law that had begun as a simple ordinance giving the board of health the authority to quarantine people had developed into a policy that reinforced social boundaries of race, class, gender, and sexuality in Kansas.

CHAPTER 3

"ANYTHING TO PLEASE THE LADIES"

THE ACTIVIST WOMEN WHO FOUNDED THE KSIFW

Before World War I and the national focus on venereal disease, before states across the country began passing American Plan laws like Chapter 205, before women like Hattie Campbell were sent to Lansing to be quarantined, the site that would become the Kansas State Industrial Farm for Women was a farmhouse in a field next to the men's prison. The story of how this site became a separate women's prison that would come to house thousands of women for no other crime than having a venereal disease starts with a group of women set on taking a role in shaping the future of Kansas. These women earned their political stripes during several statewide campaigns for suffrage, and, after finally winning the vote in 1912, they declared creating a separate women's prison in Kansas a top legislative priority.

The successful campaign to establish the KSIFW came at a crucial time for white activist women in Kansas. The eyes of liquor companies, conservative politicians, and journalists were watching to see what Kansas women would do with the vote, particularly as the national campaign for suffrage became more militant leading into World War I. Women invested their time, energy, and political capital into this campaign, and they emerged victorious. Yet their respectability as public actors was still very much in question. In 1917, shortly after the KSIFW was established, activist Lucy B. Johnston gave a speech to the Kansas chapter of the General Federation of Women's Clubs to celebrate their victory. No newcomer to lobbying for women's interests in the state, Johnston noted a shift in the attitude of male legislators toward clubwomen: "There is no longer derision or that mock chivalry attitude of 'anything to please the ladies' which is even harder for an earnest intelligent woman to bear. In its stead we found not only respectful attention but an honest desire for conference and cooperation with the new voters." Johnston reveled in the newfound influence that the vote gave women in Kansas, assuring her listeners: "The influence of women in the Kansas legislature before and after the year 1912 is in about the same ratio as the oxcart to the automobile."[1] Johnston's comments highlight the victory that the KSIFW represented to activist women in Kansas at the same time that they show the constraints of women's public role. The KSIFW symbolized the type of reform that these suffragists had been hoping for in fighting for the ballot. At the same time, though, Johnston's comments reveal how tenuous activist women's public role was: they were not far away from this attitude of "mock chivalry" on the part of male legislators, and had not yet won the right to vote on the national stage. Their respectability as public actors was still in question.

Besides giving them a topic around which they could organize, the fight to establish a separate women's reformatory in Kansas touched on issues that were intimately connected with white activist women's own social positions. Lobbying for a place to reform women who had strayed from middle-class notions of sexual propriety tied into larger cultural anxieties about evolution, sexuality, and the place of white women in the advancement of civilization. Between 1870 and 1920, Darwin's theory of evolution became increasingly influential in scientific and popular understandings of social conditions and the human race. Departing somewhat from Darwin's original theories, a wide range of people, from social scientists to newspaper reporters, began to understand the differences between the races in evolutionary terms. This framing of human civilization placed particular significance on the sexual behaviors of different groups of people, leading some reformers to seek ways to shape the reproductive potential of various racial groups to "improve" the evolutionary trajectory of the country. Known as the eugenics movement, this way of thinking informed public policy, reform work, and popular understandings of social conditions. When Lucy B. Johnston advocated for a place to reform her "lost sisters" in Kansas, then, it was not just about finding a cause that women could champion. Establishing the Farm was also about containing the threat that poor women's sexuality posed to the moral order and future genetic makeup of the state.[2]

Activist women in Kansas were not alone in trying to harness the power of the state to control women's sexual behaviors. The social hygiene movement sought to contain the threat that venereal disease and prostitution posed to the physical and moral health of the country through strategies such as sex education and passing laws to repress vice. Together with the eugenics movement, which came to encompass a variety of strategies to define and control the racial makeup of the country, the social hygiene movement infused many social policies and aspects of everyday life in the United States during the interwar period. Kansas emerged as a proving ground for many of these ideas. Fitter Families contests, in which families competed to see who best lived up to a "normal" (i.e., white) family ideal, debuted at the Kansas State Fair in 1920 before taking off across the country. More drastic measures to control the genetic makeup of the country were also tested out. Kansas had the third highest rate of involuntary sterilization in the United States, with the hospital at the KSIFW serving as a main site to conduct the operations on women and girls. In 1936 the Beloit Industrial School sent sixty-two girls to the hospital at the Farm to be sterilized, amounting to nearly half the population of the school at the time. From everyday events like state fairs to more draconian policies like forced sterilization, the social hygiene and eugenics movements permeated many aspects of life in the state of Kansas.

This chapter traces white activist women's involvement with key movements in Kansas—women's suffrage, women's prisons, social hygiene, and eugenics—to explore how anxiety about the future of the white race informed their activism and own social position. First, the chapter explores Kansas women's campaign for suffrage, a movement that was pivotal for their future political activism and established a racially informed identity for white women as public actors. Next, the chapter traces white activist women's actions to lobby for a separate women's prison in the state of Kansas. Fueled by their desire to do "women's work for women" and anxieties about the sexuality of poor women, activist women were successful in lobbying state legislators to establish the KSIFW as a separate institution in 1917, marking one of the women's first major legislative victories since gaining the right to vote in the state. This focus on controlling the sexual behaviors of young women continued as activist women moved on to other issues after establishing the Farm. Through their advocacy for social hygiene and promotion of eugenics in the 1920s and 1930s, activist women continued their efforts to define the bounds of proper sexual behavior.

This chapter explores activist women's involvement with women's suffrage, the KSIFW, social hygiene, and eugenics in relation to their own contested role as public actors. Within the framework of eugenics, these issues were not just about containing the sexual behaviors of young women. They resonated with the basis of white activist women's own social authority. Cultural associations between whiteness, purity, and self-control were crucial to white women's own respectability as public actors. As they made public arguments about the need for a women's reformatory, sex education, or stronger sterilization laws, these women also made arguments about the meaning of white womanhood and their own proper place in society. The boundary work that was accomplished through their activism reinforced their racial privileges and helped define a respectable public role for white women. This group of activist women were pivotal in creating a separate women's prison in the state of Kansas. At the same time, women's prison reform and social hygiene work were pivotal for them as they sought issues they could lobby for that would fit within ideas of white women's proper role in society.

Winning the Vote in Kansas

The life of Lucy Browne Johnston illustrates the typical biography of the women involved with creating the KSIFW. Born in Ohio in 1846, Johnston attended the Western Female Seminary in Oxford, Ohio. Following graduation, she taught grade school for four years before marrying an aspiring Kansas lawyer and politician, William A. Johnston. While William served in the Kansas legislature, Lucy settled down in Minneapolis, Kansas, with their two children. When Johnston arrived in Kansas, she would have found a state more receptive to women's participation in politics than many places during this period. Thanks largely to the efforts of journalist and women's rights advocate Clarina Nichols, the first legislature of Kansas granted women the right to vote in school board elections in 1861, making it only the second state in the country to do so. It was in Minneapolis that Johnston began her involvement with women's clubs and community activism. She was active in several women's clubs, campaigned to gain state funds for a traveling library, lobbied for the prohibition of alcohol in her hometown, and served on the local board of education for three terms. Johnston soon gained leadership experience in statewide and national organizations, serving as president of the Kansas State Federation of Women's Clubs from 1901 to 1903 and on the board of directors for the General Federation of Women's Clubs starting in 1906. William pursued a career in public service, serving in the Kansas House

Photo of Lucy B. Johnston from between 1911 and 1915. KSHS, "Lucy Browne Johnston," https://www.kansasmemory.org/item/208042.

and Senate before being elected to the Kansas Supreme Court in 1884 and as chief justice starting in 1903. Several aspects of Lucy Johnston's life history were typical of the clubwomen who would later lobby for the KSIFW: she was educated, had a well-connected and politically active husband, lived most of her life in cities or large towns, and had legislative experience in statewide and national campaigns.[3]

For Lucy Johnston, like many others, the campaigns for women's suffrage served as an introduction to political organizing. Women gained the right to vote in municipal elections in Kansas in 1887, but ballot measures to grant full suffrage to women failed to pass in both 1867 and 1894. The most powerful women in the state, including those who would later be instrumental in the fight for the KSIFW, pushed again for full suffrage in 1911. Active in the earlier statewide campaigns for suffrage, Lucy Johnston took a leading role in the third referendum on women's voting rights, serving as president of the Kansas Equal Suffrage Association. The much larger Woman's Christian Temperance Union (WCTU) lobbied hard for the measure as well, boasting that they had sponsored 509 suffrage essays by students, 1,294 lectures, and 1,728 columns submitted to newspapers, and had distributed 1,043,600 pages of literature.[4] The petitions, letters, and organizing paid off: the measure for women's suffrage passed the legislature (getting the bare minimum of twenty-seven votes to clear the Senate), was signed by the governor, and went up for popular vote on November 5, 1912. The suffrage amendment passed by sixteen thousand votes, making Kansas the eighth state in the country to grant women full suffrage.[5]

In their arguments for the vote in Kansas, suffragists drew on ideas of race and self-control that would also inform their later activism for the creation of the KSIFW, social hygiene, and eugenics. Nationally, many white female suffragists understood the capacity to participate in a democracy in racial terms, and this understanding informed their activism surrounding the fight for women's suffrage. Many women employed cultural associations between whiteness and civilization in order to argue for a more expansive role for white women in society. Their understanding of political self-governance as a trait unique to whiteness was widespread. Historian Matthew Jacobson argues that the capacity for self-governance was central to the definition of whiteness during the period between 1880 and 1940, and that critiques of such groups of "probationary whites" as the Irish and Italians frequently charged that they lacked the discipline and self-sacrifice necessary to be a voting citizen in a democracy.[6] This capacity for reason and self-governance was viewed as a racial trait unique to the white race, a result of generations of evolution and a symbol of the superiority of white civilization. The words "citizen" and "civilized" were loaded with racial meaning during this period in history in ways that are less visible today.[7]

Just as the abolition movement informed an earlier generation of suffragists, the white women who fought for women's suffrage between the 1870s and the 1920s drew from eugenicist and imperialist discourses to inform their identities and strategies for getting the vote. This was particularly visible in the struggle over the Fifteenth Amendment (ratified in 1870) and the debate about whether white women should support Black men's right to vote. Causing major divisions within the women's suffrage movement, many white suffragists struggled to reconcile their racial privileges with demands from a well-organized Black suffrage movement. White women's reticence was informed by the growing understanding of white people as the most evolved racial group and white women as particularly endowed with the qualities of white civilization. Some post-bellum suffragists drew on evolutionary discourses to argue for the vote, pointing out the absurdity of denying the ballot to white women while granting voting privileges to the supposedly "less-evolved" men of other races who lacked the self-governance needed to properly participate in a democracy. In 1869 Elizabeth Cady Stanton reasoned: "Think of Patrick and Sambo and Hans and Yung Tung, . . . who do not know the difference between a monarchy and a republic, who cannot read the Declaration of Independence or Webster's spelling-book, making laws for Lucretia Mott, Ernestine L. Rose and Anna E. Dickinson."[8] While early scholarship interpreted the racism in the suffrage movement as an unfortunate tactic used strategically to argue for the vote, more recent scholars have pointed to larger discourses of evolution, citizenship, and whiteness to show how central these beliefs were to white women's identities and social positions.[9]

Echoing the racial underpinnings of the national suffrage movement, white women in Kansas based their arguments for women's suffrage on evolutionary understandings of citizenship and race. Indeed, some of the racial tensions in the national campaign for suffrage emanated from early campaigns fought in Kansas. During the 1867 Kansas campaign, Susan B. Anthony and Elizabeth Cady Stanton upset much of the national movement when they allied themselves with George Francis Train, whose smooth talk and racist jokes made him a controversial proponent of suffrage.[10] Another example comes from a painting copyrighted in 1893 by Henrietta Briggs-Wall of Hutchinson, Kansas. Titled *American Woman and Her Political Peers,* the image featured WCTU leader Frances Willard in the middle surrounded by supposedly less evolved men. The painting was later turned into a flier, with this message printed on the back: "No one can fail to be impressed with the absurdity of a statutory regulation that places woman in the same legal category with the idiot, the Indian, and the insane person."[11] The juxtaposition of Willard, with her glasses and tidy appearance, as the symbol of white civilization, next to the unkempt and vacant looks of the other men intentionally drew on these evolutionary discourses to argue for women's right to vote. A member of the Kansas Equal Suffrage Association in the 1890s was quoted as saying: "Our cause represents what is right. It represents moral progress, the forward movement of civilization. It cannot be denied."[12] These examples from the failed 1894 campaign for women's suffrage (in which

American Woman and Her Political Peers, *a painting by Kansan Henrietta Briggs-Wall from 1893. KSHS, "American Woman and Her Political Peers," https://www.kansasmemory.org/item/208011.*

many women who would later advocate for the KSIFW were intimately involved) illustrate that the language of racial progress and the inherent capacity for self-governance among whites informed many women's understandings of themselves in Kansas.

For the women who would later lobby to create the KSIFW, the successful campaign for suffrage developed their organizing skills as well as their sense of identity as political actors. Another leader of the 1912 campaign for suffrage, Lillian Mitchner, became so well known in Kansas that she had to issue a statement denying that she was considering a run for the US Senate. Mitchner, who became president of the Kansas chapter of the powerful WCTU in 1909 and held that position for twenty-nine years, was an active presence in legislative affairs in the state. One political adversary lamented: "Lillian Mitchner can make the best chocolate pies you ever tasted, and I wish to Heaven she would stay home and make pies."[13] The suffrage movement not only developed women's political acumen; it also solidified their sense of efficacy and identity as political actors. As Lucy Johnston wrote in 1926, "I've always been interested in the betterment of humanity, and this has led me into work along church, school and political lines. Perhaps political I should put first, for I soon learned that the vote was more helpful than argument, so I soon became an advocate of political freedom for women."[14] Johnston was later quoted as saying, "The suffrage thread has run through all my work."[15] Kansas suffragists gained concrete lobbying experience and active social networks through their fight for the vote, tools that would be needed as they sought to use those newfound voting powers in the state.

Lobbying to Create the KSIFW

The Kansas Council of Women

After the successful campaign to win the vote, Kansas women wanted to capitalize on their voting rights to advocate for women's issues in the state. Together, a group of women that included Lucy B. Johnston formed the Kansas Council of Women, an umbrella organization for all of the white women's clubs in the state that would later spearhead efforts to establish the KSIFW. The council was founded in 1911 by women who were interested in turning Kansas women's newfound access to the vote into concrete social action. They wanted to unify the activities of state women's organizations in order to promote the greater good of the community.

Of particular interest were issues related to the status of women and children in the state. All presidents and past presidents of white Kansas women's clubs were members, as were female representatives from the state universities. The Kansas Council of Women was in many ways a lobbying group that represented state women's clubs. They had committees on such topics as education, citizenship, student housing, better films, and public health. The council also worked to try to get more women appointed to public office, such as the State Board of Regents. During the 1910s the council usually selected between two and five legislative priorities for the year. Once these goals were established, individual organizations were expected to mobilize in support of these measures.[16]

Given the breadth of the council, mobilizing this many women was no small matter. The Kansas Council of Women represented a host of women's groups (a 1915 report counted twenty-nine member organizations), including the General Federation of Women's Clubs, the WCTU, the Kansas Native Daughters, and the Kansas chapter of the American Association of University Women. The largest of these organizations, the WCTU, boasted ten thousand members and five hundred chapters in Kansas in the early 1910s. Altogether, organizations in the Kansas Council of Women represented approximately forty thousand women, according to a 1917 newspaper account. By 1928 another newspaper reported the membership as being closer to a hundred thousand.[17]

The Kansas Council of Women incorporated a variety of white women's organizations from throughout the state. As white women settled in Kansas in the late 1800s, they brought with them patterns of social involvement and knowledge of how to run women's organizations; Kansas women promptly started local clubs that were similar to organizations they had been involved with before moving to the state. Taking off in the 1870s and 1880s, white women's groups initially focused on self-education and created spaces for women to read the classics, discuss social issues, and gain practice in public speaking. White women's clubs united under the General Federation of Women's Clubs in 1890, providing them with national leadership and institutional support, though the topics studied by individual clubs remained locally controlled. White women's clubs transformed from groups focused primarily on self-education to groups centered on social activism in the 1890s. Clubs around the country began to take on such projects as establishing libraries and public parks, passing ordinances for food safety, and raising money for orphanages. This public work placed them at a crossroads in terms of their position within the gender order. They relied on traditional constructions of femininity based around motherhood and domesticity, but their public actions took them far outside the four walls of their homes. Employing the term "social housekeeping," these clubwomen used the language of the home to justify their involvement in areas that otherwise might have been considered off limits for women. The priorities of the Kansas Council of Women reflected this shift from self-education to social activism.[18]

While the Kansas Council of Women represented a variety of women's organizations, it did not include Black women's clubs.[19] This reflected national patterns of women's organizing along lines of race and class: while most women's clubs had a primarily elite and middle-class membership, there were also clubs for working-class women, and separate local and national clubs for women of different races. Black women in Kansas led a comprehensive and active statewide organization of women's clubs that paralleled the activities and priorities of white women's organizations. Importantly, however, these Black women's clubs were separate from white women's organizations and lacked the financial and political resources that white women could draw on to affect social change. The lines of racial segregation in women's clubs were often unstated but clear to everyone involved. Following a controversy about Black women wanting to attend the national convention of the all-white General Federation of Women's Clubs meeting in Milwaukee in 1900, a white clubwoman published an article in the *Topeka Daily Capital* praising Black women for working within their own race and not attempting to racially integrate the women's organizations in Kansas. A Black clubwoman published a response in the Black newspaper, the *Plaindealer*, commenting: "In localities where women are estimated by their intelligence, refinement and ability to do good club work, it may be [a] common sight to see a colored woman a member of a white woman's club, but it is not at all likely that we will see such a site as that in Kansas soon."[20] In her comment, this Black clubwoman argued for respectability, rather than race, to be used as membership criteria for women's clubs. However, it appears that this vision was far from reality. Black women's clubs in Kansas highlighted the arts, charity, and programs for Black youth, taking on fewer social issues than some national Black women's organizations. They lacked the financial and political resources to mobilize for the types of larger policy changes that the Kansas Council of Women undertook.[21]

Thus, the Kansas Council of Women represented a particular subset of women in the state, those who were advantaged along lines of race and class. Even within the council, there were important divisions between the leadership and the rank-and-file clubwomen that it represented. The fact that the council was made up of presidents and past presidents of women's clubs meant that only the most dedicated and career-like women were part of the council. These were not the women who showed up once a week to discuss Aristotle; these were the women who spent hours and hours organizing statewide campaigns, managing budgets, arranging for speakers, and lobbying legislators. When interviewed in 1928 about why she enjoyed working with the Kansas Council of Women, former president Mrs. C. C. Goddard stated: "Because the women of the Council are all trained workers and I do not have to coax and plead with them to act for they appreciate the big things that are being accomplished and are glad to do their part."[22] As "trained workers," these women were much more involved in the public sphere and more removed from domesticity. They were more fully committed to social issues such as suffrage than some of the rank-and-file members of their organizations.

The women of the Kansas Council of Women fit within a national movement of female activists who lobbied for women's prison reform. Due to their relatively small numbers, female prisoners across the country were often housed in men's facilities, exposing them to sexual violence and leading to few services or programs of reform that catered specifically to women. Agitation to improve the conditions for female prisoners came primarily from elite and middle-class women. Starting in the Northeast and other progressive strongholds, women spearheaded campaigns to lobby state governments to establish separate women's prisons. The general biography of the women who agitated for prison reform was similar to the members of the Kansas Council of Women: they were active in club life, well connected, and politically experienced, and they had the time, resources, and energy to devote to social change. Some of these women were more committed to prison reform in particular as an issue, taking over as superintendent or serving on the board of directors after the institution was founded. For many women, though, including most of the women who lobbied for the KSIFW in Kansas, founding a women's reformatory was one of a series of social issues that their organizations took on, with the women moving on to other issues after the reformatory was founded. In Kansas women like Lillian Mitchner bridged these two camps: she had a long career in public life in Kansas as head of the WCTU, yet she had more ties to the reformatory movement than most activist women in Kansas, having served as the superintendent of the Industrial School for Girls in Beloit from 1915 to 1919. Thus, the choice of lobbying for a women's prison in Kansas was partially a reflection of national patterns: women's prison reform was a common cause taken up by female reformers across the country.[23]

The Campaign to Establish the KSIFW

With a desire to capitalize on their newfound voting rights, the Kansas Council of Women set out to establish a women's reformatory as one of their first legislative priorities. In January 1914 the council tasked Mrs. J. S. Simmons with investigating the prospect of a separate women's reformatory in the state. At the time, female prisoners were held at the men's state prison in Lansing. Simmons prepared a four-page report that detailed some potential problems and guidelines for establishing a separate reformatory for women in Kansas. Of principle concern to Simmons was the low number of female convicts in the state and the challenge of finding an efficient way of providing services for such a small number. She considered the men's reformatory in Hutchinson, which housed men ages eighteen to twenty-five, a good model, yet there were only ten to twelve women in that age range at the state penitentiary at the time. One possible solution was to find ways to increase the number of female inmates in the state, an option that Simmons pointed out would involve creating or enforcing new categories of deviance specifically for women. Noting that there were few "thieves, murderers, and perjurers among young women," Simmons noted that "violation of laws governing Social Conduct is the most common crime among women."[24] Though there are no indications that the Kansas Council of Women sought out a policy like Chapter 205 directly, Simmons's discussion of the "violation of laws governing Social Conduct" anticipated how the facilities of the KSIFW would later be filled through the enforcement of Chapter 205. Simmons suggested that the women's reformatory be an annex to either the men's reformatory in Hutchinson or the Girls' Industrial School in Beloit as a way of consolidating bureaucratic structures to make the small number of female inmates more feasible. The location should be determined by the intent of the institution and whether it would focus on protecting society from more serious criminals or protecting vulnerable women from society while they were reformed. Again anticipating issues that would later arise with the KSIFW, Simmons commented: "It is possible that an institution might be built that would accomplish both objects, but I hardly see how it could be done without placing on a level the young woman who is preyed upon, the victim of harsh circumstance, and the young woman who is actually wicked and preys on others, and the murderer and thief."[25] Simmons's depiction of inmates as either victims of society or "wicked" women who preyed on others fit within larger patterns of classifying women as either sinners or saints. Women with more ambiguous relationships with middle-class notions of sexual propriety did not fit neatly into her framework. Despite these early hesitations about the purpose and feasibility of a separate women's prison, the Kansas Council of Women moved forward with advocating for a women's reformatory in the state.

On December 19, 1914, Arthur Capper wrote letters to women's organizations across Kansas. He was newly elected as the governor of Kansas and sought out the legislative priorities of this newly enfranchised block of voters, pledging to the recipients of his letters: "I shall be guided in no small measure, I assure you, by the views of the thoughtful women of Kansas."[26] What he received back from the women of Kansas was a well-coordinated and consistent message. Dozens of letters repeated a list of women's legislative priorities word for word. Julia Perry, who would later become the superintendent of the KSIFW, wrote to the governor-elect as a representative of the clubwomen of the Eighth District. Her letter listed fourteen legislative priorities, including one that called for "the enactment of a law establishing a detention home to shelter, protect, and reclaim delinquent women more than 18 years old."[27] Though some women wrote back only endorsing a smaller number of the statewide issues, the consistent message conveyed in these letters illustrates the political discipline that Kansas women had acquired during their fight for suffrage.

A few women elaborated on this call for a women's reformatory. Magdalen Munson, writing on behalf of the Kansas Good Citizenship League, urged that the women of Kansas and the legislature slow down to give careful consideration to a series of women's priorities. In reference to a women's reformatory, she wrote: "I am not in favor of a law that will commit women for moral delinquencies, that would not apply with equal force to men. Women cannot be legally committed for moral lapses unless it would include men also." Munson's hesitation partially stemmed from the limited time that was given to debating the measure before it was endorsed. She noted: "We did not have time to go through the details of this proposed legislation and I am not sure those present had a clear idea of what the legislation was meant to be."[28] Munson's comments reveal that many of the limitations and issues outlined in Simmons's earlier report were not necessarily common knowledge among the clubwomen who went on to endorse the measure to establish a women's reformatory in Kansas. Part of Munson's caution about moving too quickly on women's legislative priorities stemmed from her awareness of the larger political consequences of women's lobbying in Kansas. She closed her letter with the statement: "I am very anxious that Kansas women should do something to show that they have made good with the vote. It is the best thing that we can do to help the disenfranchised States."[29] While Munson was concerned about the equity of laws that might punish women for offenses that did not apply to men, other clubwomen in Kansas had no such reservations. Mrs. C. W. Smith of Stockton, Kansas, wrote to Capper: "There is a feature of our laws that I have long deplored. I think that we do not care enough for the protection of young boys—boys just entering manhood. If a law could be enacted providing for the severe punishment of a woman who enticed a boy into lewdness or lasciviousness—to put the term mildly—I should strongly favor such a measure."[30] Whether they favored careful deliberation and equitable laws or sought legal changes to punish women in order to protect "young boys," the women of Kansas made their endorsement of a women's reformatory clear to the incoming governor of Kansas.

In 1915 the Kansas Council of Women officially declared the creation of a separate women's reformatory as one of two pieces of legislation that they would prioritize for the year. They went about systematically investigating the prison conditions in the state and developing a plan for a reformatory. Similar to many other progressives during this time, the Kansas Council of Women wanted to utilize the methods and expertise of social scientists and take a thoroughly modern, objective position on this issue. They embarked on what Kansas Council of Women member Mrs. C. C. Goddard later called a "long study of prison conditions" in the state, systematically collecting data about women's rate of imprisonment in local jails and state prisons.[31] Lucy Johnston was intimately involved with these investigations into women's prison options through her role on the legislative committee of the Kansas Council of Women and her position as head of the legislative committee for the Kansas Federation of Women's Clubs. In a series of letters between Johnston and Frank Blackmar, a sociology professor at the University of Kansas, Johnston sought Blackmar's advice about the latest social science recommendations for the name, location, design, and overall philosophy for a women's reformatory in Kansas.[32] Mostly following Blackmar's advice, Kansas women advocated for an institution designed to rehabilitate women, rather than punish them, through hard work and the development of job skills. The clubwomen envisioned this reformatory as a place for everyday offenders rather than a place to house sexual deviants in particular. They sought a location that was far from the vices of the city, hoping that fresh air and hard work would help women prepare for life outside an institution.[33]

In other parts of the country, female prison reformers cited sexual abuse of female prisoners by male guards as a motivation for reform. This critique of men was largely missing in Kansas, however, where activist women worked closely with male politicians and prison officials.[34] In arguing for a women's prison, Kansas women emphasized the need for women to be truly reformed through serving longer sentences rather than the potential for victimization by men. In a newspaper article published shortly after the passage of the bill funding the KSIFW, the clubwomen praised the "clean-minded, intelligent men from country, town and city districts" who made up the Kansas legislature. The article argued: "Sometimes it is because of a spirit of chivalry or mistaken kindness on the part of judge or jury" that women were "passed on to the next town or given a light jail sentence and later paroled." This hesitation to commit women to prison left communities vulnerable to "the evil wrought by women criminals who are let at large."[35] Under this understanding of the conditions of female prisoners, it was male chivalry, as seen in men's tendency to give women light sentences, not outright abuse of male power, which was the problem. This more agreeable attitude toward male politicians and prison officials was likely due to clubwomen's close social ties to these men. For example, the husband of a member of the committee to establish the KSIFW for the Kansas Council of Women, Mrs. J. K. Codding, was the warden of the state men's penitentiary at Lansing in 1917.

Once committed to establishing a women's prison in Kansas, members of the Kansas Council of Women got to work. According to a 1917 report of the Kansas chapter of the General Federation of Women's Clubs (KGFWC), which was particularly involved with advocating for the Farm, "the club women of the entire state were urged to begin a systematic educational campaign in each county immediately following the Fall election, to the end that no member of the House or Senate could come to the legislature without a definite knowledge of the . . . important measures which the club women wanted passed."[36] They went on to initiate a letter-writing campaign, schedule meetings with the board of management, consult with an attorney to draft the legislation, and select Rep. A. M. Keene in the House and Sen. Charles S. Hoffman in the Senate to introduce their bill. The reformatory bill made it through the Senate with relative ease despite some opposition from newspapers. After stalling in committee in the House, the bill was finally put to full vote and passed with only three dissenting votes on March 8, 1917. The final bill, which went into effect April 5, 1917, allotted $75,000 for a reformatory. Considering the fact that the Farm had fewer than twenty inmates at the time, this was an impressive expenditure of state resources.[37]

Arguments for the Farm

In their arguments for establishing the KSIFW, the clubwomen of Kansas repeatedly stated their responsibility to share their values and way of life with those women in the state who had lost their way. The Kansas Council of Women envisioned their work to establish the KSIFW as, in the words of one 1916 newspaper article, "primarily a work of women for women."[38] In an undated speech about the KSIFW given before the legislation was passed, Lucy B. Johnston argued that "the care and handling of the criminal woman, be she old or young, good or bad, weak or strong, should be in the hands exclusively, of women. A woman Board, a woman superintendent, and woman keepers and teachers; the handling of the woman problem is a woman's job." Johnston envisioned clubwomen as the natural people to take the lead in reforming female criminals in the state. Her speech went on to say: "This problem of the care of dependent, delinquent and penalized girls and women is as old as humanity. . . . Shall the women of Kansas solve the conundrum? I believe they can if they will."[39] By portraying clubwomen as the natural leaders for women's prison reform, these activists carved out a space in the public sphere not only for themselves, but also for the professional women who would later staff the KSIFW.

The public reaction to activist women's efforts to establish the KSIFW indicates how successful this strategy of "women's work for women" was for establishing a respectable public role for white women. Newspapers in Kansas widely reported on the bill to establish the KSIFW as the "women's bill" and credited the establishment of that institution to clubwomen in the years following its passage.[40] A 1920 article about the Farm declared: "Kansas women decided that women no longer should be kept in the barred cells behind the high walls of the state penitentiary at Lansing." The article went on to argue that "the urgent request made by hundreds of Kansas women" was a significant influence in the legislators' decision to establish the KSIFW.[41] Johnston's report to the Kansas chapter of the General Federation of Women's Clubs about the 1917 campaign to establish the KSIFW indicated that clubwomen's letter-writing campaigns received some degree of attention from lawmakers: "These letters began coming in to the members early and continued to come until the last day. It was not unusual for a member or senator when approached by a friend of the bill to draw a letter out of his pocket and say 'Yes, I will vote for that bill. The club women of our town are for it.'"[42] The sponsor of the bill, A. M. Keene, stated that the measure to create the women's prison was "one of the few measures that all the women of the state are asking of this legislature. One hundred thousand club women are back of it."[43] This recognition of the KSIFW as being within the jurisdiction of white female activists granted a respectable public role for these women to play in public life.

Though the Kansas legislature passed the bill creating the KSIFW during the same legislative session as Chapter 205, no records have been found to indicate that these pieces of legislation were connected at the outset. Chapter 205 came to be implemented in a way that populated the facilities at the KSIFW with women quarantined for venereal disease, yet the legislation itself was very broad, simply giving the board of health the power to quarantine individuals in circumstances that it deemed necessary for the protection of public health. Similarly, the legislation to establish the KSIFW does not explicitly mention venereal disease, only the typical female inmates of the state who were convicted of a crime. The Kansas Council of Women had been working on this legislation for several years leading into the 1917 legislative session, long before the nation sat on the precipice of World War I and national attention came to be focused on venereal disease.

While no evidence has been found to indicate that these legislative measures were connected from the outset, there are hints that the women who lobbied for the Farm anticipated that the women who would be detained there may need specialized medical care. A 1916 newspaper article detailing women's arguments for a separate women's reformatory mentioned that the institution should be located close to a hospital.[44] Similarly, a newspaper article written by activist women in May 1917, which was after the passage of both pieces of legislation but before the state had started enforcing Chapter 205 on a large scale, provided as a justification for the establishment of the KSIFW that girls and women would not be admitted to the Girls' Industrial School if they had an infectious disease, and thus they would have nowhere else to go without this new institution.[45] These statements indicate that, regardless of how they felt about the way that Chapter 205 came to be implemented in the state, many activist women in Kansas understood this new institution as a place that may house women for sexuality-related offenses or venereal disease. Though it does not seem that Kansas activist women envisioned the Farm as being primarily defined by its treatment of women with venereal disease, the focus on imprisoning women who violated sexual norms was consistent with patterns of female imprisonment and the growing state regulation of women's sexuality during this period.

This conflation of female prisoners with sexual offenders was consistent with widespread beliefs about the importance of sexual behavior to a woman's respectability. It also drew on wider discourses about evolution and the role of different racial groups. The fact that reformers' and legislators' focus came to rest on the sexual behaviors of poor and racial minority women was no accident. An evolutionary understanding of race relations differed from earlier conceptions of race because of the possibility, and, indeed, inevitability, of change. Earlier groups of whites may have viewed other racial groups as being inherently less intelligent in a similar way as someone in the late 1800s would, but Darwin's theory posited that these groups had the possibility of evolving. The flip side of this was that the white race also had the possibility of *devolving*, adding a sense of anxiety to the category of whiteness that was not there before. Women played a particularly important role in this drama of civilization since, in the words of historian Wendy Kline, their ability to reproduce made them "responsible not only for racial progress but also for racial destruction."[46] Writer and reformer Charlotte Perkins Gilman highlighted this important role for women when she wrote in the *North American Review* in 1927: "The business of the female is not only the reproduction but the improvement of the species."[47] Cultural anxiety around the future of the white race focused on women's reproduction, and, more specifically, which women were reproducing.[48]

This angst around the category of whiteness and female reproduction can be seen in the way that Kansas activists constructed female inmates as a hazard to the future of the white race. Their discussion of the need to truly reform female offenders rather than let them off with light sentences stressed the domino effects women's morality could have on the community. As Lucy B. Johnston said in a 1913 report on the Girls' Industrial School, women had "an influence for weal or woe on the future citizenship of Kansas."[49] Insufficiently reforming female offenders was a threat not only because of the moral dangers it posed but also because of the possibility of reproduction. Indeed, a major way that activist women articulated this anxiety about poor women's influence on their communities was through concerns about the reproductive potential of female prisoners. In a newspaper article published shortly after the KSIFW was established, representatives from the Kansas Council of Women justified the need for the Farm by stating: "All girls leaving the Beloit school [the girls' reformatory] at 21 years are not fit for citizenship, so she and the diseased girl are turned back into the community to degrade and pollute our young people, or to marry someone of her own kind and bring more of the unfit into the world, thus refilling our jails, penitentiary, imbecile asylums, insane asylums, reform schools and poor houses." This statement constructs young women's sexuality and ability to reproduce as being at the heart of the threat that they pose to the community. The article went on to argue: "It takes many hundred thousand dollars every year to feed, clothe, house and manage this ever increasing number of unfit. Is it not wise to cut off the supply by segregating at least those who violate the criminal laws of the state?"[50] While the newspaper article pointed to the alleged drain on state resources as a reason to fear these women's reproductive potential, prisoners' racial similarity to the clubwomen was another factor in why this was so threatening. Clubwomen viewed this group of women as being from a distinct "other" (as indicated by the comment that they would "marry someone of [their] own kind"), yet the boundaries surrounding whiteness were blurry, and there was often very little stopping an average person from thinking that the elite clubwomen from Topeka and the inmates from Lansing were from the same racial stock. As Karin

Zipf notes in her study of North Carolina's efforts to control syphilis, the very presence of promiscuous white women threatened the "foundational association between chastity and whiteness" that informed white activist women's own social status.[51] Activist women were invested in protecting the purity of whiteness, both in ideological terms as well as at the level of human reproduction. Creating a prison to reform these wayward women not only provided an issue around which white activists could respectably lobby; it sought to change the behaviors of those "less civilized" groups that potentially threatened the purity of the white race.

The ultimate effects of activist women's efforts to create a separate women's prison in Kansas began to unfold as the institution became established. Prior to the passage of the legislation that offiically established the KSIFW, female prisoners were already being moved from the men's state penitentiary to a farmhouse on the prison grounds. Perhaps influenced by his wife's activism to lobby for a separate women's prison, Warden J. K. Codding ordered that twelve women be moved to the farmhouse in 1916, soon making Julia Perry the supervisor of this annex to the men's prison. When the legislation officially establishing the KSIFW went into effect in April 1917, it formalized this arrangement and officially made the Farm a separate institution. The location of the Farm in Lansing was supposed to be temporary. The legislation establishing a women's prison in Kansas called for the institution to be at least seventy-five miles from a city in an effort to distance the inmates from the suspect morals of modern life. Individuals across the state were eager to bring the women's reformatory, along with the jobs and economic impetus it could provide, to their cities; newspapers reported Beloit, which was the site of the Girls' Industrial School, and Hutchinson, which housed the men's reformatory, to be strong candidates for the permanent location of the institution. As late as March 1919, Julia Perry wrote to the governor to inquire about the permanent location of the KSIFW, noting that the women at the Farm were "feeling very blue" about the prospect of staying in Lansing and had hoped for a new location.[52] The rapid influx of women detained under Chapter 205 beginning in the fall of 1917 cemented the location in Lansing, however. Prison officials built facilities to house the quarantined women, and soon the KSIFW had expanded beyond the original farmhouse and established the physical structures that made moving the institution more challenging. Like many other aspects of the institution, the large number of women detained under Chapter 205 drastically changed the trajectory of the KSIFW.[53]

Following the passage of the legislation that established the KSIFW, clubwomen were not intimately involved with the day-to-day functioning of the institution. Immediately after the legislature approved the measure, eight women issued an article in the *Topeka Capital* justifying the necessity of having a separate women's prison for such a small number of female convicts in the state, but their activism around the issue of a women's prison seems to have trailed off after this.[54] There are a few references to clubwomen in documents related to the KSIFW in later years, such as a note about Mrs. J. K. Codding (the wife of the warden of the men's prison) giving a sermon at Sunday service to inmates in 1918 or to clubwomen donating books to the library at the Farm in 1940.[55] Nationally, the political influence of white activist women was recognized in the 1929 *Handbook of American Prisons and Reformatories*, which lamented the lack of resources given to women's prisons and identified clubwomen as the ones that should take up their cause.[56] However, clubwomen in Kansas were not major players in the day-to-day operations of the Farm.

Containing the Threat of Poor Women's Sexuality

In the state of Kansas, as well as nationally, women's organizations like the Kansas Council of Women became less active and influential in the 1920s. The decline in women's clubs reflected several trends: the opening up of other professional opportunities for women, the loss of a unifying cause after suffrage was passed, and the growth in government responsibility for many issues that women had originally championed.[57] Though Kansas activist women were less organized and influential in the 1920s and 1930s, their understanding of female deviance, the sexual behavior of different groups of people, and their own positions along racial and class hierarchies continued to shape their actions. Activist women in Kansas sought to contain the threat that they perceived poor women's sexuality as posing through two strategies: promoting social hygiene and eugenics. Given their understanding of the types of women who might be imprisoned in the state, activist women made an easy transition from their advocacy for the creation of the KSIFW to their promotion of social hygiene and eugenics legislation in the 1920s and 1930s.

Social Hygiene

In the 1920s many of the organizations that had been involved with founding the KSIFW turned their attention to social hygiene work in Kansas. They joined a national social hygiene movement that had been shaped by female reformers from its outset. Female moral reformers were some of the founding members of the American Social Hygiene Association (ASHA). Their desire to promote a single standard for sexual behavior was initially promoted through ASHA, yet as the unequal enforcement of venereal disease laws along lines of gender—what came to be known as the American Plan—emerged during World War I, many of these female activists expressed concern about the direction that the movement was taking. Women like Maude Miner and Ethel Sturges Dummer began the war working for the federal government to do social work with young women, yet they quickly found that their original goal of reforming wayward women was a lower priority than protecting the health of male soldiers. Dummer, a wealthy Chicago elite, funded some of the protective work for girls herself after the federal government failed to invest; she became so disillusioned with the way the American Plan developed that she later offered to finance a lawsuit on behalf of quarantined women. Dummer wrote in a letter to a fellow reformer in 1918: "Why should a woman be imprisoned for a disease when the man, as responsible, goes scot free?"[58] Like Miner and Dummer, the League of Women Voters was complicit in promoting the American Plan before gradually becoming aware of the problematic nature of their work. Founded in April 1919, the organization quickly established a Social Hygiene Committee and pushed for the adoption and enforcement of American Plan laws across the country. Yet by 1920 this committee endorsed a resolution that stated: "We urge the impartial administration of all laws and regulations, since when they are enforced more vigorously towards women than towards men, it seems to give governmental sanction to the double standard, and also fails adequately to protect the health of women, who constitute one-half of the entire public."[59] By 1927 the committee was actively lobbying against American Plan laws and gender discrimination in health regulations. What began as an effort to promote women's rights through endorsing a single standard for sexual behavior had quickly ballooned into a repressive system of controlling women's sexual behaviors.[60]

Other women had less ambiguous relationships with the American Plan. Doctor and reformer Katharine Bushnell was a vocal critic of the

American Plan from the outset, writing a report titled *What's Going On?* in 1919 that recounted her undercover investigations of American Plan enforcement in California. In a letter to a federal official in 1920 that opposed the ways that American Plan laws were being enforced, Bushnell proclaimed: "Soon every woman who is not at heart a prostitute to the task of pleasing the male sex at cost of the virtue of other women will rise against your measures."[61] Bushnell was acutely aware of the gendered implications of the American Plan and spoke out forcefully to try to oppose it. Other women wholeheartedly endorsed social hygiene initiatives that placed the blame for sexual behaviors on women. The General Federation of Women's Clubs collaborated with the Public Health Service in 1922 to develop sex education materials for girls. One pamphlet warned young women that any careless enticement of a man's sexual desires made them "responsible for his temptation and mistakes."[62] Whether they brought a gendered critique to their work or not, women shaped the national social hygiene movement from its very beginning.

In Kansas activist women advocated for sex education and venereal disease control in the years following World War I. Like many of their counterparts nationwide, it does not appear that Kansas female reformers were particularly aware of or concerned about the endorsement of the sexual double standard that the social hygiene movement often entailed. Despite the fact that one of their main initiatives, the KSIFW, was drastically changed by the influx of women detained under Chapter 205, no records have been found of activist women publicly critiquing the uneven enforcement of Chapter 205 along lines of gender.[63] In the web of social hierarchies that Kansas activist women navigated as they tried to stake a claim to a respectable role as public actors, the implications of their activism for the gender order were not at the top of their minds. Informed by ideas of evolution and eugenics, these women's positions along hierarchies of race and class situated them to claim social hygiene work as being a particular responsibility for white women.

Claims that public health work fell under the purview of white clubwomen came from multiple sources. A 1925 article in the publication of the Kansas State Federation of Women's Clubs, the *Federation News,* called for women to get involved with social hygiene work in the state, querying, "We are told that without the intelligent cooperation of an educated public, the success of the physician and public health worker is practically valueless. Who is going to be the educated public in Kansas? Who indeed if not the club women?"[64] Documents from the board of health reinforced this idea that clubwomen were a close ally in the fight against venereal disease. The secretary of the Kansas State Board of Health, Samuel J. Crumbine, repeatedly asserted his appreciation for clubwomen in Kansas and his regard for them as an important educational and lobbying force within the state.[65] In an undated article (likely from the early 1910s), Crumbine expressed gratitude "for the moral support as well as the active co-operation of the Kansas Federation of Club Women," noting that the board of health would get in touch with women's clubs before bringing a speaker or exhibit to a town and that clubwomen would "lend their influence in getting" people to attend.[66] Crumbine later turned to clubwomen for help as state funding for venereal disease work declined in the early 1920s. He published a letter in the May 1922 edition of the *Federation News* imploring clubwomen to lend their "energetic support" to lobbying legislators to provide more funding for venereal disease control.[67]

Educating clubwomen was an explicit part of the board of health's campaign to eradicate venereal disease in Kansas. An organizational chart printed in the board of health's 1926 biennial report listed "women's clubs" alongside such things as films, newspapers, and public speakers under the category of "Public Health Education."[68] The board put on several conferences about social hygiene in the 1920s that were specifically targeted to activist women in the state. One "Lay Woman's Conference on Social Hygiene" that was put on by the Kansas State Board of Health and the US Public Health Service in April 1922 had more than 150 women enroll.[69] A similar event held the next year reportedly attracted seven hundred.[70] An article in the *Federation News* promoted one such event in March 1924, detailing how it would "be in the nature of a clinic where club women may bring their Public Health troubles for diagnosis and suggested treatment." Members of the state board of health and leading medical authorities would be on hand to answer clubwomen's questions. The article assured clubwomen that the meeting would "offer an opportunity to discuss [their] local health problems, to hear 'boiled down' stories of successes and failures in other towns, and to secure advice and guidance from experts who have been all over the ground and are still looking for the ideal solution."[71] Clubwomen took ownership over "their Public Health troubles," claiming this issue as something that was solidly within their jurisdiction as public actors. Though other documents indicate that these meetings may not have resulted in much concrete action on the part of clubwomen, the fact that the board of health hosted these events indicates how seriously clubwomen were taken.[72]

The educational campaign for clubwomen extended to the written form as well. In 1924 the Kansas State Board of Health produced a pamphlet about venereal disease that was specifically targeted at clubwomen.[73] Put together by Buena Burr, the educational director for the Division of Venereal Diseases within the board of health, the pamphlet included a plan of study for clubwomen, lists of the laws and policies in the state of Kansas that related to venereal disease, legislative priorities, and things that could be done at the community level to prevent the "social diseases." The primary goal of the document was to educate clubwomen about the current policies of the state of Kansas and enlist their support for future action. What is perhaps most notable about this pamphlet is that it did not even mention the fact that hundreds of Kansas women were being sent to the KSIFW each year to be quarantined for venereal disease under Chapter 205. The pamphlet listed the laws regarding quarantine and the procedures to be followed by health officers in quarantining women, but it did not mention the fact that women, but not men, were being quarantined for venereal disease or the numbers of women detained. This reflects a general lack of coordination between government divisions, with the board of administration being in charge of the KSIFW and the board of health in charge of the venereal disease campaign. It also indicates that clubwomen in Kansas may not have been aware of how Chapter 205 was being implemented in the state and the numbers of women being detained. Regardless of the extent to which activist women were aware of what was happening at the KSIFW, the fact that the board of health produced a document specifically for them indicates the level to which others viewed social hygiene work as being a part of the public role of white women within the state. In a 1924 report the board of health listed the fact that "all of the women's organizations carry some type of social hygiene program" as part of their accomplishments for the biennium.[74]

Venereal Disease and the Threat to White Racial Progress

The social hygiene work that Kansas women undertook in the 1920s had clear implications for their positions as white women within the framework of eugenics. Physicians and social hygienists frequently constructed venereal disease as an ailment of the "other," a disease born of the lack of sexual restraint among minority groups. If immorality was inherited, as many eugenicists claimed, then it would only follow that venereal disease would be more prevalent among "lower" social groups.[75] From these poor and working-class roots, venereal disease would then find its way into the "respectable" white middle class. This line of thinking was particularly apparent in discussions of the asexual transmission of venereal disease. The concern that shared drinking cups or restrooms could transmit venereal disease revealed anxieties about increased contact between social groups. Ignoring the reality of sexual relations between social classes and extramarital sexuality within the middle class, many social hygienists conceived of the spread of venereal disease as emanating from lower social groups into the respectable white middle class. As gynecologist Howard Kelly stated in 1910:

> The personal services of the poor must daily invade our doors and penetrate every nook in our houses; if we care for them in no wise beyond their mere service, woe betide us. Think of these countless currents flowing daily in our cities from the houses of the poorest into those of the richest, and forming a sort of civic circulatory system expressive of the life of the body politic, a circulation which continually tends to equalize the distribution of morality and disease.[76]

In richly metaphorical language, Kelly constructed venereal disease as originating in the lower classes and ultimately threatening white, middle-class families.

The understanding of venereal disease as an ailment of the lower classes had several implications for the social position of white women involved with the social hygiene movement. This interpretation of the origin of venereal disease made a direct connection between the sexuality of the "other" and white women's own fertility and capacity to reproduce the white race. As family sizes grew smaller around the turn of the twentieth century, politicians and journalists worried about the declining fertility of white women. President Teddy Roosevelt attributed women's declining fertility to personal choices, accusing white women of committing "race suicide" by refusing to take on the responsibilities of motherhood. Others placed the blame for smaller families on the menace of venereal disease. Between 1900 and 1920, advocates for sex education, journalists, doctors, and the military all constructed venereal disease as posing a particular threat to the biological capacity of white women to bear children. These "experts" told the tale of venereal disease as originating from "loose" women, being passed on to innocent wives through their cheating husbands, and ultimately resulting in infertility, miscarriage, and infantile blindness. Ignoring the use of birth control within middle-class families, social hygiene activists argued that venereal disease had resulted in the sterility of its true victims: white middle-class women. A 1920 report from the Kansas State Board of Health warned that "the widespread prevalence of venereal disease has attained such magnitude as to make it a race peril."[77] Social hygienists often framed their arguments for public health measures to control venereal disease in evolutionary terms, stressing the need to protect future generations and innocent (white) wives from the ravages of these diseases. As historian Julian Carter argues, "The tale of venereal contagion was a story of the downfall of white civilization."[78] This reasoning provided a direct link between the lives and respectability of activist white women to the sexual lives of the "other." Constructing venereal disease as a threat to white women's fertility gave white female activists the motivation and justification to become publicly involved in regulating the sexual lives of other women, providing a connection to this social issue that touched on the heart of white women's own status in a society understood along evolutionary lines: their ability to reproduce.[79]

This construction of venereal disease as emanating from the lower classes and ultimately impacting white, middle-class fertility related to white female activists' social position in another way: it reinforced the idea that sexual self-control was a property of whiteness and that white women in particular embodied this trait of advanced civilization. Similar to the view that white people were the only ones capable of political self-governance, Julian Carter argues that sexual self-governance was part of the construction of whiteness during this period: "The passions that could destroy the republican experiment were the passions of the bedroom as well as of the marketplace and the ballot box."[80] In these narratives about the spread of venereal disease, white women embodied the sexual self-restraint characteristic of advanced civilizations, restricting their sexuality to heterosexual marriage. The public battle against prostitution and venereal disease did more than just try to control the sexual behaviors of lower social classes: it held up these white female activists as models of sexual self-restraint and reinforced associations between whiteness, purity, and sexual propriety from which white activists gained a sense of respectability.

Eugenics

Though educating the public about sexual self-restraint was a major tactic of social hygiene work in Kansas, activist women also lobbied for a variety of legislative measures that took a more coercive approach to controlling the racial makeup of the state. Kansas women joined eugenicists across the country in advocating for policies that would "improve" the racial stock of the United States. American eugenicist Charles Davenport defined eugenics in 1911 as the "science of the improvement of the human race by better breeding."[81] By the 1920s, eugenics had reached its heyday in the United States. Congress passed the Johnson-Reed Immigration Act in 1924, imposing quotas that encouraged immigration from England and western European countries and restricted it from other areas. Over 350 colleges and universities offered courses in eugenics by 1928.[82] Other efforts to "improve" the racial stock in the United States took a decidedly more draconian tone. Between 1907 and 1937, thirty-two states passed laws legalizing sterilization, leading to more than 63,000 Americans losing their ability to have children.[83] Eugenicists did not just try to prevent the "unfit" from procreating; they also sought to encourage white, middle-class women to have more babies. One such initiative had roots in Kansas. The first Fitter Families contest debuted at the Kansas State Fair in 1920. Modeled on livestock competitions, families underwent physical and mental examinations and provided accounts of their family history in an effort to prove their pedigree. Winners of the contests were held up as models of the type of white, rural family that eugenicists hoped would produce more babies.[84] Whether it was through sterilization or encouraging model families to procreate, eugenicists advocated for a variety of policies to shape the racial makeup of the country.[85]

The eugenics movement fed on the same cultural anxieties that fueled campaigns for social hygiene—concern about the devolution of the white race, questions about sexual morality in a modern era, and a particular emphasis on the role of women as reproducers of the human race. Leadership of the two movements also overlapped; many figureheads of the ASHA were also active in eugenics organizations.[86] The easy transition between social hygiene work and eugenics is apparent in the resolutions of the National Social Hygiene Committee of the League of Women Voters from 1920. The committee proclaimed that they believed in "the right of the individual to knowledge of laws of physical, mental and racial health, and

The Fitter Families contests, in which families were encouraged to have children that met the highest standards of evolutionary advancement, took off across the nation after debuting at the Kansas State Fair in 1920; this 1929 photo was taken in Topeka, Kansas. American Philosophical Society Library, "Eugenic and Health Exhibit, Kansas Free Fair, 1929," http://www.amphilsoc.org/mole/view?docId=ead/Mss.575.06.Am3-ead.xml.

stands ready to lend its support to public appropriations for agencies qualified to disseminate such education."[87] For these women, promoting sex education was part of the same overall goal of promoting "racial health." This concern about the future of the white race can be seen in who was targeted for sterilization. Though Black and other racial minority women were also sterilized during the 1920s and 1930s, many of the women forcibly sterilized through state institutions in this time period were white. Social hygienists and eugenicists both focused their attention on the figure who posed the greatest threat to cultural constructions of whiteness and stood to degrade the white gene pool: the young white woman who refused to accept middle-class norms for sexual behavior.[88]

In Kansas activist women had a long history of advocating for eugenicist policies. One example comes from a series of institutional review letters written by Lucy B. Johnston in the midst of the successful 1912 campaign for women's suffrage. Between 1911 and 1913, Johnston worked with another clubwoman to visit various state-run institutions and write a report on their conditions for the governor. These short reports repeatedly called for more restrictive marriage laws, emphasizing how the population of "feeble-minded" people in Kansas drained state resources. In her 1912 letter concerning the State Home for the Insane, Johnston wrote: "Here, as in other institutions, we learn that a very large per cent of the patients did not have the chance that every child is entitled to—that of being born well. They have a bad heredity." Her report on the State Home for the Feeble Minded stated: "If any of our farmers had, upon their estates, a herd of deteriorated, deformed and unhealthy animals that for good reasons he could not get rid of, his first thought would be for the protection of every good animal and, his second, to prevent any increase in the infected herd." She went on to write, "Can not Kansas have control over her degenerate citizens to the end that they may not perpetuate their kind?"[89] Of the seven institutions that Johnston evaluated, she mentioned the need for restrictive marriage laws in six of the reports.[90] Johnston's general feeling about the population housed in Kansas's state-run institutions can be summed up in her statement that what was really needed was "more prevention, less cure."[91]

Clubwomen's support for legislation aimed at preserving the white racial makeup of Kansas can be seen through a variety of documents during the interwar period, particularly in the late 1920s and 1930s. In 1924 the Kansas Council of Women passed "a resolution stressing the need for selective immigration for the United States."[92] In that same year, the venereal disease pamphlet published by the Kansas State Board of Health for clubwomen urged that the women of the state "[confer] with recognized authorities on eugenics, [read] recommended literature, and [draw] up suitable legislation."[93] A list of legislative agendas for the Kansas Federation of Women's Clubs in 1927 included the proclamation: "Legislation aimed to decrease hereditary evils resulting from the mating of the physically or mentally unfit has the support of the Club women of Kansas."[94] Women's endorsement of eugenics was not unique to Kansas, as women's organizations across the country embraced the ideas of eugenics and advocated for stronger state policies to prevent the "feebleminded" from having children.[95]

The ease with which eugenicists, reformatory officials, and clubwomen transitioned between discussions of different groups of people demonstrates the boundary work that took place through conversations about who needed to be sterilized. As historian Wendy Kline argues, eugenicist discourses combined with the growth in psychological testing during this period to produce such terms as "feebleminded" and "moron"; these terms gave reformers medicalized categories through which they could clump together such diverse groups as poor people, people who had venereal disease, and sexual deviants.[96] The minutes of a 1935 meeting of the Kansas Council of Women provide one example of how discussions of sterilization could lump together these different populations. The discussion began with the chair of the public health committee bringing up "the dire need of public care of the unfit, and the successful use of sterilization for persons unfit for reproduction." The conversation then turned to a discussion of the need for good administration at the girls' and boys' industrial schools, since "sexual development appears earlier in subnormal children." Mention of the sexual abnormality of children caught up in the state's correctional facilities prompted two women to share "shocking illustrations of cases which have come within their personal knowledge." The committee then resolved to study sterilization laws and propose legislation that might strengthen them and, in some cases, make them obligatory. The discussion ended with another member suggesting "that more restriction be made in the admission of immigrants who bring with them their morals and lower standards of living."[97] The turns in this conversation, from sterilization of the unfit to juvenile delinquency to the moral threat posed by immigrants, reveal the various social categories that got caught up in discussions of sterilization and sexual immorality. The ease with which these women moved between sexual danger, the criminal justice system, and the threat of immigration shows how connected these things were in their minds. As clubwomen discussed the need to sterilize the feebleminded as well as the sexually immoral, they created an amorphous sense of the "other" that encompassed various social categories yet placed all of them squarely out of the bounds of respectability.

The conflation of inmates with people at the bottom of the evolutionary ladder led to some conflicts between the reformatory ideal that Kansas women had lobbied for at the KSIFW and their beliefs about inmates' capacity to be reformed. The reformatory model implied that women were able to be changed, but biological understandings of inherited "feeblemindedness" and "imbecility" led to a belief that some people were not capable of being rehabilitated. The tendency to classify inmates as being biologically inferior and the quandary of what to do with them at the Farm can be seen in a 1921 report to the Kansas State Board of Health by Darlene Doubleday Newby. Newby made explicit connections between poverty, sexual delinquency, and the physical characteristics that were markers of these women's status on the evolutionary ladder. A social worker who did an undercover stint at the KSIFW to understand the social conditions leading to imprisonment, Newby commented on the change in character of the women interned at the Farm in 1920 compared to during World War I: "The visitor at the Farm in 1920 notes a change in the type of girl. Now there is a predominance of stupid-looking, listless girls, such as one sees in reformatories and in psychopathic wards of city hospitals." While the inmates of the Farm during the war years might have been able to be reformed, Newby expressed doubts about these inmates. She made connections between these women's delinquency and poverty, noting, "Some of them formed a part of the little procession that winds its way to the county courthouse and stands outside the door marked 'Commissioner of the poor.' They were all part of the group which experts classify as dependent, defective or delinquent children." Newby also commented on inmates' biological deficiencies, viewing them as indications of their lower racial stock, class status, and moral standards: "Some of them are cross-eyed, some of them have adenoids, some of them have been sex offenders since they were six years old."[98]

Newby's growing concern about the capability of the women at the Farm to be reformed was consistent with national trends in the women's reformatory movement. Just as being a prostitute was evidence enough for a diagnosis of syphilis in Kansas, eugenicists' framing of the "girl problem" led reformers to classify violations of middle-class sexual norms as indications of "feeblemindedness." Sexual impropriety was medicalized and could lead to drastic medical procedures being forced on inmates. While reformers in the 1910s might have argued that long-term imprisonment was the most realistic method to contain the innate moral depravity of some groups of people, prison officials in the 1920s began to see sterilization as the best solution to prevent women from passing on their propensity for crime and immorality to the next generation.[99]

Clubwomen in Kansas were enthusiastic supporters of stronger sterilization laws in the 1920s and 1930s. This fear of the reproductive capacities of the "other" was consistent with the sentiments clubwomen expressed during the campaign to create the KSIFW: a woman who lacked sexual self-restraint was all the more dangerous because of her capacity to have children. This fear of the reproductive danger of female prisoners can also be seen in Newby's 1921 report. She argued: "The line is sharply drawn between the dangerous lunatic who might cut his own throat and the feeble-minded prostitute who gives birth to a child every year. The lunatic is locked up; the promiscuous woman is allowed to roam the streets." Newby argued that the state needed to intervene earlier in the lives of "wayward" girls before they ended up at the KSIFW, making clear that these women's danger to society was intimately bound up in their capacity to have children. Within the larger context of anxiety about whiteness and the future of the race, this specter of the fertile prostitute seemed particularly dangerous to activist women in the state. Newby went on to comment: "The antisocial conduct of one feeble-minded prostitute will cost the community irreparable damage in diseased young manhood and in a future sickly citizenry. The woman's illegitimate children are likely to become an additional contribution to the criminal population of the state. Thus it will be seen that she is a menace to the future as well as to the present generation."[100] Though Newby argued for more preventative measures to keep these "feeble-minded" prostitutes from falling into a life of immorality, many activist women in the 1920s thought that sterilization was a more realistic approach to controlling the fertility of the "other." Clubwomen in Kansas firmly backed state-mandated sterilization, discussing strategies for increasing the use of sterilization in their organizational meetings and officially declaring that stronger sterilization laws were legislative priorities for their organizations.

Clubwomen were not alone in their support for sterilization in the Sunflower State. Kansas was a leader in efforts to sterilize those deemed "unfit" for reproduction. The first records of state-enforced sterilization in Kansas date from 1894, when the superintendent of the Kansas State Asylum for Idiotic and Imbecile Youth sterilized many of the inmates in his institution. The Kansas legislature officially passed a sterilization law in 1913. The state board of administration thoroughly endorsed such measures to control reproduction. In its 1920 biennial report, the board listed restricted marriage laws among a series of requests to reduce the population at the state's institutions, commenting that "Kansas has given statistical study to the improvement of its livestock, but has been too busy or too heedless to give thoughtful care to improve its breed of men."[101]

The board of administration required that wardens of penitentiaries wanting to sterilize its inmates submit a statement to the board outlining an argument that the inmate's condition would be improved by the operation or that "procreation by such named inmate or inmates would be likely to result in defective or feeble-minded children with criminal tendencies."[102] Once approved by the governor, inmates (or their legal guardians) would be notified before the operation was performed. The constitutionality of this law came before the Kansas Supreme Court in 1928, one year after the US Supreme Court upheld Virginia's forced sterilization law in *Buck v. Bell.* In the Kansas case, *Smith v. Schaffer,* the court analyzed the problem of reconciling government powers and personal liberty by focusing on "the two functions indispensable to the continued existence of human life": nutrition and reproduction. The court upheld the state's sterilization law, arguing, "Without nutrition, the individual dies; without reproduction, the race dies. Procreation of defective and feeble-minded children with criminal tendencies does not advantage, but patently disadvantages, the race."[103] Overall, Kansas was one of the leading states performing involuntary sterilizations in the 1920s and 1930s. A 1937 report from the Human Betterment Foundation reported that 1,915 people had been sterilized in Kansas up to January 1, 1938, giving Kansas the third-highest number of involuntary sterilizations in the country.[104]

Across the country, state institutions became pipelines for sterilizing those deemed unfit for reproduction, and Kansas was no exception. The hospital at the KSIFW became a central site in the state's efforts to sterilize girls and women in the 1930s. The eugenicist-minded superintendent of the Girls' Industrial School at Beloit, Lula Coyner, ordered the forced sterilization of sixty-two girls (almost half of the number of inmates at the time) in 1935 and 1936. The girls were sent to the hospital at the KSIFW, where doctors performed the operations to sterilize them. The sterilizations came to public attention after former congresswoman Kathryn O'Loughlin McCarthy spoke out in 1937. McCarthy had been elected as a Democrat to one term in Congress in 1932, and she was outraged that the state had sterilized girls as young as nine years old as a form of punishment. The sterilizations at the KSIFW drew national media attention, prompting magazine headlines such as "Sterilization: The Unholy Horror of Lost Motherhood." The public scrutiny that McCarthy incited apparently caused Kansas officials to think twice about sterilizing girls from

Beloit at such a scale. After the brief spike in 1935 and 1936, the number of sterilizations performed at the KSIFW dwindled.[105]

Though the exact number of sterilizations is not clear, officials sterilized at least some women and girls who were sent to the KSIFW under Chapter 205. Historian Scott Stern has identified at least four inmates who were sterilized among the girls from Beloit who were originally sentenced under Chapter 205. One of these girls, age fourteen, was originally sentenced to the Farm under Chapter 205 after authorities discovered that her mother had been hiring her out for sex. Once treated for disease, the girl was transferred to Beloit, then shipped back to the Farm for sterilization even though her IQ tested well above the range for being classified as "feebleminded."[106] Outside of the group of girls from Beloit in 1935 and 1936, the records are less clear about which procedures doctors performed for the explicit purpose of sterilization and which ones may have been a legitimate part of medical treatment for inmates. For example, the 1922 physician's report from the KSIFW listed two operations performed to remove the fallopian tubes, but no explanation as to why these procedures were conducted.[107] Doctors who sterilized the girls from Beloit listed these operations in the 1936 medical report as salpingectomies, the surgical damage or removal of the fallopian tubes, which was a common method of sterilizing women during this period.[108] The 1938 report listed eleven of these operations, and by 1940 the number was down to zero.[109] Thus, it does not appear that sterilization was a major focus of the KSIFW except for the large number of girls sterilized from Beloit in 1935 and 1936. The laws permitting the state of Kansas to sterilize inmates remained on the books until 1965.[110]

Activist women's support of social hygiene and eugenics in Kansas built on the same cultural anxieties around race, class, and sexuality that informed their arguments for the need to establish the KSIFW. Whether it was framed through the lens of the need to reform "wayward" young women, the dangers of venereal disease, or the threat of procreation, the challenge that sexually active young women posed to the moral and social order envisioned by white female activists in Kansas was consistent. The social influence that clubwomen and organizations like the Kansas Council of Women wielded in the state declined through the 1920s and 1930s, yet they remained a voice in the state that argued for the need to reform women and contain the threat of sexual immorality.

Conclusion

When Lucy B. Johnston told her fellow clubwomen in 1917 that male legislators were growing away from the mocking attitude of "anything to please the ladies," she recognized both how far women had come in Kansas and how far they still had to go to be taken seriously as public actors. Activist women in Kansas sought an expanded role for women in the public sphere, yet the landscape of social boundaries that they navigated was rapidly shifting. While women in the late 1800s often drew on the ideology of the home and separate spheres to justify their involvement in social issues, changing gender ideals meant that this basis for public authority was eroding by the 1910s.[111] As historian Louise Newman argues, the loss of public authority based on the image of the home was largely replaced by a new public authority based on an evolutionary conception of white women's role within the progression of civilization. In a sense, white women traded a political role based on their (supposedly racially neutral) gender position to a political niche based explicitly on their role as white women.[112] These uncertainties about the respectability of female public actors and the future of the white race were intimately bound up with each other in the lives of white female activists in Kansas.

This chapter has shown how understanding these women's actions in light of eugenicist discourses turned this questionable public role into a respectable one. Through their work to establish the KSIFW and to advocate for social hygiene and eugenics, white female activists in Kansas found a political niche for white womanhood. These topics opened up paths for social action that were seen as within the jurisdiction of white women in the state. A eugenicist understanding of gender roles, racial progress, and the values of civilization tied these seemingly disparate political activities together.

However, these were not just issues around which female activists could lobby: being involved with women's prison reform and social hygiene work had connections to white activist women's own sources of social advantage. Part of women's ability to claim a respectable public role was their status as "ladies," a status imbued with understandings of their moral purity. The presence of sexually promiscuous women in society, particularly when they were white, threatened this source of respectability. As Nicole Rafter argues in her discussion of female prison reformers during this time: "Indeed, if the fallen woman was *not* a victimized 'sister' but rather an autonomous, deliberately sexual being, then the *raison d'être* of social feminists—their concept of womanliness and, with it, the justification for their work—was built on air."[113] The inmates of the KSIFW thus presented a challenge to one source of activist women's social advantage: associations between moral purity and femininity. As this chapter has argued, the inmates of the Farm and sexually active women in general presented another challenge to white activist women's social position: their racial privilege. Through inmates' ability to reproduce and the construction of venereal disease as making its way from diseased prostitutes to innocent wives, the purity and future of the white race was put into question. Anxiety about poor women's sexuality and the future of the white race fueled white women's activism in Kansas, from their campaign to create the KSIFW to their support for stronger sterilization laws.

Lucy B. Johnston remained involved with women's clubs and was consulted for her lobbying expertise until her death in 1937. Organizations like the Kansas Council of Women continued to lose momentum and social influence in the 1930s, and by the eve of World War II were far less influential in state politics than they had been at the time that the KSIFW was established. Yet the legacy of these women for state control of women's sexuality had been firmly established. They had created an institution that housed female prisoners in the state, and it quickly filled with women detained under Chapter 205. Now it was up to the professional women who would run the Farm to define its day-to-day operations.

CHAPTER 4
TRAINING INMATES FOR RESPECTABILITY
THE PROFESSIONAL WOMEN OF THE KSIFW

On November 23, 1918, social worker Darlene Doubleday Newby went undercover at the KSIFW to investigate the causes of moral delinquency among the inmates. She arrived at the Farm in what the inmates referred to as the "hoodlum wagon" along with fourteen other women from Junction City, Kansas. The women were quarantined in the "hospital," which was really a makeshift structure unsuited for medical treatment, for a five-day period in an attempt to avoid spreading the deadly flu epidemic that was sweeping the nation. Though the facilities were basic, with not enough beds for everyone, Newby was impressed with the inmates' adaptability. When breakfast was brought in and there was not enough room at the table for everyone, several women filled their plates and "sat around the wall, 'like society dames at a tea,' one of the girls remarked." The inmates were provided gingham dresses and basic necessities, like drinking cups and soap; the superintendent also sent over some books and magazines, of which Newby commented that "the girls were more interested in the knitting and crochet patterns and in the advertisements than they were in the stories." Newby was impressed with the influence that the professional women who staffed the Farm had over the inmates they worked with. She noted: "Mrs. Perry and her matrons put a great deal of their personality into the daily life at the Farm; contact with the girls is close." Newby saw the close relationships that the staff formed with inmates as a key part of their reform, commenting that the inmates were "morally bolstered up in the belief that they have made good with somebody that counts."[1] Newby's observations point to the pivotal role that the superintendents and matrons played in the daily operation of an institution like the KSIFW. Through their actions and their ability to model respectability for the inmates, the professional women who staffed women's reformatories were key to the success or failure of these institutions.

The women that Newby observed interacting with inmates at the KSIFW were just some of an emergent class of professional women who found employment in the growing state institutions that regulated women's sexuality in the first few decades of the twentieth century. Following the initial founding of women's reformatories in the United States in the 1860s, the women's reformatory movement flourished between 1900 and 1935. While only four reformatories were founded between 1870 and 1900, seventeen separate women's institutions were established between the years 1900 and 1935.[2] The women who staffed these institutions found new avenues for professional employment and positions of authority over other women. Yet these opportunities did not come without their drawbacks: low pay, limited prestige, and poor working conditions were realities for many superintendents and matrons who worked at women's reformatories.

This chapter explores the social position of the women who worked at the KSIFW and how their lived experiences informed how they ran the institution. The staff at the Farm faced competing expectations. As an institution, the KSIFW was supposed to reform women, yet they were also supposed to keep costs as low as possible. As individuals, the staff of the Farm were supposed to be models of femininity while maintaining a professional status. While the superintendents and matrons of the Farm gained jobs and some degree of status from their roles at the Farm, their positions were wrought with contradictions that complicated their relationship to respectability. The philosophy of reform that they brought to their work at the Farm was informed by these competing expectations. The idea of reform, rather than punishment, infused every detail of life at the KSIFW. From the physical layout of the buildings to the teaching of domestic skills, professional women set up daily life at the Farm in a way that sought to help inmates lead a better life once leaving the institution. At the same time, the emphasis at the Farm on domesticity and reform brought some reconciliation to the competing expectations of the institution and to professional women's roles. Inmates could accomplish the work of the institution at the same time that they were being reformed if it was through domestic training, just as professional women themselves could be models of femininity for the inmates at the same time that their very working conditions prevented them from leading a normal family life of their own. While the KSIFW reflected national best practices in women's reformatories, it also reflected the complicated social positions of the women who ran the institution.

The Superintendents of the KSIFW

The person who most influenced the KSIFW during its early years was Julia Perry, superintendent of the KSIFW from its opening in 1917 until her death in 1932. She was born as Julia Bailey in Stewart, Ohio, and went on to attend Marietta College and the National Normal University and teach school for several years. In 1885 Julia moved to Kansas to teach school in various towns around the state. In 1901 she became superintendent of the Girls' Industrial School in Beloit, Kansas, a position she held for twelve years. Following her departure from Beloit, Perry worked at various state institutions throughout the East to learn best practices and methods of management, working in six different states before returning to Kansas to take the helm at the KSIFW. As a young woman, Julia had married John B. Douglas, who died a mere six months after their marriage. Julia gave birth to one son, also named John Douglas. She later married Newton Perry, a teacher.[3]

Julia Perry was in charge of the KSIFW from the start, guiding it through the initial influx of women quarantined under Chapter 205 and setting the tenor for the institution as it became established. Perry's approach to the Farm is apparent in an account from Newby's undercover report. Shortly after a group of inmates arrived at the Farm, Perry reportedly told them: "Now that you are here, we are going to see that you have good treatment, good medical treatment, and in addition to that the best care in every way that kindness and love can give." She went on to offer them one narrative of how they contracted a venereal disease: "Most of you have known love at some time; you have all been loved by some one, and you have all loved some one. That is one reason why you are here. Women are not always wise in their affections; they are not always fair to themselves." In this interaction, Perry expressed attitudes that would define the approach of the KSIFW during her tenure as superintendent: the desire to reform inmates rather than punish them, to see the inmates' better natures rather than their faults, and to offer them a path forward that would lead to an upright life after leaving the institution. Newby reported that the inmates appreciated Perry's approach: "In the days that

Julia Perry, longtime superintendent of the KSIFW from its opening until her death in 1932. Courtesy of KSHS.

followed the girls commented frequently on this talk of Mrs. Perry's. They agreed that 'she is an awful good woman,' and the new girls were hearing constantly from the old girls that Mrs. Perry was 'kind and square.'"[4] This congenial attitude between prison staff and inmates was foundational to the reformatory ideal that activist women in Kansas had lobbied for and professional women tried to implement.

Perry's biography illustrates the national ideal for having professionally trained superintendents of women's reformatories. Unlike many of the female reformers who lobbied to create separate women's prisons, the superintendents who ran the institutions typically had high levels of formal education and professional experience for women during this time. Among the twenty superintendents that Eugenia Lekkerkerker was able to gather data on for her 1931 study of women's reformatories, nine had college training, two had a doctor of philosophy, five were physicians, and one was a lawyer.[5] Professional women's social authority came to be based less on ideas of benevolence and charity and more on progressive ideas of professionalism and social science as their roles changed going into the 1910s and 1920s. This was apparent in the qualifications of superintendents at women's reformatories nationwide, as they increasingly distinguished themselves from their nineteenth-century peers through their educational achievements and professional identification. Julia Perry's long career in public service in Kansas was quite typical of her peers across the country.[6]

Like her counterparts nationwide, Julia Perry benefited from the professional opportunities opened up to middle-class women through the growing state bureaucracies that regulated women's sexuality. Most laws establishing women's reformatories (including the one in Kansas) explicitly stated that a woman should be the superintendent, in part as a method of protecting female inmates from the abuses of male officials, and in part under the assumption that a woman would be better equipped to reform other women's character.[7] The creation of jobs for superintendents of women's reformatories was part of a larger growth in professional women's opportunities during this period that was directly related to the authority professional women derived over the working-class women they were "helping." Julia Perry noted this connection between jobs for professional women and services for poor women in a speech given at a Topeka social workers' conference in 1918. Commenting on the changing role of women in public, Perry noted that the modern woman "spurns the idea of dependence, and is no longer willing to play the part of a helpless being; but is everywhere recognized as a co-worker with man, and with him has a sphere whose boundaries are unknown." She went on to say that professional women could not "afford to neglect the unfortunate women of our state" and that it was "up to the thinking women of Kansas" to take action to save these women from the "tide that is bearing them swiftly to destruction."[8] Through their responsibility for the "unfortunate women" of Kansas, the "thinking women of Kansas" gained an opportunity to prove their equality with men. The growth and institutionalization of professional positions for women clearly benefited educated, middle-class women like Julia Perry.[9]

Though professional women found jobs in the growing state bureaucracy to regulate women's sexuality in Kansas, they still reported to male officials and relied on them for their jobs. These male officials did not always treat women with the respect that their status as professionals might warrant. The condescending attitude that Darlene Doubleday Newby's supervisor, Samuel J. Crumbine, displayed toward her is apparent in his account of her decision to go undercover to investigate conditions at the KSIFW. Crumbine, who described Newby as "a distinguished social worker who was resourceful and dignified, as well as unostentatious and likable, both in manner and appearance," made Newby promise that she would ask her parents' permission before going undercover. Apparently sharing Crumbine's concerns for Newby's reputation, her parents objected, "but they agree[d] that this was for [her] to decide."[10] With this paternalistic attitude, Crumbine disregarded Newby's judgment and ability as a professional.

These condescending attitudes could combine with the political nature of superintendents' positions to create uncertainty about their jobs. As appointed public boards, both the board of administration and the board of health were subject to the political maneuverings of state political parties. For example, Governor Henry Allen came under fire from the Ku Klux Klan in 1922 for appointing a Catholic woman to head the Beloit Industrial School.[11] In 1923 much of the board of health, including Samuel Crumbine, was replaced or forced to resign for political reasons, ultimately leading to a Kansas Supreme Court battle over which of two competing state boards of health was the legitimate one.[12] These political appointments had the potential to make their way down to institutions that reported through these boards.

Julia Perry was fully aware of how vulnerable her job might be as a result of changing political winds. In 1913 Perry was forced to resign from her position as superintendent of the Girls' Industrial School at Beloit, an apparent casualty of political maneuverings in Topeka that were unrelated to her job performance. In a private letter sent from Perry to Lucy B. Johnston, with whom she had a very friendly professional relationship, Perry wrote: "It is hard after all the years of service I have given the State to have to be attacked in the manner I have been. The great pity is that we do not have men at the helm of State that are able to appreciate good loyal service." The gendered dynamics of the situation were not lost on Perry, who noted: "The trouble is there is not <u>one</u> there that appreciate women—they tolerate them but would down them any minute if they could. I know whereof I speak."[13] Perry's situation highlights the tenuous grasp that professional women had on a respectable public role. Professional women, though the head of women's reformatories across the country, were mostly reporting to men in positions of power who determined whether they could keep their jobs.[14]

In her role at the KSIFW, Julia Perry was able to avoid such political drama, serving as superintendent from the inception of the institution until her death in 1932. Following Perry's death, however, the KSIFW went through a series of superintendents in a relatively short period. Between the years of 1932 and 1942, five different women headed the institution.[15] During these same years, the governor's office transitioned between Democrats and Republicans three times.[16] These political changes influenced decisions to retain or replace the superintendent at the KSIFW.[17] Changes made for political reasons could trickle down past the superintendent; one former employee of the Farm later reported: "I was matron of the womans [*sic*] penitentiary from October 1936 to April 1937. I happened to be a Republican and went in about ten days before Election and of course was let out the following April."[18] The influence of politics on the administration of state institutions drew the attention of reformers during the 1920s and 1930s, leading at least one governmental report to recommend that state institutions switch to a civil service system rather than a system of political patronage.[19] In her 1931 study of women's reformatories during this period, Eugenia Lekkerkerker indicated that political appointments were not as much of a problem in women's reformatories as they were for men's prisons, a fact that she attributed to less competition for the positions among women and the "higher type" of women attracted to reformatory work.[20] Perry's dismissal in 1913 and the high turnover of superintendents at the Farm in the 1930s indicate that politics were very much at play in Kansas, however.

Considering the political vulnerability of their positions, it is no surprise that the superintendents of the Farm made few public statements criticizing state laws or the men who made them. There are, however, a few examples of Julia Perry speaking publicly against the sexual double standard that was enforced through the implementation of Chapter 205 in Kansas. In response to a query from the national League of Women Voters' Social Hygiene Committee in 1920 about women's recommendations for social hygiene work from Kansas, Julia Perry responded: "I believe it to be the consensus of opinion of thinking women that any bill, presented to be enacted into law, should apply to both sexes equally. Here I refer especially to freedom from venereal disease." Perry, who the article stated was "deeply impressed with the necessity of writing sex equality in the laws," went on to argue that health certificates should be issued prior to marriage testifying to both men's and women's overall health. In a statement that indicates she had witnessed abuses of physicians' authority in Kansas, Perry argued that the Public Health Service should finance doctors' positions, lamenting that "a physician dependent on the public for patronage will always be biased in his decisions." Perry also advocated for better training for doctors in treating venereal diseases, noting: "I find, too, that a great many physicians do not acquaint themselves with venereal diseases, or at least do not recognize them when they exist." Though Perry may not have been free to express these frustrations in the biennial reports that she submitted to the all-male board of administration every two years, she found an outlet through the national League of Women Voters.[21]

Julia Perry again turned to other women as allies in 1924 and, in a move that tested the boundaries of her political position, included the text from a speech that she gave to the Kansas chapter of the Woman's Christian Temperance Union in the 1924 KSIFW biennial report. In this speech, Perry gave a much more pointed critique of the gender dynamics behind the campaign to eradicate venereal disease in Kansas:

> The number of young persons that are becoming infected is alarming and many times they are pursued by married men with families. I took the trouble to notify one such to not send any more correspondence to the institution. His wife received the letter and wrote: "My dear Mrs. Perry: In our town there are so many by the same name as ours and when I showed your letter to my husband he said: 'Isn't that a good joke on me that she thought I would mix myself with the likes of those girls.'"[22]

Here, Perry portrayed the young women sent to the KSIFW as victims of male lust, a sentiment she repeated when she called on "the splendid womanhood of our state to . . . throw every possible protection around our young girls." This portrayal of women as victims of male sexual excess stands in contrast to most of the depictions of women in the KSIFW biennial reports, where they are typically presented as women capable of making their own sexual decisions who need a "reforming" experience to help them make better choices. In the speech, Perry went on to explicitly criticize the state's unequal enforcement of Chapter 205:

> We are sorry to say that nothing is being done in the way of quarantining the men of Kansas who are afflicted with venereal disease. We surely know that so long as they are permitted to spread infection, that

> we are failing in wiping out the most deadly diseases that flesh is heir to, and that they continue their nefarious work of wrecking the lives of young girls and enticing them into lives of shame.[23]

This larger political critique of the enforcement of venereal disease control laws was absent in the rest of the KSIFW biennial reports.

This Kansas Woman's Christian Temperance Union (KWCTU) speech and Perry's choice to include it in the 1924 biennial report illustrate the political tensions that superintendents of women's reformatories had to navigate. In the speech Perry appealed to clubwomen to lobby to make changes in the enforcement of Chapter 205. Politically, Julia Perry was not in a position to directly challenge male legislators and administrators on the sexual double standard that was being enforced through Chapter 205. Her choice to include the speech in the 1924 biennial report was a very indirect way of criticizing men in power, showing that Perry herself may have had relatively little influence with decision makers in the state.

Professional women like Julia Perry gained employment and authority over other women through their roles in state institutions, yet their authority was not without limits. From the laws that determined who would be sent to the KSIFW to the budgets that would dictate what they could accomplish, the superintendents at the Farm were reliant on male legislators and government officials to dictate the parameters of their work. In her article on social service delivery in Kansas between 1916 and 1930, Mary Scott Rowland notes the gendered power dynamics as the state began to take over many social services. Jobs that men typically filled had more social influence and respect, while women's positions were usually subservient to men's: "The doctor and the accountant were still more important than the social worker, and they all knew it."[24] Women in public roles during this period often found themselves jockeying for power against institutions that were dominated by men. Professional superintendents' social position was thus bolstered by their role in the reformatory, but they had limited authority, respect, and control outside of a specified realm within the institution.[25]

The Matrons and Officers of the KSIFW

While the women who served as superintendents were able to gain status over female inmates through their position with the KSIFW, the women who worked as lower-level matrons and officers of the institution had less physical and social distance between themselves and the female inmates who were their charges. The KSIFW employed men and women in a variety of positions. A 1933 account reported twenty-nine employees of the institution (ten of whom were men): "the superintendent, a stewardess, physician, nurse, 17 matrons, 1 guard, a chaplain, priest, farm supervisor and 2 engineers."[26] The largest group of these workers, the matrons, performed and supervised much of the everyday work of the institution, including cleaning, cooking, farm work, and supervising inmates. The 1938 KSIFW biennial report began referring to matrons as "officers," reflecting a national trend to try to give more professional status to this group of workers and change their job duties to be more like teachers and social workers.[27] This higher level of responsibility envisioned for "officers" reflected prison reformers' ideal matron: a woman who was capable of aiding in the mission of reform, rather than merely supervising inmates.

In practice, however, the low pay and poor working conditions for matrons in women's reformatories meant that superintendents struggled to attract and retain qualified employees; the ones they did get were typically women with relatively low levels of training. Nationally, the pay was quite low in women's reformatories. Lekkerkerker's 1931 survey of institutions reported that the average matron earned $900 a year, compared to the average superintendent's salary of $3,430. Matrons in Indiana and Ohio were paid only forty to fifty dollars per month, which Lekkerkerker noted was "about what a good domestic may earn in the larger cities." She went on to say: "Considering the fact that the working conditions are often less attractive than in a private position, one cannot expect to get for such salaries well-educated, capable women who can give intelligent co-operation in the difficult work of adjusting delinquent women."[28] Consistent with this national trend, a matron's salary in 1933 at the KSIFW was seventy to seventy-five dollars a month, compared to $190 a month for the superintendent.[29]

This low pay was accompanied by less-than-ideal working conditions. Matrons at many institutions lived in the same buildings and ate their meals with inmates, leaving them little time "off work." The KSIFW had a separate dining room for matrons, but for much of the 1920s and 1930s the matrons either lived in the cottages with the inmates or in an older building with few amenities. The isolated locations of most women's reformatories and the need to staff the institutions twenty-four hours a day meant that matrons worked long hours, with few opportunities to experience life outside their institutions. Lekkerkerker commented: "On the whole, then, the number of hours on duty of this class of workers is high, twelve hours a day not being exceptional, and—what is also important—they are often distributed in a way which is not convenient to the worker." In addition to the low pay and long and irregular hours, matrons faced a variety of restrictions: "Sometimes she cannot receive male callers, or have any relatives live with her, and many other 'cannot's' which do not exist for the outside worker who at least in her free hours can do as she pleases."[30] Working as a matron at a women's reformatory was anything but ideal.[31]

Other conditions of the job of reformatory matron posed challenges as well. High numbers of inmates could make the mission of reforming women rather than just detaining them difficult to achieve. Kansas had a relatively low staff-to-inmate ratio compared to other women's reformatories. Among the ten institutions for which Lekkerkerker provided a snapshot of data, the average ratio was 18.5 inmates for every matron, whereas in Kansas the ratio was 11.6 inmates per matron.[32] Even so, a 1938 report stated: "The present staff is so swamped with the problem presented by the continual stream of venereal cases, most of whom average less than six months in the institution, as to make any more constructive program with present personnel impracticable."[33] Despite the image of the ideal worker as being trained in social work, matrons were generally not treated as professionals. There was little formal training available for matrons at women's reformatories. Several institutions had policies that forbade matrons from viewing inmates' files, a practice that Lekkerkerker argued was demoralizing for matrons, at least "to those more intelligent social workers who bring to the work a genuine interest in human lives."[34] Women's reformatories provided a workplace that offered low pay, a high level of restrictions, and little respect to the matrons they employed.

Under these conditions, women's reformatories failed to attract the type of female professionals that would have been best equipped to aid in the reforming mission of the institutions. Lekkerkerker commented: "The work of the cottage matrons should be considered a 'key-position' only to be trusted to the best. Unfortunately, rather the opposite meaning seems to prevail in many institutions, if one considers the low salaries of the matrons and the position these officers occupy."[35] Women's reformatories struggled to adequately staff their institutions, and the education level of the matrons they could retain usually fell below what was considered ideal. Kansas was a good example of this: a 1933 report gave information about the educational background of ten of the seventeen matrons, indicating that one had only an elementary-level education, five had attended high school, and four had some level of college or teacher training. The report went on to comment: "It would seem obvious that women with some background in social case work, abnormal psychology, and probation work might be better suited to looking after such women, than the untrained staff who are there."[36]

Since they could not necessarily require the level of formal education and professional background they wanted, the matron's respectability became a central qualification for the job. In the 1924 KSIFW biennial report, Perry commented: "It is a matter of the greatest consequence that the officer, who is the pattern, be a person of the highest type of character."[37] A 1933 independent evaluation of the Farm listed "knowledge of human nature; Christian character," and "moral and spiritual guidance; helping girls to find their better selves" under a column titled "Training, Experience, and Duties."[38] Matrons were not only required to be upright citizens; they also needed to be somewhat knowledgeable about the types of problems inmates might be facing. Lekkerkerker noted: "It is especially important that the officers have a wholesome and objective understanding of and attitude towards sex, for they will often have to deal with sexual problems, and it is almost entirely through the attitudes and reactions of the officers that the inmates have to gain a correct interpretation of sexual questions which many of them so badly need."[39] Echoing larger cultural discourses about sexuality that emphasized a rational, controlled approach to sexual matters, matrons were supposed to be knowledgeable about sex, not piously above it.[40] Through these descriptions of the moral character desired for reformatory matrons, respectability became an important qualification for the job. Given their low salaries, matrons were in similar social class positions as many of the women they were trying to reform; their respectability was often the only thing differentiating them and putting them in a position of authority over the inmates.

Tensions at the Farm

Tensions around the working conditions of matrons at the KSIFW spilled over in 1931 and 1932 when two former employees rallied clubwomen and ministers in a campaign with the governor to oust Julia Perry from her position. Evelyn Woodruff and Emma Sells Marshall were both former employees of the Farm who were frustrated with what they viewed as intolerable conditions there. Woodruff first wrote to Governor Harry Woodring in March 1931. She was upset that women sentenced to the Farm under Chapter 205 mixed freely with other inmates and were involved with the preparation of food. Given that the facilities would have allowed for the interned women to be separated from others, Woodruff viewed their integration with other inmates as an indication of "a disregard for subjecting clean inmates and officers to the liability of contracting one or more of the loathsome diseases." Woodruff also lamented the lack of respect given to employees of the institution, noting that "officers are not allowed to take the initiative in the slightest degree, and yet, are held responsible for good deportment in the various departments." Woodruff was particularly critical of the leadership of Julia Perry, warning the governor that the eighty-three-year-old Perry was "old, feeble, lame and forgetful."[41] Marshall later sent a document endorsed by eight matrons at the Farm to the governor that echoed these concerns. They added, "Most Matrons are now working from 15 to 17 hours a day—some of them getting up at 4 to 4:30 A.M., having breakfast at 6 and on duty until 9 P.M., with only 1 day off each month."[42] The poor working conditions noted at women's reformatories across the country were clearly an issue at the KSIFW as well.

Of particular concern to these current and former employees was the fact that Julia Perry had hired former inmates who were on parole to work at the Farm. In many ways, hiring former inmates reflected the highest ideals of the reformatory model: seeing inmates' potential, giving them a second chance, and offering them concrete paths of employment so they could lead a respectable life. Yet the women who wrote to the governor deeply resented the authority given to former inmates at the Farm. The document that was endorsed by several matrons complained that one former inmate who was hired on as a matron was sometimes drunk while on the job, used excessive force with inmates, and carried a razor with her wherever she went. The women went on to comment on what they viewed as Perry's overly friendly relationship with former inmate Effie Beverly, a woman who lived in nearby Leavenworth after serving a sentence for killing her two children. Saying that Beverly was Perry's "best friend," the matrons were upset that Beverly advised Perry "concerning the management of the institution."[43] The influence that former inmates had at the KSIFW was troubling to Evelyn Woodruff as well. In a letter to Emma Sells Marshall in January 1932, Woodruff stated: "Three convicts, all murderers, had been paroled, and were all on the payroll as officers. . . . I soon learned to take censure from these convict officers without remonstrating for when I appealed to the Supt. I was told that common sense should have shown me the right way, while the fact that a convict was being allowed to censure a respectable citizen was ignored." Given matrons' low pay, their social status was not all that different from the inmates that they supervised. Having former inmates serve as matrons blurred the line around one of the few things that differentiated inmates from matrons: their respectability. The inversion of this moral hierarchy troubled Woodruff, who went on to comment about a former inmate turned matron whom she referred to as her "monitor": "From the first the monitor assumed the air of a superior. She even tried to advise in matters of discipline—but just there I drew the line. While she might give me the rules pertaining to the bath-room and so forth, I made her understand that I should manage the inmates without being subject to anyone but the Supt."[44] In a situation where the social distance between inmates and matrons was minimal, the blurring of these categories threatened the sense of authority that matrons' supposed moral superiority brought to their role.

Governor Woodring largely disregarded these initial warnings about the Farm, yet the situation again came to his attention in the fall of 1931 when a clubwoman, Mrs. Robert D. Blair, learned of Woodruff's complaints and began to lobby other women and ministers to write to the governor to urge him to take action. Blair's involvement in the issue reflected a widespread understanding of activist women as arbiters of women's issues in Kansas. The document from the group of matrons at the Farm stated: "It is our opinion the Club women would not object to Mrs. Perry being removed if they knew a little of the inside workings of this institution."[45] Attorney H. C. Castor wrote a letter to Governor Woodring to express his support of Perry, commenting that the matrons were just unhappy because Perry had fired them for incompetence. Like the disgruntled matrons, Castor saw clubwomen as being key players in this situation; he sent a copy of his letter to Lucy B. Johnston.[46] In several letters that he sent out on October 20, 1931, Governor Woodring assured several ministers that the institution was in good hands, noting in one letter: "I do not know Mrs. Blair nor her reasons for sending out what has developed into propaganda. My investigations have convinced me that the institution is well-managed."[47] In several of his responses, Governor Woodring referred people to Lucy B. Johnston for more information about management at the KSIFW. He also corresponded directly with Johnston about the complaints, assuring her of his confidence in Julia Perry and stating: "I am happy to know that my attitude in this matter is approved by you."[48] The success of activist women's casting of the KSIFW as "women's work for women" was apparent in how many people viewed this dispute between supervisors and staff at the Farm as being of concern to clubwomen in the state.

The complaints quieted down again until former matron Emma Sells Marshall began organizing clubwomen in early 1932. Marshall resigned from her position as matron at the Farm in January, telling Perry in her resignation letter: "Your insults, and persecutions are unprecedented; your absolute unfairness, your spy system, your methods of address and reprimand—very simply suggest a czar."[49] Marshall then drafted petitions calling for investigations into the conditions at the Farm and gathered the signatures of more than thirty Kansas clubwomen. Comments on the petitions and some accompanying notes took a decidedly partisan tone, calling on Governor Woodring, who was a Democrat, to replace Perry, a Republican. One woman signing the petition wrote: "Any statement Mrs. Marshall makes can be accepted as truthful, and there are many Republican women who think it is time to change superintendents at the Womens Farm."[50] Evelyn Woodruff had made a similar partisan pitch in her original letter the previous spring, writing: "I know that several Republican officers here voted for you, hoping that your election might make a change here."[51] Emma Sells Marshall reported that only two women that she asked refused to sign her petition, one of them giving as her reason that she felt "that the democratic women should see that [Perry] is removed." Marshall commented that this woman forgot that it was "the Republican women who have helped to keep her there, and allowed a more deplorable state of affairs at The Lansing Farm for Women."[52] Marshall herself seemed to be angling for the position of superintendent. Writing on the letterhead of the Kansas Federation of Women's Clubs, Mrs. F. W. Boyd wrote to the governor to encourage him to believe Marshall's reports. She added: "That she is true to her convictions, is shown by the fact that she was one of the very few women in Topeka, who was always and consistently <u>a democrat</u> when it was quite unpopular to be one."[53] Another woman wrote next to her signature on Marshall's petition: "I feel a change should be made at the Lansing Ind. Farm for the welfare of the inmates and I know of no one to fill the position better, than Emma Sells Marshall."[54]

These appeals to Governor Woodring's political loyalties missed the mark. The governor stood by Julia Perry throughout the complaints against her. In one letter he wrote: "Mrs. Perry is superintendent of the Farm and is a Republican and not of my faith, so the charge can not be made that she is being retained for political reasons. It is my desire to remove the State Institutions as far as possible from politics."[55] In another letter Woodring commented: "It is my contention that efficiency and management of these state institutions is more to be desired than that they be made a means of political debts."[56] Woodring retained Perry in her role as superintendent of the Farm, but her death in April 1932 opened up the Farm to a series of changes in leadership that proved less resistant to changes of political parties in Topeka.

This controversy about leadership at the KSIFW in 1931 and 1932 reflected several aspects of working conditions at the KSIFW: the political nature of the superintendent's position and vulnerability of her job, the poor working conditions of matrons at the Farm, and the tenuous nature of the social boundary between matrons and inmates that was based on matrons' respectability. Thus, the KSIFW created opportunities for the women who worked there at the same time that it set up problematic working conditions. Both the superintendents and matrons of the Farm gained validation and a bolstering of their respectability through their roles at the Farm, as being respectable was a requirement of their jobs. For the matrons, their respectability was sometimes the only thing that distinguished their own social position from that of the inmates. The rest of this chapter will explore the ways that the conflicted social positions of the superintendents and matrons of the KSIFW informed the way that they set up daily life at the Farm.

The Farm under a Mission of Reform

The matrons and superintendents of the Farm drew on an emerging national women's reformatory movement as they established the daily schedules and overall philosophy guiding the KSIFW. Starting in areas where progressive ideals were strong, such as the Northeast and the Midwest, a standard for women's reformatories developed during the early years of the twentieth century. Most reformatories, including Kansas, were founded by legislative action and governed by a central board that also supervised other penal institutions in the state. The laws establishing most women's institutions typically gave more direction about the management of the institution than did laws establishing men's institutions, such as statutes that stated a woman should be the superintendent. Overall, the KSIFW was typical of women's reformatories across the country. From the philosophy of reform to the architecture of the institution, the professional women who set up daily life at the Farm did so in accordance with national best practices. Where Kansas differed was in its emphasis on venereal disease. The sheer number of inmates going through the Kansas reformatory as a result of Chapter 205 led to some key differences in the degree to which the KSIFW could achieve the ideal model for women's reformatories.[57]

A Mission of Reform, not Punishment

The defining characteristic of women's reformatories, their emphasis on reform rather than punishment, guided multiple aspects of life at the KSIFW. The philosophy that women's prisons should reform inmates, rather than merely punish them, was reflected in the names of the institutions themselves: women's institutions during this period rarely had the word "prison" in the name, instead using the terms "home" or "farm" in combination with "industrial" or "state." The emphasis on reform was part of a general tendency to think of women's reformatories as more similar to schools for delinquent youth than to men's prisons. The women lobbying to create the KSIFW in Kansas fully endorsed this philosophy of reform in their arguments to establish the Farm. An October 1917 WCTU report about the reasons for founding the Farm highlighted the "wholesome and healthful work" that would be done at the institution, stating: "It will not be the purpose of this institution to merely deprive women of their liberty, or to see how much the state can punish them, but the purpose will be to furnish an environment where they can be reformed, built up, as it were, and made ready for citizenship."[58] Women's reformatories took on a much larger task than merely protecting society from criminals; turning female offenders into people "ready for citizenship" took a considerably more demanding and expansive approach.[59]

Classifying Inmates

One strategy for reforming inmates was to use the methods of social science to accurately classify women in order to cater to their specific needs. Classifying inmates became an increasingly popular idea within women's reformatories nationwide as the movement took on a more professional tenor in the first few decades of the twentieth century. Using a variety of tests, including intelligence tests and physical exams, psychologists, social workers, and prison officials worked together to group inmates by various criteria to facilitate the most effective plans for reforming their character. In doing so, they reinforced emerging ideas of "normalcy" against which inmates would be compared. Those deemed subnormal might be labeled "feebleminded" or a "moron," opening up doors to sterilization or institutionalization.[60]

Fueled by this national trend to categorize inmates and funded by the Public Health Service and the Children's Bureau, a team of psychologists and social workers conducted an in-depth study of the psychological well-being and social histories of women detained under Chapter 205 in Kansas from June to October 1918. Finding 114 of the 206 women studied to be affected with some form of "mental disorder," the team of researchers proposed different types of treatment for the groups of women diagnosed with various psychoses.[61] Many of these diagnoses pathologized deviant behavior, turning what might have been a simple moral transgression into an indicator of feeblemindedness. Psychologist Walter L. Treadway reported that a mere 19.9 percent of the 206 women detained under Chapter 205 that he examined had "a normal personal make-up." The inmates' sexual behaviors factored into Treadway's diagnoses. Of one group, he commented: "As a rule their love affairs were very perfunctory, as they did not show the tenderness, self-sacrifice, and self-subordination that one would naturally expect in a genuinely deep love."[62] Casual sex was not only against the moral order of society but was medicalized as a psychiatric disorder. As historian Wendy Kline has noted, this tendency to categorize moral deviations as signs of mental maladjustment led to many women being diagnosed as "feebleminded" whose only "symptom" was their promiscuity.[63]

The desire to classify inmates was apparent in statements from the matrons and superintendents of the KSIFW. With such comments as stating the need to "measure carefully the possibilities of the one worked with," to closely grade and classify inmates, and to conduct a "patient, intelligent study of the individual," matrons at the Farm repeatedly referenced this idea that they could better reform women by classifying them into groups.[64] In 1920 Julia Perry commented: "The classification of individuals in any institution has much to do with the success of the work. Segregation is the first essential, and as we segregate we find three classes: First, those who should never have been sent; second, those who through misfortune or misguided justice need medical care; third, those who should never be released, because of inherent weaknesses, viciousness, depravity and defectiveness."[65] While Perry's groupings of women had more to do with their guilt and relative respectability (i.e., those who were innocent, those who were victims, and those who were too mentally ill-adjusted to be safe for society) than with an official psychological evaluation, her emphasis on the need to separate inmates in order to more effectively reform them reflected the prevalence of this ideal in the national movement.

In practice, however, the KSIFW and most women's reformatories across the country lacked the resources to implement a system of classification for inmates. The idea of classifying female inmates was brought to its fullest realization through the Bedford Hills Reformatory in New York, whose generous funding from the Rockefeller family allowed it to have a large staff to classify inmates and separate facilities in which to group the different classes of offenders. Most women's reformatories in the United States did not have the psychological staff to systematically diagnose inmates or implement such an individualized, psychological model of reform. Another barrier to effectively implementing a classification system in women's reformatories was the small number of female inmates in most states: while there was usually more than one men's prison in a state that allowed for the classification of inmates, most states only had one female reformatory for the entire state. While superintendents at women's reformatories often tried to classify inmates based on the severity of their crime and their psychological makeup, there was only so much that they could do with limited resources. Outside of the initial in-depth psychological evaluations that Treadway and his colleagues carried out in 1918, the KSIFW did not have enough money to hire even one psychologist for the institution. Thus, the idea of classifying inmates to facilitate effective plans for reforming them remained more of an ideal in the women's reformatory movement than a reality.[66]

Architecture and Location as Opportunities for Reform

The overarching ideal of reform that guided women's reformatories was reflected in their physical location and the architecture of their buildings. Women's prison reformers advocated for a different type of architecture that was closer to a home environment than an institutional prison. Thus, the cottage system became a hallmark of women's reformatories of the period. Under this plan, female inmates were housed in a series of smaller buildings, where they would ideally live with a smaller group of women and a matron and take care of all of the needs of their individual cottages, such as cleaning and cooking. Inmates could recreate the dynamics of a home to facilitate their reform, making the cottage system, in the words of historian Nicole Rafter, "an architectural embodiment of the notion that criminal women could be reformed through domestic training."[67]

The physical grounds of the KSIFW in many ways reflected this national ideal. At first, however, this was far from the case. The location for the Farm was initially meant to be temporary, but the huge influx of women quarantined under Chapter 205 during the war led to a rapid expansion of the facility. The original small farmhouse was insufficient to house the women, and temporary tents and makeshift buildings were erected almost overnight. As the institution developed, brick buildings replaced the temporary structures built during the war. By 1940 the KSIFW included an administrative building, three cottages, a library, a hospital, a laundry, custodial buildings, a dairy barn, a horse barn, and poultry houses.[68]

In addition to architectural elements that more closely resembled homes than institutions, women's reformatories were ideally located in a country location, where there was little risk of escape and women could enjoy the rehabilitating effects of outdoor exercise and farmwork. Rooted in anxieties about modern urban spaces and the poor and racially and ethnically diverse people who lived there, national calls to have female prisoners perform farmwork in rural locations drew on idealized notions of the purity of nature and the construction of a rural, hardworking whiteness. This rural ideal was reflected in the original legislation that established the KSIFW, which stated that it should be located at least seventy-five miles from any city. Though the Farm ended up being quite close to Kansas City, the grounds of the Farm were situated in a country setting, with ample room for the inmates to garden and have livestock. Having

Photo of the original farmhouse and buildings of the KSIFW. The building to the right was at one point a hospital. Eugenia C. Lekkerkerker, Reformatories for Women in the United States *(Groningen: J. B. Wolters, 1931), 48.*

the institution be physically located in the country had great symbolic power besides its physical distance from the people and modern influences of the city. Perry noted the beautiful views and setting at the Farm in the 1930 biennial report, highlighting the importance of nature for the mission of the institution: "There is no broader field of research than nature, and our women need to be taught the lessons that nature holds."[69] In this description, nature fit neatly within the overall mission of reform of the Farm. Descriptions of the Farm from outside sources consistently remarked on the beauty of the grounds, from a 1917 newspaper article about the Farm that referred to it as "The Biggest Garden in Kansas" to a 1920 board of health inspector who described the Farm as having the "appearance of a substantial country home."[70]

Creating a truly homelike atmosphere in a prison setting was a challenge, but the professional women who ran the KSIFW tried to construct and run their facility as a home rather than an institution. Statements in the KSIFW biennial reports repeatedly mentioned steps that the superintendent and matrons took to try to create a homelike atmosphere at the Farm. Matron Agnes Lundstrom commented in the 1940 report that the inmates took great interest in decorating their rooms, adding pictures, doilies, pillows, and homemade bedspreads to recreate the comforts of

Photo of women standing by the pergola west of the old administration building at the KSIFW. Eugenia C. Lekkerkerker, Reformatories for Women in the United States *(Groningen: J. B. Wolters, 1931), 441.*

home. She noted approvingly, "There are very few girls who do not have the home-making instinct."[71] This analogy of the "prison as home" was taken even further by Perry in a comment from the 1924 biennial report: "The knowledge they gain here will serve as an aid in keeping strong and well themselves and caring for the inmates of their own homes."[72] By referring to inmates' future family members as "inmates of their own homes," Perry sought to create a parallel between the KSIFW and the home.[73]

Reporters and chaplains who visited the KSIFW were receptive to this analogy of the "prison as a home." A 1920 newspaper article by Mildred Reed titled "A Prison without Walls Is Women's Industrial Farm!" repeatedly commented on the warm atmosphere of the KSIFW. Reed reported that she was confused when she first arrived at the institution, as the lack of fences made her think that the place was "too attractive to be a penal institution." After describing a dance held for the inmates while she was there, she again commented: "They seemed too happy and carefree to be in a penal institution."[74] Another newspaper article reflected on the experiences of the first few inmates of the Farm: "When these first 16 women were moved to the hill they found themselves suddenly transferred from

The library in Cottage A of the KSIFW, 1936. Like many buildings at the Farm, this library was decorated in a fashion more typical of a home than a prison. KSHS, "Views of the Kansas Women's Industrial Hospital and Library," https://www.kansasmemory.org/item/229176/page/2.

the cheerless, depressing routine of the prison to conditions closely resembling those of normal home life."[75] These perceptions of the KSIFW as having a homelike feel were echoed in comments from the chaplains of the KSIFW, who were only at the Farm on a part-time basis. The chaplain in 1922 commented that "the spirit of the Industrial Farm [was] unlike that found in a woman's prison."[76] In the 1926 biennial report, Chaplain Charles A. Hatfield wrote: "Instead of feeling that one is in a prison or a reformatory, it seems to be more of a home where the very best of relations exist."[77] Though still very much a prison, elements of daily life at the institution sought to replicate the feeling of home.

Part of the superintendents' efforts to make the KSIFW a "homelike" atmosphere was its use of the cottage system. Striving to meet the national reformatory model, the KSIFW called each of its housing units a "cottage" and designated a matron to manage each building. In Kansas, however, calling the buildings "cottages" was more a name than a reflection of the actual architectural ideal. While the ideal cottage in the national women's reformatory model would house twenty-five to thirty inmates, "cottages" at the KSIFW housed two to three times that many.[78] Kansas also had a centralized dining room, whereas the national cottage model entailed each cottage doing its own cooking in order to replicate typical home life. The degree to which Kansas "cottages" strayed from the national ideal can be seen in photographs of Perry Cottage, built in the early 1930s. This large building was meant to house many inmates and was a far cry from the smaller ideal of the cottage model. The high number of inmates going through the KSIFW made the true cottage system a challenge to implement. The larger buildings and centralized dining facility of the KSIFW set them apart from the cottage model, yet these were much more economic ways to organize an institution. The KSIFW superintendents and matrons, however, continued to emphasize the value of home and refer to their buildings as cottages. In the 1938 biennial report, the matron of Perry Cottage, Kathleen M. Mottin, stated: "Those who have come to Perry Cottage as housekeepers have been taught the art of keeping a home as it should be kept at all times. As a rule I find them quite willing to take advantage of this opportunity and to appreciate the fact that in learning to do for others they are really improving themselves."[79] Though housekeeping for a large building like Perry Cottage was far removed from the housekeeping duties that inmates might face in their own homes, officials with the KSIFW claimed that doing this type of work would reform inmates' character by teaching them the value of the home and the feminine duty of "learning to do for others."

Domesticity as a Tool for Reform

This desire to create a homelike atmosphere at women's reformatories led to an emphasis on teaching domesticity as a way to reform inmates. Women's prison reformers as early as the 1870s had called for femininity and domesticity to be used as tools for reforming female inmates. The superintendents and matrons of the Farm described domestic work as a central feature of their plan to reform inmates, as it taught both appropriate feminine behavior and the concrete job skills women would need in the outside world.

A picture of Perry "cottage," built in the early 1930s. This photo features the four large sleeping porches. Eugenia C. Lekkerkerker, Reformatories for Women in the United States *(Groningen: J. B. Wolters, 1931), 272.*

The biennial reports of the KSIFW talked at length about the reforming power of domesticity. The teacher of the homemaking department, Eleanor Robson, wrote that the aim of her department was not just to teach basic skills but to get inmates to "learn that home making is an art not to be despised." Getting inmates to embrace the value of the home was an important component of their moral training. Robson went on to proclaim that when inmates recognized the value of housework "and the sacredness of the home, they are on the path of uprightness and virtue."[80] Like Robson, other staff at the Farm imbued the daily work of the institution with several layers of meaning. Doing housework taught inmates to be properly feminine and to value the home, both of which worked to reform their character so they could lead a respectable life once they left the institution.

The professional women who worked at the KSIFW not only imbued domestic work with larger meaning; they also positioned domestic work within the language of the home economics movement to give it added legitimacy. The matrons of different departments frequently talked about the lessons they taught through the course of carrying out the work, sometimes referring to "classes" or a "curriculum."[81] The 1920 biennial report includes Perry's description of the work carried out in the homemaking department. She reported that inmates took two classes daily, each one being half a day. Inmates first learned the "theory or science" of home economics, followed by time to apply those principles. Similarly, cooking was divided between coursework and practical application: "The study of foods by classes is then taken up, together with their nature and composition. Food values and cookery are discussed. Practical work in cookery follows each lesson."[82] As the combination of coursework and daily tasks shows, the staff at the KSIFW sought to impart general knowledge about housework in addition to the daily requirement of getting needed work completed. Descriptions of the work of the different departments in the KSIFW biennial reports generally included instruction beyond the basics that would have been required to complete the tasks at hand. For example, a description of the "laundering" department included this statement: "Along with this practice work information is given concerning the proper laundering of cotton, linen and flannel, and the removing of mildew, rust and staining of various kinds."[83] Matron Eleanor Robson described the work in her homemaking department: "Our forenoons are mostly devoted to classwork. Each girl prepares a notebook for each class. They put forth extra effort to finish these books and wish to take them home with them."[84] In her study of women's reformatories, Eugenia Lekkerkerker cited the KSIFW as one of three examples of institutions that taught good domestic science courses.[85] The KSIFW attempted to add a layer of education to the everyday work that needed to be done to run the institution.

The staff at the KSIFW emphasized how the skills that inmates learned at the Farm would transfer to their lives as homemakers once they left the institution. The matrons of the kitchen and bakery departments wrote in 1938: "We find the majority of the girls willing and eager to learn, as they realize the knowledge gleaned here will be of great benefit to them when they go back to their homes."[86] Superintendent Perry frequently spoke of the value of having crude facilities at the Farm in order to make the inmates' work more transferable to their life outside the institution. A 1929 description of the Farm commented: "The industries consist primarily in institutional work which is organized to give training in Home Economics. The equipment as a whole is of a type used in homes rather than in institutions, so that this work has real vocational value."[87] Lekkerkerker's 1931 book emphasized a similar point in her description of the KSIFW. As examples of ways that the Farm had retained "some of its pioneer crudeness," she noted that "the plainest utensils are used for cooking and serving the food, and all the laundering is still done by hand in old-fashioned

This picture of the "shack in which domestic science" was taught features "girls dressed in white muslin, ready for their period in class." Note the child in the front who is holding a doll and freely mixing with other inmates; having children at the Farm was one of the more controversial aspects of the institution. Eugenia C. Lekkerkerker, Reformatories for Women in the United States *(Groningen: J. B. Wolters, 1931), 217.*

wash-tubs." Lekkerkerker commented that the Farm was rather proud of these rustic methods: "The superintendent considers it a great asset to develop resourcefulness and practical ability in the inmates, who nearly all are, or will be, the heads of a household. It should be remembered that Kansas is a rural state where the homes which the majority of the Farm girls will later have to conduct offer few of the modern conveniences."[88]

A strong current of the logic for teaching domestic skills was the idea that inmates of the Farm would go on to be "the heads of a household." In this way, the Farm served to facilitate middle-class ideals of femininity and the proper place of women as being within the home.

At the same time that the professional women who ran the Farm emphasized inmates' future roles as housewives, though, they also acknowledged that many of these women would need to be able to financially support themselves and their families. Nationally, many women's prison reformers advocated for job training in skilled trades that would equip women to get well-paid jobs once leaving the institutions. However, this type of job training was rarely realized in women's reformatories, as lack of funding and institutional commitments got in the way. In lieu of training in more skilled occupations, women's reformatories emphasized teaching domesticity as the best route to both reforming women's character and teaching them viable job skills. Teaching domesticity was much less threatening to the overall gender order than training women for better-paid professions, keeping working-class women in a position of economic dependence on both their husbands and the middle-class families for whom they might work as domestics. As Lekkerkerker commented in her 1931 study of women's reformatories: "A domestic position offers experience similar to what the woman would meet in her own household so that there is no conflict between the woman's task as wage-earner and as a housewife, which is not true of other positions."[89] Several comments from superintendents and matrons at the Farm portrayed domestic work as an important set of skills that would be required for a woman to be economically self-sufficient once leaving the Farm. In discussing the sewing department, Perry commented that "a thorough knowledge of this department lays the foundation for a future livelihood to the one who tries to become efficient."[90] Similarly, Daisy Sharp, the superintendent writing the 1932 report, commented: "The institution has been made, not only an industrial farm in name, but a place where the industries pursued may be so competently mastered that a girl or woman going out into active life may have the ability to do her work well and be of service to society as well as to her employer."[91] Having the only job training offered through the institution be as a domestic reinforced inmates' position as working-class women. The 1922 biennial report listed teaching women about "the duties of mistress and maid" as one of the valuable things that inmates learned at the Farm.[92] Most reformatories, including Kansas, emphasized the teaching of home economics as the primary means of providing inmates with job skills, in turn reinforcing gender and class hierarchies.[93]

This emphasis on domesticity reflected the contradictions in professional women's own relationship to femininity. In women's reformatories across the country, women were explicitly hired as superintendents and matrons based on the assumption that their femininity would have a positive influence on the inmates. At the same time, however, the superintendents and matrons who worked at these institutions were straddling the transition from a Victorian version of femininity that idealized the "angel in the house" to an updated conception of the "modern woman" who worked and had a greater level of independence. Many of the superintendents and matrons did not have families of their own, and those that did would have had a nontraditional living arrangement due to the work requirement of living at the reformatory. Indeed, social commentators at the time often voiced concern about professional women's sexuality, seeing many professional women's lack of interest in heterosexual relationships as a sign of lesbianism or an overly developed sense of Victorian prudery, often called "frigidity." Basing their public authority on their embodiment of Victorian femininity was what landed professional women their jobs, yet the conditions of their jobs prevented them from fully realizing this feminine ideal.[94]

The emphasis that KSIFW staff put on domesticity allowed them to identify with elements of femininity and construct themselves as the models of domestic skill and proper feminine behavior. Before the KSIFW was established, Lucy B. Johnston gave a speech to Kansas clubwomen to convince them of the need for a women's reformatory in Kansas. She emphasized the need for staff who would model femininity and respectability for the inmates, noting that when an inmate left the reformatory, "she has not only been trained in right living by skilled and able teachers, but for months and years she followed the leadership of strong, clean and balanced womanhood. Her teachers, keepers, superintendent, and governing board should be the best and strongest women that can be found; they are the models each day for her." In Johnston's view, the respectability of the staff was a critical component of the reformatory mission of the institution; she went on to state, "There is nothing so potent in the re-moulding of the deficient woman as the leadership of clean and wholesome women."[95] Similarly, physician Sherman L. Axford wrote to Julia Perry in the 1918 board of administration report: "Ofttimes there are ailments among the inmates at the Farm that neither medical skill nor surgery will reach. In such cases the true-hearted womanhood of yourself and your capable assistants has been invaluable."[96] Thus, despite the fact that these professional women were working and often did not have families of their own, this construction of their role at the Farm as providing a model for femininity and respectability brought some resolution to their claims to femininity.

This resolution of professional women's relationship to femininity was taken even further in several comments that created parallels between the professional staff/inmate and mother/daughter relationship. Whether it was referring to the Farm as "a happy family," the matrons as "housemothers," the nurse as a "big sister," or the inmates as "girls," the language used in documents related to the KSIFW continually evoked familial relationships.[97] Perry directly made this connection between the role of a mother and the role of the professional staff at the KSIFW in this comment from the 1922 biennial report: "It is not more true that 'the hand that rocks the cradle rules the world,' than that the one who works patiently and persistently with those who need help, molds and makes characters that in turn bless the world."[98] Here, Perry quite explicitly identified the role that professional women played at the Farm with ideals of Victorian motherhood and femininity.

Inherent in this construction of professional women as proxy mothers for the inmates was a critique of the inmates' own biological mothers. Similar to social workers and female reformers across the country, staff at the Farm were able to position themselves as "mothers" precisely because they viewed the inmates' biological mothers as inept.[99] A 1920 social worker's report on the social backgrounds of women imprisoned at the Farm stated that the majority of the girls had "been handicapped by lack of proper home training and discipline." The report went on: "One mother seemed astonished because the agent assumed that she might know what her children were doing when they were away from the house. Another mother stated that she had never spoken upon sex matters to her daughter until the latter, illegitimately pregnant, was about to give birth to a child."[100] This criticism of inmates' mothers was also apparent in a speech from Julia Perry to the WCTU that was included in the 1924 biennial report. Perry asked her audience: "What about the mothers of these girls? There is something radically wrong when a daughter of fifteen years is beyond the mother's control." She went on to say: "The factor most potent in the home is the mother. She is the loadstone to all hearts and the loadstar to all eyes."[101] These critiques of inmates' mothers were rooted in perceptions of their respectability, or lack thereof. The superintendent and matrons of the KSIFW contrasted their own respectability with that of the inmates' mothers, even if they themselves were not biological mothers.

The irony of this construction of motherhood was that many of the inmates themselves had children. Though the biennial reports of the KSIFW do not provide information about inmates' pregnancies and births, social worker Alice Hill's report included information about the women she studied in 1918. Of these women, 69 percent had at some point been pregnant. While many of these pregnancies had ended in miscarriage or the children had died at young ages, this still left a large number of children whose mothers were sent to the Farm. While the sentence to the KSIFW surely created childcare issues for many women, the women in Hill's study reported that most of their children were not living with them in the time leading up to their arrest. Of the 114 children born to the inmates in her sample, only nineteen (17 percent) were living with their mothers. Most were living with other relatives, in foster homes, in state facilities, or with a charity organization. Though it is not known whether this pattern continued through the rest of the interwar period, the lack of involvement of many of the inmates in their children's lives speaks to their inability to live up to the expectations of motherhood espoused by the staff at the Farm.[102]

The superintendents and matrons of the Farm made explicit connections between inmates' morality, their own mothers, and their lack of training in domesticity. Several superintendents and matrons commented that the domestic training provided at the Farm was filling a gap in the inmates' domestic education. Cora M. Smith, instructor in the art department, commented: "Many of the girls who come to us cannot use a thimble and do not know the first principles of sewing, and before they leave us are able to do the finest embroidery."[103] These sentiments are echoed in a comment from Kate Hooven, instructor of the sewing department: "Many of the women and girls have never had the opportunity to know home-making in the finer sense, and they come to us not knowing what they are capable of doing."[104] The idea that inmates had been denied the opportunity to develop proper domestic skills in their lives prior to coming to the Farm was a continued theme in the biennial reports; the 1938 report quoted superintendent Sara Mae Cain as saying "that many girls learn their first lessons in cooking, housekeeping, sewing, laundry work, and gardening" while at the Farm.[105] Inherent in these comments about inmates' domestic ineptitude was a critique of the inmates' mothers and the idea that this lack of domestic training was part of the reason for the women's moral downfall. Agnes Lundstrom, an officer in Perry Cottage, commented that many girls were grateful for the opportunity to learn domestic skills. She commented: "One often feels if the girls had had the counsel and understanding she duly receives from our Superintendent and officers here prior to her difficulties these same difficulties might have been avoided since so often society at large condemns before hearing."[106] These comments echo the logic of reform that ran throughout the

KSIFW's philosophy for running the Farm. Inmates' lack of a respectable female role model and proper training in domesticity were the root of their poor choices in life. With the proper training and "mother" figures provided through the Farm, they could be reformed. Thus, the professional women who worked at the Farm were able to rewrite themselves as mothers and be a model of domesticity, reconciling to some degree their problematic relationship with femininity. The emphasis on domesticity had layered meanings for the inmates and staff alike.

Reforming Inmates and Controlling Costs

In many ways, the language about the reforming power of domesticity was just making a virtue of necessity. While the professional women who ran the KSIFW tried to provide an education beyond that entailed in completing the work, the fact remains that, as an institution, the KSIFW had to complete much of this labor in-house in order to remain financially solvent. Comments about the reforming power of hard work brought together the sometimes-competing demands of reforming inmates and keeping institutional costs to a minimum. The staff at the Farm were particularly likely to use heightened language about the reforming power of work when they talked about domesticity. This can be seen in a comparison of how professional women talked about homemaking and farmwork in the 1922 biennial report. The report described work carried out in the homemaking department:

> In general, we teach all home work at all times, emphasizing the word *home*. At the same time we distinguish it from housework; that in the home is the woman's work, and no part of it should be considered beneath a woman's notice and knowledge, from fancy sewing and cooking to the cleaning of the kitchen sink and cellar stairs. The great lesson we try to impress upon the minds of these future home-makers is the usefulness, the beauty and sanctity of the home.[107]

Idealized notions of home and connections to femininity add layers of meaning to the daily work of washing dishes and sewing clothes. Compare to this the description of the work involved with caring for livestock in the next section of the same report: "The past biennium we have raised a thousand chickens. We expect our eggs to entirely supply our institutional needs. Our cattle, our hogs and horses come in for their share of attention. The dairy products, the meat we put away for winter use, both help to place us on a self-supporting basis and reduce our per capita cost."[108] The work of caring for animals was presented merely as work that needed to be completed, devoid of the added meaning imbued in work more closely associated with the idea of home. In practice, the inmates involved with caring for the livestock probably learned just as much as the women working in the homemaking departments, despite the lack of language about an intentional educational program for those working with animals.

The reforming power that KSIFW staff imbued in different types of work was consistent with gendered ideas about women's labor in the national reformatory movement. Lekkerkerker's 1931 book spoke to the different domestic standards maintained at men's and women's correctional institutions: "As cooking, cleaning and other acts of housekeeping have no educational value for men, the tendency in men's prisons is always to do the minimum of this work that is compatible with accepted standards of hygiene." A women's reformatory, however, "which attempts to be a school of domestic science for its inmates, cannot afford to give a minimum of physical care only; it will rather have to set an example."[109] The fact that both men's and women's institutions completed similar types of domestic work, but it only had "educational value" for women, shows that the conflation of domestic training with reform was largely a matter of language.

The superintendent of the Farm had to balance financial pressures and the desire to reform inmates from the outset of the institution. Though the initial appropriation of $75,000 for the creation of the KSIFW was generous considering that there were fewer than twenty inmates at the time, the huge influx of women into the institution within just a few months of its opening completely overwhelmed the facility. The 1920 report of the state board of health praised the way that Julia Perry handled the situation: "The story of how the Farm came into existence reads almost like a fairy tale; it is a story of providing housing facilities and food for an increasing population of infected women without money with which to purchase such necessities."[110] The report went on to account how Perry arranged with the warden of the men's prison for male laborers to cut down trees and erect makeshift buildings and tents to house inmates and how she made sure that gardens were planted immediately so that inmates would have enough to eat. Despite the board's assertion that this was "like a fairy tale," the reality of the situation was that the state sentenced several hundred women to an institution and provided no additional financial resources to care for them. How Perry was supposed to accomplish her mission of reform in these conditions is a mystery. Though the KSIFW received regular funding and appropriations for new buildings throughout the interwar years, the Farm was not allotted as much as would have been necessary to truly achieve the reformatory ideal, particularly in terms of the funding to pay well-trained staff.[111]

These competing expectations about reforming inmates and keeping costs low reveal some of the contradictions imposed on the Farm. The original legislation establishing the KSIFW stated that inmates' labor at the Farm should be used to reform character, not for profit. At the same time that Kansas pushed this mission of reform on state prisons and reformatories, it also pushed institutions to be as economically self-sufficient as possible. This escalated in 1926, when the state legislature mandated the creation of a budget director position, who asked all state institutions to begin reporting their expenses on a per-client basis. Kansas institutions completed as much of the work of the institutions in-house as possible, with each having farms, laundries, and kitchens staffed by prison labor. With such tight budgets, there was little room for the KSIFW superintendent to allot much staff time or resources to anything outside of the basic work that needed to be done to keep the institution solvent. Amid these financial pressures, the mission of reform was sometimes lost. A 1933 independent report critiqued the KSIFW for lacking a serious educational program outside of the basic work that had to be completed at the Farm.[112] Despite all of the rhetoric about the reforming power of training in domestic science, the KSIFW was largely in line with national trends in women's reformatories in that the work of the institution took precedence over a serious educational program.[113]

Female superintendents may have had control over women's reformatories themselves, but they had little control over the legal and funding decisions that had a huge impact on their institutions. With separate cottages rather than a central building, high staff-to-inmate ratios, and extensive educational and parole missions, the women's reformatory model was an expensive one to implement. In practice, women's reformatories rarely had the funding to truly live up to their aspirations. The 1929 *Handbook of Prisons and Reformatories* commented: "The defects of the women's reformatories are not defects of spirit and purpose. . . . They often have insufficient appropriations and their interests are subordinated by legislators to those of the state prisons."[114] As states tightened their belts during the Great Depression of the 1930s, the gap between what women's reformatories needed and what male-controlled legislatures would actually allot widened, resulting in many women's reformatories that lacked any sort of professional or educational training at all.[115]

Ideal Inmates and Sentences for Reform

Another barrier to being able to achieve this ideal of reform was the type of inmates that were sent to the Farm and the duration of their internment. Unlike men's prisons, women's reformatories were not designed for hardened criminals. Instead, the reformers' ideal inmate was someone who was on the brink of diving into a life of crime but was still capable of being reformed. Thus, reformatory officials preferred younger women convicted of minor offenses. They also tended to prefer white women, as women of color were thought of as being less capable of being reformed and were often sent to regular women's penitentiaries in states that were large enough to have both types of facilities, and in states across the South. Together with increasing state regulation of women's sexuality, the emphasis on minor offenses meant that most of the women sent to women's reformatories were there based on sexuality-related offenses, such as prostitution, or generic convictions, such as vagrancy, that, in practice, were used to convict women guilty of some type of sexual misconduct.[116]

Though the ideal inmate was a younger woman capable of being reformed, male-controlled legislatures inadvertently sabotaged the mission of women's reformatories nationally by sending them the "wrong type" of women. The small number of female convicts in most states meant that, in practice, women's reformatories received all women in the state convicted of a crime, hardened criminal and novice alike. This had enormous implications for the mission of reform. By the early 1930s felons began to constitute most of the inmate populations at reformatories as states consolidated women's penal institutions. Superintendents of women's reformatories across the country complained that they were unable to realize the ideal of the reformatory model with such a diverse set of inmates. This was the sentiment behind a comment by Perry in the 1920 KSIFW biennial report saying that women with extreme discipline problems "do not belong in our reformatory class."[117] Thus, there was a gap between the ideal inmate of women's reformatories from the superintendents' viewpoint and the reality of the types of inmates committed to the institutions.[118]

Like reformatories across the country, the KSIFW had a particularly high population of young women who were sent to the reformatory as a result of sexual misconduct. Where it differed was the convictions under which women were sent to the institution. The Kansas reformatory was one of only a few across the country, including those in Nebraska and Wisconsin, that focused almost exclusively on women sentenced under a venereal disease control law. The fact that the majority of the inmates at the Farm were sent for venereal disease was, in and of itself, a decision of enormous impact that was made outside the institution. The 1926 KSIFW biennial report commented: "The original plan of the institution was to care for the sentenced women of the state, but, to better protect the public from ravages of infection from exposure to venereal disease, we have received and cared for the interne girls and women."[119] Activist women founded the KSIFW with the idea of reforming women, and the superintendents held this same philosophy as well. Yet the high number of women sent to the Farm under Chapter 205 meant that, in some ways, the institution functioned more like a hospital than a prison. It also meant that, due to the way Chapter 205 was enforced, there were a fairly high number of inmates going through the KSIFW. While the average population size was consistent with other reformatories, inmates at the Farm did not serve very long terms, so there was a high turnover rate among inmates. Such high numbers of women going through the institution meant that parole work was nearly impossible, particularly because the KSIFW did not have the money to hire a parole officer.[120]

However, this difference between the KSIFW and other reformatories should not be overstated. In terms of race, class, and age of the inmates, as well as the average number of inmates at the institution at a time, Kansas was fairly typical of other reformatories in the country during this period. Most women's reformatories routinely gave Wasserman tests for syphilis to all inmates, with one conservative estimate showing that 20 to 30 percent of inmates at reformatories not explicitly focusing on venereal disease tested positive.[121] Whether they were convicted of violating a law associated with sexual morality or quarantined under a venereal disease control law (such as Chapter 205 in Kansas), inmates of reformatories across the country were coming under the control of state authorities based on their perceived sexual misconduct. The populations of different types of reformatories were actually quite similar, as were the functions performed by the KSIFW and other women's reformatories. Indeed, there was a general blurring of distinctions between the roles played by private organizations, penal institutions, and medical treatment facilities for women during this period. In her 1931 study Eugenia Lekkerkerker noted the overlapping missions and functions of these types of institutions in light of the fact that "sexual misconduct constitutes such a large part of women's criminality in America." She noted: "There is no province in which the lines drawn between law and morals, between what is to be considered as a public offense or as a private sin, are so vague and vacillating as in the domain of sexual morality, and it is not surprising that this vagueness also blurs the distinction between the measures to be applied."[122] Women's reformatories, medical facilities, and private organizations performed similar functions, such as treating physical ailments, reforming character, and providing job training. For many social reformers and prison officials, diseased women and sexual delinquents were essentially the same. The underlying accusation of sexual impropriety supported the imprisonment of women under a vagrancy charge or under Chapter 205 in Kansas; it was just a different legal mechanism that gave the state authority to detain them. However, women sentenced under a quarantine law were not guaranteed due process, and, particularly since the diagnosis of venereal disease was so ambiguous, the burden of proof was often lower for women sentenced under venereal disease laws.

The high number of inmates going through the KSIFW and their relatively short sentences had enormous implications for the mission of reform of the institution. Julia Perry continually lamented in the biennial reports that she did not have a long enough period of time to truly reform the women sentenced under Chapter 205. Though, by the nature of the source, the biennial reports rarely directly criticized male officials or the state, they did repeatedly point out that the time of detention for venereal disease cases was incompatible with the ideal of reform and asked for longer sentences for interned women. In the 1922 biennial report, Perry wrote: "It is all wrong to send young girls to the Farm merely to be cured, when they need training and direction fully as much as to be cured of disease. As it is, they do not have time enough to catch a new viewpoint and become established in right living."[123] Julia Perry also appealed to clubwomen to lobby for inmates to be convicted under charges other than Chapter 205 so they could serve longer sentences at the Farm and more fully benefit from the reforming elements of the institution. In her speech to the KWCTU that she included in the 1924 biennial report, Perry argued that if women could be sent to the Farm under convictions that carried "a definite sentence of not less than a year's time for the first offense and a longer period if repeated, [Kansans] would begin to see results worth while."[124] In urging clubwomen to lobby for inmates to be detained under other sexuality-related charges, like lascivious conduct or vagrancy, to detain similar populations of women, Perry sought to bring the KSIFW more into line with other women's reformatories and extend the amount of time women spent at the Farm.

Longer sentences were an important part of the national women's reformatory model. Many reformers advocated for indeterminate sentences for female prisoners. If the point of incarceration was to reform women, rather than merely punish them, then prison officials needed to be able to keep female inmates in their institutions until they were truly reformed, regardless of the severity of their original offense. In a 1919 article about combatting prostitution, women's reformatory champion Martha Falconer highlighted the importance of detaining women for extended periods. She criticized facilities that kept women for short periods of medical treatment as ineffective, noting: "Of course these girls, when leaving after thirty days' intensive treatment, with instructions for the next six months, would each one assure you, 'Sure, I've had my lesson. I'm going to get a job and stick to it!'"[125] Falconer viewed these claims with skepticism, instead arguing that many women would needs months, if not years, of time at a reformatory to learn the value of hard work and regain their moral compass. The practice of giving women indeterminate sentences, even for relatively minor offenses, was commonplace in women's reformatories across the country. The time of incarceration became divorced from the nature of the original offense, investing great authority in the social workers, psychologists, parole boards, and superintendents who made the decision about when an inmate was "reformed" enough to be released into society. Besides fitting within the larger idea of reform and investing them with a high level of discretion in their jobs, having indeterminate sentences also gave women's prison officials very practical leverage to use against inmates in their institutions in order to maintain discipline. KSIFW superintendent Daisy Sharp commented in the 1932 biennial report: "While every possible privilege is accorded, at no time are the girls allowed to forget that their future depends upon the rectitude of their own conduct."[126] Because women sent to the Farm under Chapter 205 were there under a quarantine charge, they were supposed to be there until deemed noninfectious. Given the fact that there was no cure for syphilis or gonorrhea at the time, the length of their detention was highly subjective and amounted to an indeterminate sentence. Yet the high number of women continually entering the institution meant that the facility would have quickly become overwhelmed if the superintendents had kept women for longer periods. The relatively short time that inmates were at the KSIFW was a barrier to achieving the type of reform envisioned by the women's reformatory model.[127]

Physical Health as a Component of Respectability

The high percentage of inmates detained under Chapter 205 meant that the KSIFW was primarily providing medical care in an institution intended to provide moral reform. To reconcile these competing missions, the superintendents and matrons at the Farm constructed respectability and reform in such a way that included physical health.

The professional women who staffed the KSIFW continually referenced the need for inmates to be cured physically before they could be reformed morally in the institution's biennial reports. In 1918 Julia Perry commented: "Suffice it to say that it is absolutely necessary that the individual be built up physically before she can be reached otherwise."[128] Perry repeated this idea in the 1920 biennial report: "Our first thought is to let everyone grow physically well. As they do this their physical development is reinforced by mental development, and then is the time that we make appeals to their moral nature."[129] Assertions that physical and moral rehabilitation were part of the same overall process brought together the competing missions of the KSIFW to treat venereal disease and morally reform the inmates. Superintendent Sara Mae Cain articulated this connection in the 1938 report: "We feel that our hospital and dental departments contribute greatly to our work of rehabilitation. Only through a healthy body can we work to create a healthy mental attitude, which is necessary if these women are to become useful citizens."[130] In these statements, the superintendents attempted to bring physical care in line with the institution's overall mission of moral reform.

One way that KSIFW staff emphasized this connection between physical care and moral reform was through highlighting the parallel natures of physical, mental, and moral development. In the 1926 report, teacher Eleanor Robson wrote: "But my greatest aim is to send our girls out clean. Clean in body, mind and soul. Equipped for higher duties of life."[131] Superintendent Etta Beavers commented: "The general policy of this institution can be best expressed by our program of rehabilitation—which is, strive to improve, physically, mentally and morally."[132] The task of the female administrators of the Farm was to facilitate the development of these parallel facets of human development in order to cultivate an inmate's potential. In an oft-repeated statement, Perry commented in the 1918 report, "The delinquent woman is, without contradiction, the product of disproportionate development. In her you discover the lack of parity of growth between the physical, mental, and moral parts of her nature. . . . So the person that develops physically and mentally, but *not morally*, becomes a criminal." Here, Perry cautioned against the dangers of young women who have developed physically (i.e., become sexually mature), yet lacked the moral development needed to keep pace. Whether inmates were physically marked with the stigma of venereal disease or were more sexually developed than their morals were prepared to regulate, the professional women at the Farm constructed their bodies as being out of control and an important component of their reform. Through such language as referring to the Farm as a "moral hospital," professional women made explicit connections between their tasks of reforming women physically and morally.[133]

Tied to these connections between physical bodies and respectability, officials connected with the KSIFW frequently asserted that the inmates who were sent to the Farm on state criminal charges were of a higher type than the women sent to the Farm under Chapter 205, also called interns. Responding to a report on the Farm that suggested that venereal disease patients would be better served outside of a penal institution, Perry argued for the importance of moral training as part of interns' plan of treatment. She commented: "As a rule, the sentenced women are a much higher type than the intern," noting that she "would be glad if the intern woman could stay with us much longer and get more training than she does."[134] In these comments, Perry reinforced the connection between physical and moral retraining, insisting that both were necessary for the full rehabilitation of diseased women. While there were times when Perry expressed frustration with the sexual double standard enforced through Chapter 205, she still viewed most of the women sentenced to the Farm under Chapter 205 as being in need of moral reform. The perception that state charges were of a "higher type" than interns was also apparent in the autobiography of Samuel J. Crumbine. He recalled an incident from the initial influx of women at the Farm during World War I in which a matron asked one of the state charges why they treated the interned women poorly and refused to share the dining room with them. The inmate, who was serving a life sentence, reportedly replied: "I know I killed my husband. However, I did it under great provocation. Anyway, I'm paying for it now. But I have never sold my body and soul for a piece of filthy money, nor interfered with keeping our boys fit to fight for our country! So I despise these vile creatures."[135] The perception that state charges were morally superior to women sent to the Farm under a venereal disease charge reveals the way that the association between bodies and respectability influenced administrators' perceptions of moral worth.

The fact that prison administrators made a distinction between the state charges and the intern population is made more remarkable by the fact that many of the women who were there on state charges also had venereal disease. A 1931 newspaper article commented: "Since many, if not most of the interned women potentially are delinquent in other than sex matters and since many of the criminal women also are venereally diseased on entrance, it might be assumed that the two groups would be similar. On the whole, however, the criminal women are older and of higher grade mentally and socially than are the venereally diseased sex offenders."[136] There were surely some behavioral differences between the groups, since the state charges were older on average and would have been at the Farm long enough to fully learn the routines of the institution. Yet given the overlap between the two populations, the construction of state charges as being more respectable than the intern population had more to do with the fact that women sentenced under Chapter 205 were explicitly identified with their (diseased) bodies in a way that the state charges were not.

Newby's undercover reports on the Farm highlighted this distinction between women sentenced on state charges and women sent under Chapter 205. Though noting that "it became increasingly difficult . . . to distinguish between state charges and internes" since there was so much overlap in the populations, Newby highlighted both the disdain felt by state charges for the interns and the greater respectability of state charges. Speaking of the initial influx of women sentenced under Chapter 205 to the Farm, Newby commented, "Feeling on the part of the 'state charges' for the incoming diseased women was not friendly. A number of state prisoners, though charged with serious crimes themselves, have a contempt for loose women, and in addition feel a physical fear in associating with diseased prostitutes."[137] Newby made a distinction between those women who violated the laws of society in general (state charges) and those who violated the laws of society through their bodies (interns), with the clear implication that the "loose women" were less respectable. She had a much more favorable impression of the state charges than the women sent to the farm under Chapter 205: "In nearly every instance the state girl was cleaner and neater in appearance, more industrious in her habits, more dignified in manner; while the diseased girls, with a few noticeable exceptions, engaged in coarse talk that was so distasteful to the state girls that they were often seen to withdraw in disgust."[138] This description positioned state charges as more respectable: they had better control of their bodies ("neater in appearance") and had mastered some of the skills in domesticity that the Farm sought to instill ("industrious in her habits"). Newby also referenced different levels of cultural capital ("dignified in manner" and "coarse talk"), indicating that cultural markers of social class factored into the designation of interns as less respectable. Regardless of whether there were concrete differences in the way state charges and interns presented themselves, this indicates a perceived difference in respectability that was centered on how the two groups of inmates managed their bodies.

The perception that state charges were more respectable than interns is particularly apparent in the way Newby described two inmates at the Farm, one an intern and the other a state charge. In describing the girls with whom she shared a living space, Newby referred to one as the girl "with the bobbed hair," who seemed to take a leadership role in the group. Newby described her: "She is pretty in a hard sort of way; has a bold manner and a 'tough' walk; smokes a great deal, and uses more profanity than do the other girls."[139] From her bobbed hair to her smoking, this inmate exhibited many of the characteristics of the flapper of the 1920s, a cultural type widely associated with permissive sexuality.[140] Newby's description of the inmate's short hair and "tough" walk emphasized her masculine qualities. Compare this to the way Newby described one of the state charges, Tillie, who stopped by the cottage on an errand and asked one of the new girls about her crocheting. Tillie praised the girl's piece, though it was "coarse and soiled," and then went on to show her a "bit of exquisitely made lace which she was finishing." Newby commented: "I had been struck with the beauty of Tillie's voice the first time I heard her speak; now I noted the daintiness of her appearance in the midst of the rather untidy-looking girls in our cottage. Her hair was soft and clean; her skin pink and health-looking; her eyes were clear; her hands beautifully kept."[141] This description highlighted Tillie's respectability in a very embodied and class-specific way. Tillie had mastered many elements of domesticity and femininity that the staff of the KSIFW sought to instill. Her respectability was embodied: her voice was beautiful, her hair was soft, and Newby went on to note that she "carried herself with dignity." Tillie's respectability was also very class-specific: she had the cultural capital to be able to appear "dainty" and her hands were "beautifully kept," indicating that she had not had to work with them as a woman from the working class might. Overall, Newby's descriptions of the "girl with the bobbed hair" and Tillie reveal a particular version of respectability that was being constructed through professional women's discussions of state charges as being more respectable than interns.

Together, this emphasis on the need to build women up physically before they could be reformed morally and the assertion that state charges were more respectable than interns constructed a version of reform and respectability that highlighted the role of the body. As women whose bodies were physically marked with their (perceived) lack of sexual self-control by their illness, interns at the Farm had their bodies put front and center. Whether it was talking about teaching inmates "to get control of themselves" or to be "self-governing individuals," the professional women who worked at the Farm emphasized self-control as an important characteristic for interns to develop.[142] By learning to control their behaviors and their bodies, women sentenced to the Farm under Chapter 205 could start on the path to respectability.[143]

Discipline under a Mission of Reform

Despite the emphasis on reform in the ideals of women's reformatories, punishment and maintaining discipline were necessary components of managing these institutions. Overall, the disciplinary approach in women's reformatories was one of positive reinforcement, where good behaviors were praised and rewarded with additional privileges. Superintendents of women's reformatories repeatedly discussed the importance of keeping inmates busy and structuring the daily life of the institution so as to avoid the potential for behavior problems.[144]

Life at the KSIFW reflected this desire to maintain order at the institution through positive reinforcement rather than direct punishment. The biennial reports from the early days of the institution downplayed any direct disciplinary actions toward the inmates. In the speech that Perry gave to the WCTU that was reprinted in the 1924 biennial report, she highlighted how the institution had no walls, cells, or bars to keep the inmates in. She noted: "Not even a fence shuts them from the great outside world. Under the leafy shade of elm and birch trees they breathe the fresh air of Heaven and bask in the sunlight of God's love."[145] Nationally, women's reformatories attempted this strategy of creating a homelike environment by doing things like leaving inmates' rooms unlocked at night. Despite the lax security, relatively few women escaped from the KSIFW: Lekkerkerker reported that only twenty-three escaped from the KSIFW in an eight-year period, out of 2,960 women committed, even though "there had been no lock between the girls and the free outdoors during the night" during certain periods.[146] Direct punishment and confinement were at odds with the ideal of reform that guided the institution.[147]

Instead of punishment, the biennial reports from the KSIFW repeatedly discussed the virtues of positive reinforcement and providing a wholesome, stimulating, and homelike environment at the Farm. The KSIFW sought to provide recreational diversions, such as sporting events and plays, in order to keep the inmates busy and out of trouble. Several comments in the biennial reports claimed that simply by keeping inmates busy and appealing to their better natures, most need for direct punishment could be avoided. Julia Perry wrote in 1922: "Such a spirit of contentment prevails among our girls and women that one vies with the other to excel in any given work. Corporal punishment is not known in our correctional work."[148] This effort to appeal to inmates' better natures was a way of getting inmates to internalize the rules and expectations of the institution and society more broadly. This target of self-regulation was an important component of the overall strategy of reform. Superintendent Etta Beavers wrote in 1942: "We try to discover the good in each girl, then emphasize and build on this good in a positive way, with the idea of doing something with the girl instead of something for or to her."[149] Rather than someone imposing rules on inmates, women's reformatories sought to get women to impose rules on themselves.[150] In a section titled

"Punishments" in the 1924 biennial report, Perry emphasized that corporal punishment, scolding, and nagging were not allowed at the Farm. Instead, the professional staff were to study each inmate and create the conditions to develop her character. Perry noted: "An inmate shortens her time of detention, or stays her full time, according as her conduct shows her fit or unfit to leave the institution."[151] Throughout the interwar period, superintendents at the Farm emphasized the strategies employed by the institution to reform women's character—indeterminate sentences and the medicalized, individual model for treatment and reform—instead of direct punishment and confinement.

One behavior issue common to penal institutions was the potential for sexual relationships between inmates. Nationally, prison reformers made explicit connections between same-sex relationships and racial integration in women's reformatories. In her account of women's reformatories during this period, Lekkerkerker commented: "Another reason, however, for separating the two races in a woman's institution is the fact that a peculiar attraction has been found to exist between colored and white women in confinement which intensifies much the danger, always present in an institution, of homosexual involvements."[152] The official biennial reports of the KSIFW did not mention this concern about interracial sexual relationships, but several other documents cited sexual relationships between inmates as a problem at the Farm. A 1931 newspaper article mentioned "the ever insistent problem of homosexuality" as one of the disciplinary problems of the institution.[153] Among the complaints sent to Governor Woodring from disgruntled employees in 1932 was the assertion that "no line is drawn in the mingling of white and negro girls and they become entirely too chummy, writing one another sweetheart notes."[154] In a response typical of women's reformatories' effort to prevent behavioral issues from occurring rather than relying on punishment after the fact, the association between same-sex relationships and interracial mingling led many superintendents to segregate inmates of their reformatories based on race. The KSIFW, however, remained racially integrated, with women of different racial backgrounds living and working together.[155]

Despite all of the language about a "prison without bars," the policy of appealing to inmates' better natures did not solve all disciplinary problems. The biennial reports of the KSIFW did not mention cells until 1926, when Perry requested funding to build a separate cell house and indicated that the Farm was, at that time, using cells within each cottage.[156] The

A photo of the "Field Gang," showing Black and white inmates working side by side. Eugenia C. Lekkerkerker, Reformatories for Women in the United States *(Groningen: J. B. Wolters, 1931), 337.*

conflict between the ideal of reform and the need to maintain order at the Farm can be seen in Perry's vacillation about this cell house. She again requested funding for a cell house in 1930, but after the Kansas legislature allotted money for the purpose, she wrote to the Governor's office to say that the building was not needed since it did not "seem to be in keeping with the liberty and freedom we have here."[157] The biennial reports of the KSIFW included more comments about confinement and punishment as the years progressed. A 1931 newspaper article faulted the high number of inmates and low staffing levels as causes for the KSIFW passing "into an era of wire gratings and locks and bolts." Though inmates were not denied food or subject to corporal punishment, the article noted that "every window now is grated, every door has a key and every ward is locked." The article reported that isolation cells in the basement of each cottage were "little better than common jail cells," though these were seldom used, "and that only to enable emotionally unstable women to 'cool off' or ‘come to’ when they ‘go berserk.’”[158] An independent 1933 evaluation of the KSIFW noted that the Farm started using locks in 1925, and that “now all girls are locked in with heavy steel screens covering windows and doors separating corridors and shutting off stairways. Cells were installed recently for punishment by solitary confinement,” although talking with matrons was still viewed as the primary means of disciplining inmates. The report went on to comment: “One is impressed with an inhibiting orderliness or routine. The girls are required to sit by their bed, or by their own room door, during their leisure hours and may not visit except with the girl across the hall. Quarantined girls are rigidly controlled.”[159] This report presents a significantly different picture of life at the KSIFW than the biennial reports. While the language of the biennial reports emphasized the effectiveness of one-on-one counseling provided to each inmate by matrons and the general approach of positive reinforcement, these comments about direct punishment show what happened when this strategy failed.

Though it is difficult to determine the extent to which mistreatment of inmates occurred at the KSIFW, the record of sterilizing inmates from 1936 points to at least one example of this occurring. A comment in the 1940 biennial report praising the new superintendent from Rev. P. H. Delahunty, the Catholic chaplain, also raises suspicions: “The effects of your treatment are now beginning to show. Abuses that continued for long have been eradicated, and a better understanding has been established between officers and inmates.”[160] Exactly what these “abuses” were is not known, but it is safe to say that the ideal of reform was just that: an ideal, one that, in practice, was insufficient to maintain the order needed at a large institution.

Conclusion

The KSIFW embodied many of the ideals of the national women’s reformatory model. People from around the world visited the institution to study how a prototypical women’s reformatory operated.[161] While the philosophy of reform and the architecture of the buildings were consistent with the national ideal, the focus on venereal disease set the KSIFW apart. The high numbers of inmates who stayed for short sentences posed serious challenges to the mission of reform that the professional staff of the Farm hoped to implement. The superintendents and matrons who ran daily life at the KSIFW gained jobs and some degree of status from their roles at the Farm, yet they lacked control over several elements of the institution that had enormous impact on their ability to carry out their vision for the institution. In Kansas as well as nationally, the ideal of the women's reformatory model was not realized in the everyday operations of these institutions. Superintendents of women's reformatories often did not control the type of inmate being sent to the institution and did not have enough funding to fully implement the reformatory model or provide the type of parole work and psychiatric treatment that they would have liked. In Kansas the superintendent also had no control over how men were treated in the criminal justice system and had to sit idly by while the state blatantly endorsed the sexual double standard through the gendered enforcement of Chapter 205. While the idea of the reforming power of domesticity may have reconciled some of these competing expectations for the KSIFW, the professional women who ran the Farm faced contradictory expectations and values as they sought to implement a plan of moral reform through the daily life of the KSIFW.

The superintendents and matrons who ran the Farm had a complicated relationship to respectability. The contradictions of their social positions illustrate how their jobs were tenuous and bounded by the decisions of men. However, these women had the symbolic power to define inmates' sexuality and what respectability should look like for them. It was through their power over other women that they were able to bring some resolution to their own social position. For the matrons at the Farm, their low pay meant that they were fairly similar to the inmates in terms of social class. It was the matrons' respectability, a qualification for their job, that allowed them to be in a position of authority over the inmates and hold themselves up as models of femininity and respectable behavior. For the superintendents of the KSIFW, their ideals for reform often butted up against the reality of limited budgets and lack of control over important aspects of their institutions, such as whether quarantine patients were sent to the Farm. They sought to establish a professional role for themselves through following the ideals of the national reformatory model, yet faced limitations in the extent to which they could reach this ideal. Through emphasizing the importance of physical rehabilitation to inmates' moral reform, superintendents of the Farm attempted to bring together the competing missions of the institution into a coherent philosophy. Reforming inmates was an important part of women like Julia Perry's professional identity. While Perry spoke out against the sexual double standard enforced through Chapter 205, she also argued that interned women should receive *longer* sentences. Perry, like many of her professional counterparts nationwide, endorsed the idea that sexually promiscuous women needed to be reformed through the coercive power of the state. The work involved with reforming these women gave the superintendents and matrons of the Farm a job, and it also gave them the symbolic power to define what respectability should look like for the women under their charge.

CHAPTER 5

PATHS TO THE KANSAS STATE INDUSTRIAL FARM FOR WOMEN

In December 1923 sixteen-year-old Catherine Ward was admitted as inmate number 2045 at the Kansas State Industrial Farm for Women. Catherine was briefly married two years earlier then went back home to her mother in Arkansas City, Kansas, after that marriage was annulled. She explained: "I have never been with but two men [since] I left my husband. . . . I have never got money from either of them we just went out on parties. My mother never knew until I was sent here that I wasn't a virtuous girl."[1] Catherine's path to the KSIFW was fairly typical. She reported that a police matron visited the house where she was staying and said that someone had reported Catherine and a friend as being diseased. Along with her friend, she went in for an examination and was sent to the Farm under Chapter 205.[2]

Catherine's path to the Farm was just one of the typical ways that women ended up being detained under Chapter 205 in Kansas. Jealous husbands and concerned parents turned women in to the authorities as venereal disease suspects. Other women came to the attention of authorities through routine encounters with the law, such as liquor violations or a raid of a boardinghouse. Other inmates actually volunteered to go to the Farm, desperate to get treatment for their diseases within a public health system that offered few affordable treatment options. The enforcement of Chapter 205 was a clear example of social control, where government officials invoked the power of the state to control individual behavior and reinforce societal norms. Yet Chapter 205 also functioned laterally, with individual citizens using the law to report other people and some desperate women using the law to commit themselves to the institution in order to access health care.[3] By exploring accounts of how women were arrested, the complexities of how Chapter 205 came to control women's sexual behaviors in Kansas become apparent.

This chapter draws from interviews that were conducted with inmates as they arrived at the Farm to understand how authorities enforced Chapter 205 and the different ways that women came to be quarantined in Lansing. Women were arrested under a variety of circumstances, with many cases reinforcing existing social hierarchies. Gender hierarchies were strengthened when a husband turned in a wife for a disease while he faced no repercussions, just as class hierarchies were reinforced when some women had to submit themselves to prison in order to access health care while others were able to afford treatment from the comfort of their hometowns. Regardless of how they ended up at the Farm, the inmates' accounts offer a rich source to understand inmates' experiences and how social boundaries of race, class, and gender informed the implementation of Chapter 205 in Kansas.

Analyzing the Inmate Interviews

The primary sources for this chapter and the next are the inmate interviews that KSIFW staff conducted with women as they arrived at the Farm. These interviews are interesting to consider not only in terms of their strengths and limitations as a historical source but also for what they tell us about the philosophy of reform espoused at the KSIFW. Prison staff used a standard interview form with each inmate who came to the Farm, regardless of whether she was imprisoned under Chapter 205 or a criminal charge. The practice of interviewing inmates on their arrival at the KSIFW, as well as the types of questions asked, was consistent with national practices at women's reformatories at the time.[4]

A look at the one-page interview form for Catherine Ward reveals many details about her life. First, some basic demographic information is presented, such as that Catherine was still in school at the time of her arrest and had lived in Kansas for eight years. Like all inmates, Catherine's race was recorded next to two spots on the form, the first labeled "Color" (which was almost always "White" or "Black") and the second labeled "Nationality" (which had a variety of responses). Catherine's form listed "White" and "Dutch Indian 1/8." Women whose color was recorded as White included those who had "Indian" or "Mexican" recorded next to nationality, while women whose color was recorded as "Black" almost exclusively just had "Negro" recorded for their nationality. These categorizations speak to the primacy of the white/Black racial divide in how prison staff understood race.[5]

Other than basic demographic information, the interview form also gives factual details about inmates' life histories, such as when and where they were born, dates of marriage and children born, and where they were employed. Several questions on the form illustrate the assumptions and approach of the staff at the Farm, including questions such as "At what age did you commit your first offense against the law of chastity?" (Catherine listed age fourteen) and a short spot on the form that simply stated "Cause of downfall." Questions asking about a "first offense" or "sex delinquency" were common on reports and interview forms during this period, even for young girls who were the victims of sexual abuse.[6] In Kansas and nationally, institutional documents assumed moral faults and sexual promiscuity on the part of all inmates. Given that the same form was used for women detained under Chapter 205 and criminal convictions, this conflation of sexual promiscuity with disease and crime speaks to the centrality of sexuality to officials' perceptions of women's deviance. Two places on the form where interviewers often recorded longer answers were next to a spot that read "History of offense" and a general category titled "Remarks." The short format of the one-page form, however, left little room to record many qualitative details about inmates' lives.

The interview form tells us much about the life of Catherine Ward and how Chapter 205 was implemented in her case, but it also leaves many questions unanswered. The inmate interviews cannot be read as direct representations of inmates' viewpoints. The interviews themselves were conducted in a highly charged situation: inmates were sentenced to the Farm under Chapter 205 until they were physically and morally "cured," meaning that the women had every reason to present themselves as respectable and downplay anything that might be perceived as a moral transgression. Given this, it is likely that many women simply lied to their interviewer. In his account of the influx of venereal disease patients at the Farm during World War I, Kansas State Board of Health official Samuel Crumbine indicated that the reason he sent social worker Darlene Doubleday Newby undercover was that prison officials did not feel like the inmates were being honest with them.[7] In a description of the interview process in women's reformatories during this period, researcher Eugenia Lekkerkerker commented: "Of course, very often the women lie, consciously or unconsciously, as naturally they are not always willing to tell about certain facts in their personal lives."[8]

Besides the more blatant issue of lying, the role of the person doing the interview must also be taken into consideration. The amount of information required to fill out the form would have required a fairly extensive conversation, yet only a few sentences were written down fully as quotations. Thus, the interviewer had to be very selective about which of the inmate's words were the most important to record on the interview form. The interview form for Catherine is fairly representative of the interviews overall: while most of the fields on the form were filled out by the interviewer, some, such as the question about the "Cause of downfall," were left blank, and it is unclear why that was the case.

A woman named Effie Beverly conducted the majority of the interviews in the sample. Beverly herself had been an inmate at the KSIFW. In July 1916 Beverly was living with her father near Milan, Kansas. She had gotten a divorce several years earlier and was caring for her two children. In an act of desperation, Beverly shot and killed her daughter Hazel, age six, and son Herbert, age five, while they were sleeping, but she lost her nerve before shooting herself. She was convicted of first-degree murder and served time at the KSIFW.[9] Effie Beverly went on to work at the Farm, and her name was among those of former convicts that matrons complained held too much sway at the KSIFW in their letters to the governor in 1932 (see chapter 4). Beverly's status as a former inmate has implications for the inmate interviews. The social distance between herself and the women she was interviewing may have been closer than if she were a regular staff member, which could have resulted in greater honesty in the women's answers. However, incoming inmates likely would not have known about Beverly's past at the time of the interview.

The potential bias of the interviewer can be seen during a short period in the late 1920s when Superintendent Julia Perry conducted the interviews. These interviews conducted by Perry were much more likely to include statements saying that the woman contracted a venereal disease through a philandering husband, and they contained more detailed discussions of future plans after leaving the Farm. Perry's overall emphasis on seeing inmates' better natures and making plans for them to lead respectable lives once leaving the institution can be seen in what she chose to write down during the interview process. Whether it was a former convict or the superintendent of the Farm conducting the interview, the person typing up the inmates' responses played an important role in shaping the inmate interview documents that we have today. Given these dynamics, these interviews can be seen as co-constructed between what the inmate said and what the interviewer actually typed.

Between the potential for outright fabrication and the mediating role of the interviewer in conducting and transcribing the interviews, these documents need to be read with caution. While they cannot be read as unproblematic windows into the lives of the inmates, the inmate interviews do offer a rich source for understanding the types of narratives that inmates understood as helping them stake a claim to respectability. Given the judgmental character of many of the questions and the unequal power relationships taking place, the inmates were likely on the defensive, trying to present themselves as respectable in the midst of a situation predicated on the assumption that they were not. As historian Elizabeth Clement argues, the justifications and explanations offered in these interviews give us a unique window into working-class women's views about sexuality and their perception of what would qualify as respectable behavior for their interviewer. These interviews "force their participants to articulate their values and their understandings of community standards and traditions."[10] For the purposes of this research, these interviews tell us what inmates thought a "respectable" account of their actions would sound like. For example, when Catherine Ward contended that she "never got money from either" of the men that she had sex with, she was articulating her perception that monetary exchange was a key distinction between respectable extramarital sexuality and prostitution. Reading these interviews as articulations of community standards also helps us move from simply making sense of these particular women's lives to the larger project of understanding the cultural schemas of the working class.[11] Thus, while the concerns about the power dynamics and structure of the interview outlined above will certainly be kept in mind in analyzing these interviews, there is still a wealth of information in this source.

Chapters 5 and 6 take a close look at these inmate interviews from the years 1923 to 1933; years prior to and after this date have been lost. Of the 2,437 interviews for women sentenced under Chapter 205, I looked at every fifth interview for a total of 488, or 20 percent of the total.[12] Interviews were coded for basic demographic information, how they were arrested, and how the women narrated their sexual histories. The first two categories are treated as more factual than the latter; the interviewers would have little reason to fabricate this information, and the inmates would have less motivation to be dishonest (though there were some instances where an inmate would have a reason to lie about how she was arrested, examples of which are noted below). The rest of this chapter is devoted to exploring how women claimed that they came to be arrested under Chapter 205. Quotes about how women narrated their sexual histories will be examined in the next chapter. They are read as described above: not necessarily as accurate accounts of inmates' sexual pasts, but rather as articulations of what the women perceived as being respectable accounts of their sexual histories. Read in this light, these interviews provide a rich source about inmates' experiences and perceptions of respectability.

While this section has laid out the limitations of these inmate interviews, I do not want to overlook their strengths as a historical source. Any kind of document, produced by the state or otherwise, that preserves the perspective of those who are not often included in the historical record is valuable. The large number of interviews is also a strength. While the shortness of the interview form prevents an in-depth understanding of individual women's stories, the large number of interviews helps us understand general trends in inmates' experiences. For example, inmates' claims that their husbands turned them in to authorities are difficult to verify individually, but the fact that so many women reported a similar experience gives some confidence that such incidents did occur. Particularly because the inmates' accounts of their experiences differ so drastically from the stories told about them by the state and moral reformers, these sources provide a valuable perspective for understanding the implementation of Chapter 205 in Kansas.

Women's Accounts of How They Were Arrested

In the inmate interviews, women recounted how they came to be quarantined under Chapter 205. Though their accounts of how state authorities came to find out that they had a venereal disease varied, some clear patterns emerge for ways that Chapter 205 was implemented in Kansas. The results of the sample are shown in table 5.1.

Targeted Arrests

The most common way that women reported being detained under Chapter 205 was through a targeted arrest. Individuals could turn in someone's name to health officers or law enforcement officials as a person suspected

Table 5.1 Inmate Reports of How They Were Arrested

How Arrested	*Number*	*Percent*
Targeted arrest	118	38
Arrested for another offense	43	14
Associates	15	5
Police raids	36	11
Picked up by police	26	8
Seeking help	13	4
Volunteered	61	20

This table gives information from the 312 interviews that indicated how the woman was arrested. This is less than the total sample size (488) because some interview forms did not include information about how the inmates came to be arrested.

of having a venereal disease; the woman would often then be picked up by police and subjected to medical testing. Thirty-eight percent or 118 women reported that they were arrested after someone else turned them in to authorities.

Several interviews indicate that parents utilized Chapter 205 as a way of gaining control over daughters who would not listen to them. For example, an eighteen-year-old white woman interviewed in 1931 reported: "I wasn't staying at home, and I was running around and mother had me picked up."[13] A similar account can be found in the story of Evelyn Carter, interviewed in 1925. This fourteen-year-old girl reported that her mother sought assistance from a local judge to help locate her after she traveled with a friend to another city and was gone overnight. Reporting that she "got drunk on 'Corn' and was not responsible for what happened," Evelyn apparently contracted gonorrhea and expected to be sent to the girls' reformatory at Beloit after leaving the KSIFW.[14] Another inmate, age fifteen when interviewed in 1927, had already been married and separated from her husband when her parents turned her in to authorities. She reported that she had "been intimate with 2 boys since [her] marriage," which had apparently ended after only three months when she "'triffled' on him." Her "parents had [her] sent" to the Farm when they found out she was getting treatment for syphilis.[15] In these cases, Chapter 205 became a tool for parents to use in controlling their daughter's sexuality in an era of rapidly changing sexual norms. White/northern European inmates were more likely to report that their parents turned them in to authorities: of the seventeen inmates who reported that their parents turned them in, fourteen were white/northern European.[16] Given historical patterns of systemic racism, it is not surprising that Black and Native American parents might have been less likely to view the state as a resource to help rein in an out-of-control daughter. After all, parents had little say in what happened to their daughters once they came under the control of state authorities.[17]

Parents were not the only group who notified state officials about a possible violation of Chapter 205: many inmates reported that it was their husbands that turned them in. Mary Carpenter described how her husband used Chapter 205 to punish her for her sexual behavior. Mary, a white woman who was forty-two when interviewed in 1931, reported: "My husband and I had been separated for several months, and I had been going with different men, and I think he was jealous and turned me in."[18] Other husbands used Chapter 205 as a way to begin divorce proceedings in an era before no-fault divorce laws. Agnes Clark reported that she was only thirteen years old when her mother pressured her into marrying. She was interned at the KSIFW at age sixteen in 1924, by then separated from her husband and the mother of a seventeen-month-old boy. Agnes reported: "Husband was wanting a divorce and the only way for him to get it was to send me here through Dr. Robertson."[19] The statement that her husband had the power to "send [her] here through Dr. Robertson" illustrates at least one inmate's perception of the power that Chapter 205 gave husbands over their wives. Betsy Rogers's case illustrates how this law might have come into play once a messy divorce was already under way. A seventeen-year-old white woman working as a sales clerk at the Owl Drug Store in downtown Kansas City, Betsy reported that her husband left her after living together one and a half years. She "arrested him for non-support," and he then "reported [her] as being diseased. He was treated there. [She] was sent" to the Farm. This husband was thus able to use the gendered enforcement of the law to get back at his estranged wife while their divorce was pending. This was particularly consequential in their case because they had a baby, whom the husband had taken to his mother's house while the inmate was at the Farm.[20] As these marriages dissolved, Chapter 205 gave husbands a way to control their wives and a legal rationale to initiate a divorce.[21]

While all of these cases illustrated a husband's ability to control his wife through the law, the coercive potential of Chapter 205 was most clearly apparent in cases of domestic abuse. Only educated up to the second grade, Ruth Thomas first married at age fourteen. The marriage only lasted three months but resulted in the birth of one child, a daughter named Sarah Mason. Ruth married again in 1912 and went on to have six more children with her second husband. This second husband was physically abusive, with Ruth noting that he had spent two weeks in jail after he was "arrested for beating [her] when drunk." The situation came to a head in 1927 in the events leading to both Ruth and her first daughter Sarah being sent to the KSIFW. Ruth, now age thirty-one, reported: "Husband was so abusive to me—beat me terribly any number of times. I told him I was going to my daughters and he thought I had left and had me arrested." Sarah's account gives even more details about what transpired. Now age sixteen, she had married the year before and was the mother of a ten-month-old baby boy. Sarah described the events that led to her and her mother's arrest:

> Husband and I was going to move over to mother's house and were at the house and husband went back to our house after our clothing. During his absence father got so abusive mother and I were going to my aunts in Missouri. When we got to the car father and two policemen came up and we were arrested. Father accused mother of living with a greek. He had been to my mother's house at my father's invitation for dinners.

In a domestic dispute such as this, Chapter 205 became a legal mechanism for a husband to control not only Ruth but also Sarah. Both women were sent to the Farm under Chapter 205, with the physician's report alleging they both had gonorrhea. Sarah's baby went to live with her mother-in-law. Similar to Agnes Williams's account from above, Ruth's description that her husband "had [her] arrested" illustrates her perception of the power that Chapter 205 gave her husband over her.[22]

The gendered enforcement of Chapter 205 gave men power over the women in their lives. Whether it was a case of domestic abuse, infidelity, or an impending divorce, husbands were able to use women's diseased status as a mechanism to get law enforcement to intervene on their behalf. This is particularly troubling given the fact that many of these same women reported that their husbands were the ones who gave them a disease in the first place. While a husband turning in his wife for venereal disease would have also implicated himself, the unequal enforcement of the law merely meant that he would need to be treated on an outpatient basis while his wife was imprisoned.

Besides parents and husbands, other family members turned women in to authorities as a particularly vindictive move in an ongoing disagreement. Rose Walker, a twenty-year-old white/Irish woman, got caught in a domestic dispute in 1923 between her family, her aunt Faye, and her uncle. She explained that her uncle "was arrested once for child desertion on complaint of my grandmother and he became anfry [*sic*] at the whole family." Rose admitted that she had "lived an immoral life several months" and had been going out occasionally with her aunt Faye. Rose reported that Faye's "husband ordered me to not go out with her anymore and I did so he sent Faye and I both up here."[23] Similarly, Neita Pierce found herself at the Farm in 1932 after a disgruntled family member turned her in. Neita was a mother of four who had left her husband after finding out he gave her a venereal disease. She was taking treatments from a doctor and found stable employment as a live-in domestic worker. She reported: "I had been working in Wichita for Alta Woods and she was a respectable woman and they ran three grocery stores and I worked for her." However, a family member's knowledge of her disease led to her being sent to the Farm at the age of thirty: "But my brother-in-law was mad at me and he knew my husband gave me this disease so he turned me in to the health officer."[24] Knowledge of this inmate's diseased status was dangerous leverage that could be used against her under the gendered enforcement of Chapter 205 in Kansas.

The liability of having other people know about one's disease status was a continued theme in the accounts of women who were turned in to the authorities. Louise Clark went to the KSIFW in 1925 along with her mother and sister for a violation of Chapter 205. Given that many members of her family were committed, it may have been general knowledge in her hometown of Hutchinson that she was diseased. A year later, this knowledge caught up with her. In 1926 seventeen-year-old Louise was at her "sister's having [her] wedding clothes made." She was engaged to be married to a man who had previously been engaged to another woman. This other woman found out about the upcoming marriage and "turned Louise in as diseased." Louise's disease status thus became a weapon that others could use against her.[25] A similar dynamic took place with Bessie Carmichael, a thirty-three-year-old widow when arrested in 1931. She had four children, the first of which was born when she was just fourteen. Bessie reported: "I dont know how I got this disease. I stayed at home with my children. A man lied on me and told that I gave him a disease, but I had no dealings with him at all. He wanted me to go with him but I wouldnt." Here, the inmate's disease status became a tool that a rejected lover could use to get back at her.[26] These cases illustrate how dangerous it could be for women to let others know that they had a venereal disease.

Chapter 205 could also be used by pimps who wished to exercise control over the women who worked under them. A set of interviews from four Black women arrested at the same time in 1924 reveals one way that Chapter 205 might have influenced the outcomes of a routine encounter with the law. Between the women's accounts, it seems that all four engaged in some form of prostitution, most of them sharing their profits with the man they all lived with, Frank Baker, in Leavenworth, Kansas. Baker's eighteen-year-old daughter, Esther, was one of these women, and she gave this account of how she started working as a prostitute: "Father got cut about the head and the length of his right arm by a drunk man. Father was unconscious for two weeks and the only way I knew to help him was to hustle. I provided for father in this way about a year."[27] This group came to the attention of authorities after a dispute one night over the share of their profits that the women would give to Frank. Beulah Edwards, a twenty-eight-year-old who was most opposed to sharing her earnings with Frank, reported the night as such:

> Have lived an immoral life ever since I was grown. I had been living with Esther Baker's father about one year. He ordered me to do as the other girls do. I stayed there longer. I refused to do for him as he requested. There was a dance at his house and they had liquor there. I was "full" and told him what I thought of his asking me such a thing. I left his house and went to a neighbors. He sent the law down and found myself and May Russell with our two men friends and four boys in adjoining room. We were all arrested then I turned his house in.[28]

May Russell, age thirty at the time, corroborated this account, reporting: "I had lived at the Baker residence about 3 weeks and during that time I gave Mr. Baker a good part of the money I made. He had asked me for more. His daughter Esther Baker also gave him money. He had not worked for a year and he made his money off of us three girls."[29] Chapter 205 led to very different outcomes for the people involved with this incident. Frank Baker called the police on the women, even though that decision ended up implicating himself. He was fined twenty-five dollars and spent thirty days in jail.[30] Because the women could be detained under the venereal disease law in addition to any charges for prostitution, they were subject to another level of scrutiny that Frank Baker was not. All four women were sent to the Farm for a violation of Chapter 205.

The final group of people that inmates reported had turned them in to state authorities were doctors. Some of these cases were clearly an abuse of medical authority. Nora Brown was a twenty-five-year-old divorced mother of three who was working as a housekeeper in Wichita. The woman she was working for was sick, and the family called Dr. Bierman to tend to her. Nora reported: "He had also doctored me for my throat and he asked me if I was going to pay him. I told him I was working for my room and board and couldn't. Dr. Hobbs told me after I was picked up that Dr. Bierman had called him and said I refused to be doctored for venereal disease."[31] According to Nora's account, the doctor turned her in because she could not pay for an unrelated medical treatment, illustrating a clearly coercive use of the law.

The more typical scenario involved a woman who was getting treatment for venereal disease and stopped taking those treatments, prompting the doctor to turn her in. For example, twenty-one-year-old Dorothy Burns was quarantined at the KSIFW under Chapter 205 in May 1931. She was released early under the condition that she finish treatments with a doctor outside the institution in order to go take care of her sick baby. Dorothy reported: "I lived in Topeka Kansas and took my treatment from Dr. Goodman I failed to report and take 3 of my treatments, so he reported me to the sherriffs office, and they returned me here to finish my treatments."[32] Cases such as this were more in keeping with the intended spirit of Chapter 205, as doctors were asked to report any cases where the patient was not complying with treatment. However, some women's stories illustrate a clear disregard for the women's health, revealing a general focus on protecting the public *from* these women rather than a genuine desire to improve their physical well-being. For example, Lottie Jackson found herself at the Farm in 1925. More educated than most of the women at the Farm, Lottie had gone to college for some time and listed her occupation as "stenographer." She reported that she contracted gonorrhea from her husband and had been taking treatments from Dr. Cooper for three and a half months. She reported: "I was sick in bed and failed to let Dr. Cooper know that I was sick so he ordered me arrested. I stayed in jail 12 days without any medical attention. Have an abscess back of left ear caused by car accident."[33] Considering Lottie's report that she received no medical attention for several days, in practice this provision seems to have been more about identifying deviant women than about providing them with proper medical care. These stories illustrate the risks that women took when seeking treatment for venereal disease; if they chose to discontinue the lengthy, expensive treatment, they opened themselves up to arrest by letting a medical authority know about their condition.

From parents to husbands to doctors, a variety of people notified state authorities about women's potential disease status. Far from being a top-down, government-led effort to control women's sexuality, a range of people were involved with the enforcement of Chapter 205. Once others knew a woman's disease status, Chapter 205 gave individual community members leverage over her. Parents could try to control their daughters, and husbands could try to control their wives. Chapter 205 worked itself into the social relationships of Kansas citizens and was utilized by everyday people against each other. It was much more far-reaching than a simple board of health quarantine policy.

Arrested for Another Offense

Rather than being specifically targeted by state authorities as a venereal disease suspect, 14 percent of the sample, or forty-three women, reported that they were arrested for an unrelated offense and were then tested for disease. Many of these arrests involved liquor, though there were a variety of circumstances under which women came to be arrested.[34] Indeed, any encounter with law enforcement could result in venereal disease testing, as can be seen in the story of Flora Johnson. In the spring of 1926, this fifteen-year-old white/Irish girl had already had an eventful year. Flora got married in Texas in February, only to have her husband leave her after one week and then subsequently get a divorce. Returning to her parents' home in Hutchinson, Kansas, Flora earned ten dollars per week as a cashier at a bakery. Her situation changed dramatically after what was supposed to be a fun night out. Flora recalled: "I had been to a dance and on the way home the battery run down and we were driving without lights. Motor cycle cop arrested us and took us down. The boy Floyd Carter was released." Flora served over five months at the Farm in Lansing.[35] The different consequences that routine encounters with the law could have for men and women was also apparent in the case of Ethel King. Ethel was a white housekeeper who had served a six-month term under Chapter 205 in 1930 at the age of only fourteen. Two years later, she was sent to the

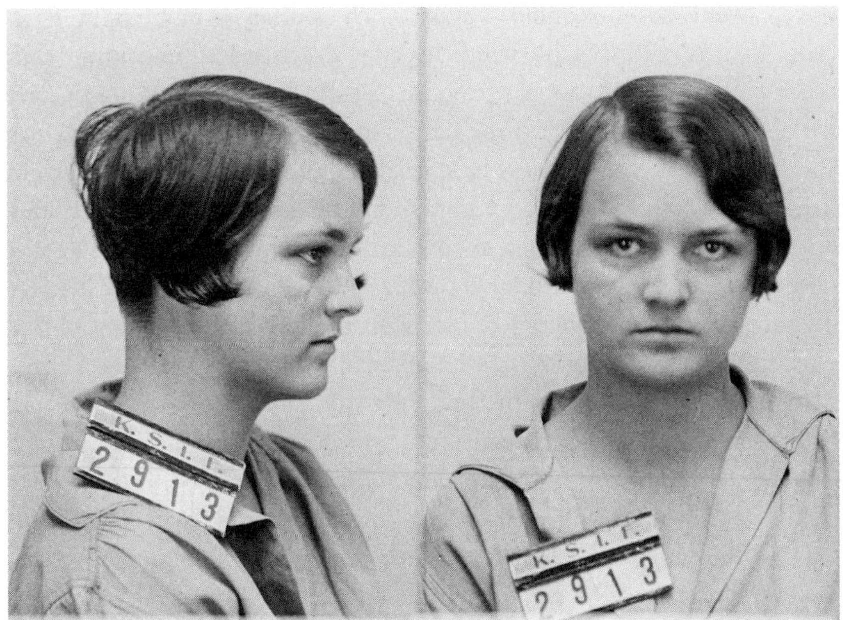

Mugshot of fifteen-year-old Flora Johnson, who was detained at the Farm under Chapter 205 in 1926. Photo has been cropped. Lansing Historical Museum, "KSIF Prisoners 2913 & 2914," http://lansingmuseum.omeka.net/items/show/50.

Farm again under a quarantine charge, this time after she attended a party thrown by her employers. Ethel reported: "I worked for a private family at Kansas City, Kansas. One evening they gave a party and we were not loud or boisterous but it was about 3 o'clock and the neighbors called the police and they took we girls to the police station. They let the boys go. They examined me and gave me a blood test and I was sent here to be treated for my blood."[36] Whether it was being in a car without headlights or at a party that went on a little too long, Flora and Ethel came to be detained at the Farm after fairly routine encounters with the law that likely would not have resulted in jail time if it were not for Chapter 205.

Oftentimes authorities were able to detain women under Chapter 205 when they had insufficient evidence to convict them under other offenses. Vera Scott, a twenty-year-old Black woman, was arrested after her former landlord reported that she and her husband had stolen some sheets from the house. The case was dismissed after the landlord failed to appear at the hearing, but Vera had already been tested for venereal disease and was sent to Lansing under Chapter 205.[37] Another inmate, Ida May Robinson, was a twenty-seven-year-old white/French woman who lived in Pittsburg, Kansas, with her husband. Ida May described an encounter with the law charged with racial tensions: "My husband, myself, and Claire Parker and a colored Taxi-driver started to Cherokee. We had a puncture and stopped. There were several special deputies come up, my husband had some booze and a gun on him so he ran leaving us two girls alone with the nigger they charged we two girls with being with the nigger. I never saw him before and dont know his name."[38] In this account Ida May describes a fairly routine encounter with the law: having a flat tire and needing assistance. Ida May saw the racial dynamics of having a Black man appear to be alone with two white women as arousing suspicion, incorrectly attributing her incarceration to that scenario rather than the Chapter 205 charge noted on her interview form. Indeed, the presence of two white women with a Black man may have aroused suspicion in an era of anti-miscegenation laws and fears about the mixing of the races. Besides illustrating the general confusion that many inmates had about their quarantine under Chapter 205 (see below), this example also shows how an everyday encounter with the police might lead to imprisonment for women. No mention is made of what happened to the taxi driver. These accounts of women's arrests highlight the variety of situations under which women might come into contact with police. In these routine encounters with the law, women found themselves being detained under a quarantine law while their male counterparts were often set free.

Associates

A smaller group of women (5 percent, or fifteen women in the sample) reported that they came to be detained under Chapter 205 because they were associating with someone who was being pursued by the authorities. In 1926 a young girl named Mary Wilson ran away from home, prompting her parents to call in local law enforcement to help locate their daughter. They focused their efforts on two of Mary's friends, twelve-year-old Frances Pearson and sixteen-year-old Rachel Miller. Frances reported: "Mary Wilson ran away from home and her folks thought I and Rachel Miller knew where she was. She did come to my house but I did not know when or where she went."[39] Rachel gave a similar account, stating: "Mary Wilson ran away with some boys. The law said I knew who with. Took me up and arraigned to send me here."[40] Though it is unclear whether

Frances or Rachel had any relevant information to help locate Mary, the end result was that they were both tested for disease and sent to Lansing.

Several women reported that they were arrested because they were staying at a boardinghouse that also lodged someone who was being pursued by law enforcement. Myrtle Harris was a fifty-year-old white mother of seven living in Junction City in 1927. She reported that a boarder at her house "had liquor on my place (15 Qts.). He was arrested and the liquor confiscated." Along with another woman who was boarding at the house, Myrtle was detained during this encounter and tested for disease, resulting in her quarantine after a gonorrhea diagnosis.[41] Another inmate, a thirty-one-year-old Black woman named Hazel Moore, reported that she was arrested after being at the wrong boardinghouse. She ran a "small confectionary" in Kansas City with her brother-in-law and took a weekend trip to Topeka with a friend. Hazel reported: "We went to Junction City from there to see some more friends of ours and we stayed at a rooming house which we supposed was a nice place, but one night the proprietor and his wife got into a fight and she called the police. The law took us down for witnesses and they interned us here." Despite Hazel's claim that she "had always worked hard" and the fact that she thought the rooming house was "a nice place," she and her friend were tested for disease and quarantined.[42]

Another inmate reported a much more dramatic encounter with the law that led to her arrest under Chapter 205 in 1927. A sixteen-year-old white/Indian-Irish woman, Mattie Davis had already separated from her husband after a seventeen-month marriage, leaving her nine-month-old baby girl with her mother. She was apparently working as a prostitute, reporting that she "had to have something to live on and had to resort to an immoral life." Mattie came to the attention of the law when they came after a man she was with. She "was sitting in the dark in Memorial Hall with 'Slim.' He was known and could be found so when the 'law' flashed light on us he ran. Got shot in right hand. Paid fine and released. I was sent up."[43] Even though "Slim" was wanted for a crime and ran from the police, he paid a fine and was released while Mattie was interned due to a gonorrhea diagnosis. These stories illustrate the danger of associating with people who might come into contact with law enforcement. Even if the woman herself had committed no offense but was merely staying at the wrong boardinghouse or had a friend who ran away from home, she was subjected to medical testing and interned if found diseased.

Police Raids

In a similar vein, women who were taken into custody during police raids, usually for liquor, were detained and tested based on their association with disreputable people and places. Of the women in the sample who indicated how they were arrested, 11.5 percent, or thirty-six inmates, reported being detained after a police raid. Annie Mitchell's account gives a sense of the experience of being in a raid. A twenty-year-old white/Irish-Indian woman, Annie had married at age sixteen and had since separated from her husband. More educated than most inmates with some high school education, she listed her occupation as a beauty operator, though she had been unemployed for three weeks prior to her arrest. Annie had been staying in a friend's apartment in Wichita, and it was through this friend that she came to be arrested:

> One afternoon she took some clothing to her brother that had left her apartment down to where he roomed. Just as we passed thru the hall some one told us to stop, and we soon found they were raiding the place, we were taken down to the jail and interviewed, my girl friend's blood was O.K. but mine wasn't as I had taken treatments before for I got this disease from my husband.[44]

Annie was simply at the wrong place at the wrong time, leading to her arrest and detainment under the quarantine law. The danger of being in a disreputable place is clearly illustrated in Lena Thompson's account. Lena had gotten married in 1916 in Kansas City, Missouri. She was married for only six months when her husband "died after falling on the street in convulsions." By 1925 Lena was twenty-four years old, the mother of a seven-year-old boy, and listed her occupation as a nurse. She came under the attention of authorities during a visit to her foster sister: "Went to Junction City to see foster sister Betsy Carter and the law came in and told me I was would have to go to station as the place I was in is not a goold plac as long as I was in such places I could expect to be arrested."[45] The only charge the police had against Lena was that she tested positive for gonorrhea, resulting in her sentence to the Farm under Chapter 205.

Sophie Hawkins also reported being initially arrested for being in the wrong place. Sophie had married at the age of sixteen and then separated from her husband. Two years later, she found herself under arrest:

I had been living with my sister in Wichita and I went to visit my mother in Arkansas while I was there I was going with a boy and was intimate with him and he gave me a disease. I came back to Wichita and did'nt want my sister to know it. So I got a job in a resturaunt and I had a room above the resturaunt, in a rooming house and it was raided, I did not know it was a disrespectfull place.

In this case, Sophie's desire to hide her disease from her sister led her to being in the type of "disrespectful place" that was often subject to police raids. Once in Lansing, she commented: "I will obey all the rules of the Farm and I will certainly be a different girl from now on."[46] The gendered enforcement of Chapter 205 meant that there were very different consequences for men and women picked up in these police raids. Gladys King, for example, reported that her landlady, two men, and four women were picked up in a Wichita hotel raid; the landlady was released on bond, the two men were released, and all four women were sent to the KSIFW.[47] There were also racial disparities in arrest patterns during police raids. Black women made up 15.6 percent of the overall arrest sample, yet they made up 42.1 percent of the women who reported being arrested during a police raid.[48] Police may have been more likely to raid Black establishments, or they may have been more likely to arrest everyone present than they did when raiding white hotels or parties. Chapter 205 increased the stakes of routine police raids for women, and particularly Black women, in Kansas.

Picked Up by Police

Some women's stories illustrate the suspicion that fell on all women in public spaces. Twenty-six women, or 8 percent of the sample who indicated how they were arrested, described being picked up by police merely for being in a public space. Angela Martinez was a white/Spanish-Indian woman who was driving through Kansas from Oklahoma City. Angela had been married twice and had a nine-year-old adopted boy with her second husband. This twenty-five-year-old woman reported: "I was going to town about 9 o'clock P.M. to get my boy some ice cream. I was picked up on the street as I was going to town." Angela's simple errand to get something for her child turned into an extended stay in Kansas when she tested positive for gonorrhea and was detained under Chapter 205.[49]

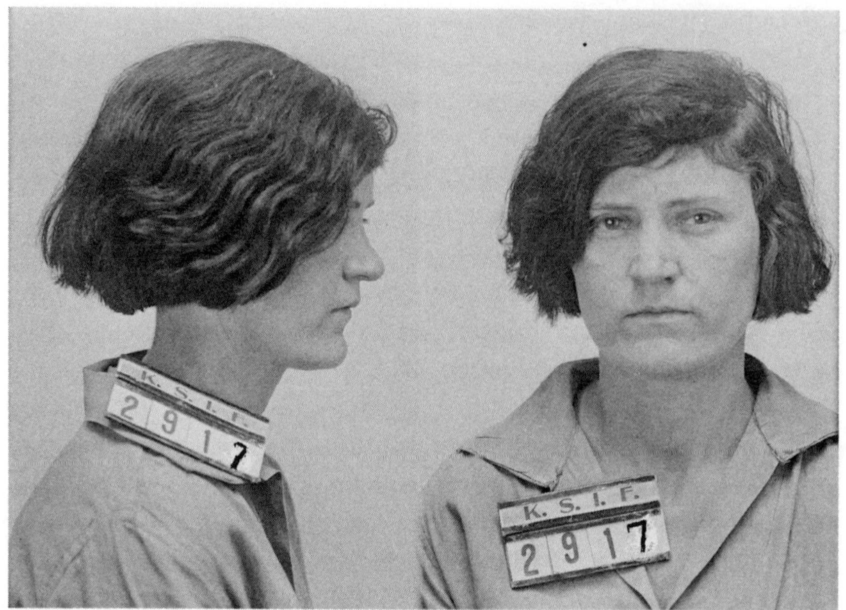

Photo of Angela Martinez, who was picked up by police while out getting ice cream for her child and then tested for venereal disease. Photo has been cropped. Lansing Historical Museum, "KSIF Prisoners 2917 & 2918," http://lansingmuseum.omeka.net/items/show/26.

Other women also reported that police picked them up and tested them for disease even though there were no obvious reasons for suspicion. Lois Anderson, age fourteen, was on probation from the Girls' Industrial School in Beloit when she was picked up by police: "Was standing on street—had been in Wichita three hours—was arrested."[50] Though Lois was on probation, there was no reason for the police to stop and arrest her other than the fact that they were suspicious of a woman being in public on her own. Similarly, Nellie Hall was arrested merely for being in public. Age twenty-one when arrested in 1929, Nellie had graduated high school and listed her occupation as "operator." She reported:

> I got this disease when I was in High School quite a while ago. I had gone to Wichita to wait for my Father. One night as I was going from home from a show, the "cops" asked me where I was going. The next day I got news that my father had been hurt, so I went out to take a walk that night the cops stopped me again and took me to the station for a blood test.[51]

Nellie's presence on a public street two nights in a row made the police suspect her of prostitution, yet these women do not report doing anything in particular to arouse suspicion. While the 1920s are often seen as the era of the "New Woman," Lois and Nellie's accounts reveal that the opportunities to establish an identity outside of the home were not yet available to all women. Merely being a woman in a public space was enough to warrant an initial arrest for these women, and Chapter 205 gave the police an easy legal mechanism to detain women they deemed suspicious.

Seeking Help

A small group of women (4 percent of the sample, or thirteen women) reported being detained under Chapter 205 after they had initially reached out to police or charity organizations for help. Dora Young was divorced with two children, age five and three, when she was quarantined in 1929 at the age of twenty-one. She reported: "I came to Kansas City, Ks. looking for an Uncle and I went to the Welfare Board for help and they had me sent here."[52] Reporting that she contracted gonorrhea from her ex-husband, Dora's disease status was completely irrelevant to the context in which she contacted the welfare board, yet it became a means to detain her. Alice and Dorothy Wilson's interactions with police demonstrate a similar application of Chapter 205 to detain women viewed as vagrants. Ages twenty and seventeen, respectively, these cousins took a train to visit relatives in Wichita, Kansas. Alice recounted:

> So we girls started to hitch hike back to Collinsville, Oklahoma, where we lived. We got as far as El Dorado, Kansas, and it was about 1100 O'Clock so we stopped to ask a man which way to go on, and he said we better stay all night. So he got an Officer who sent us to the Hotel for the nite, and the next morning he took us up to the jail and gave us a blood test, and we were sent here.[53]

This story illustrates a mix of good intentions and coercive measures by the police. Dorothy noted that the sheriff had "said we hadent better go that nite, as it was dangerous," illustrating a concern for the girls' welfare.[54] This tendency to see young women as needing protection was the same logic behind the original creation of reformatories for young women. Unfortunately for Alice and Dorothy, this concern ultimately resulted in their quarantine at the KSIFW.

Other women's stories illustrated cases in which Chapter 205 was used to detain women who came to the police for help in situations of domestic violence. Ellen Lewis had married at age thirteen and separated from her husband after seven years. A white/French-English woman, she was twenty-one when arrested in 1928. Ellen reported that she originally called in the police for their help: "I and Frank Johnson were out riding and we got into an argument. We fought and I called a policeman. He took me to the City Hall. They examined me and sent me to the Industrial Farm."[55] Though we do not know the nature of Ellen's relationship with Frank, it is clear that she was reaching out to the police for help and ended up being detained herself. Similarly, Grace Powell reported being detained after the police intervened in a domestic dispute: "Was arrested after beating husband gave me. Was not just straight, but no women are that way. Sent up for cure. Did not know I was diseased." This twenty-five-year-old Black woman was quarantined under a gonorrhea charge while her abusive husband was likely set free. Grace's interview ended with the statement that she would be "going back to husband" when released.[56]

A similar situation played out in the case of Eva Porter. Eva, whose race was listed as white/Indian-Dutch-Irish, was the mother of three children. Reporting that her husband "drinks every day, never works," Eva separated from her husband in June 1925. They got back together in May 1926, and it was at this time that the situation escalated to the point of involving the police. Now age twenty-six, Eva was working as a waitress at the Better Eats Cafe in Kansas City, Kansas. She reported: "I was working and husband came into Cafe about 10-30 P.M. My employer asked me to go outside so the laws would not interfer. After I got into street he struck me. Both my eyes were black and one is still discolored." The police were called, and Eva's husband was arrested for beating his wife. However, Eva was also detained under a gonorrhea charge. She stated in her interview: "Will go back to Kansas City when released but can not live with a drunken husband."[57] Whether it was domestic abuse or trying to find a lost relative, these women were in vulnerable situations and sought help from people in positions of authority. Instead, they found their own respectability and health under question and ended up detained under Chapter 205.

Volunteers to Go to the Farm

Unlike the women discussed above, a sizable portion of the women in the sample (sixty-one, or 20 percent of those who reported how they came to

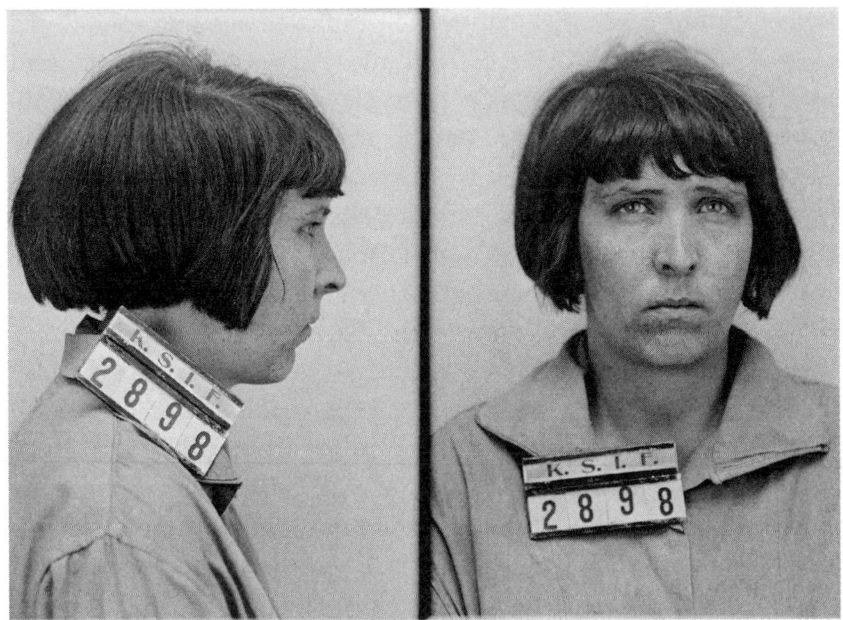

Mugshot of inmate Eva Porter, who was arrested following a domestic dispute in which her husband gave her two black eyes. Photo has been cropped. Lansing Historical Museum, "KSIF Prisoners 2898 & 2920," http://lansingmuseum.omeka.net/items/show/34.

be at the Farm) actually volunteered to go to the KSIFW. While it is unclear whether these volunteers were aware that they were not free to leave the Farm at their choosing, these women's need to access treatment for their diseases motivated their actions. The accounts of women who volunteered to go to the Farm bring us back to the core purpose of Chapter 205 in the first place: treating disease. While reformers often lamented the lack of personal responsibility that made these women unable to finish out a course of treatment, the inmates who volunteered to come to the Farm reported going to great lengths to access health care. Although there was no legitimate reason why these women could not have been treated on an outpatient basis that respected their civil liberties, the reality of their physical disease and their desire to get treatment are reminders that venereal diseases during this period could be serious conditions.

The women who volunteered to go to the Farm often highlighted their agency and their desire to take care of their health when discussing their choice to go to the Farm. Jessie Cox was a thirty-three-year-old divorced mother of three who reported: "Was in bad condition and volunteered to come to Lansing for treatment, so came to Leavenworth and was sent out."[58] Though Jessie did not say how she knew about the Farm, other inmates indicated various ways of learning that they could get treatment for their diseases in Lansing. Lola White, age twenty, reported: "I had been here before and as I was needing medical attention I volunteered."[59] Alma Taylor was a twenty-five-year-old white/Irish woman who divorced her husband due to "other women and liquor." She reported: "Volunteered. Patrice Rogers advised me to come here. I had to have blood tests. Also worked in homes, and knew my condition was not proper in caring for children. Had to do something so came here."[60] Through such language as "had to do something so came here," Alma accounted for her choice to volunteer to come to the Farm as a way of accessing the treatment she needed for her disease. Similarly, Marie Bryce discussed the Farm as a way to access much-needed health care. A twenty-six-year-old white/German-Irish woman, Marie reported that she had a disease despite never having "broken the laws of chastity":

> I have had this disease for about six years, however, I did not know it until about a month ago I have been sick more or less the greater part of my life; I had been working in Wichita, Kansas for the year and a half, and two months ago I took sick and was taken to the hospital, the Doctor there said I had a disease, my sister came and got me, and after going back to Independence, Kansas, my sister found out I could come here for treatment.[61]

Marie's statement that her sister "found out [she] could come here for treatment" shows the way that the Farm could be viewed as a resource for women with few options to take care of their health. With few affordable alternatives for treating venereal disease available in Kansas at this time, it is perhaps not surprising that women were willing to give up their freedom in order to get treatment at the Farm.

Indeed, among all the language of moral reform in the biennial reports of the KSIFW, it is easy to forget that venereal disease could be a very serious health condition during this period. The 1926 biennial report for the KSIFW included this description of a patient from the head nurse:

> A girl of eighteen years was received. She could not walk. She had a stiff knee and it was very much enlarged from gonorrhea rheumatism.

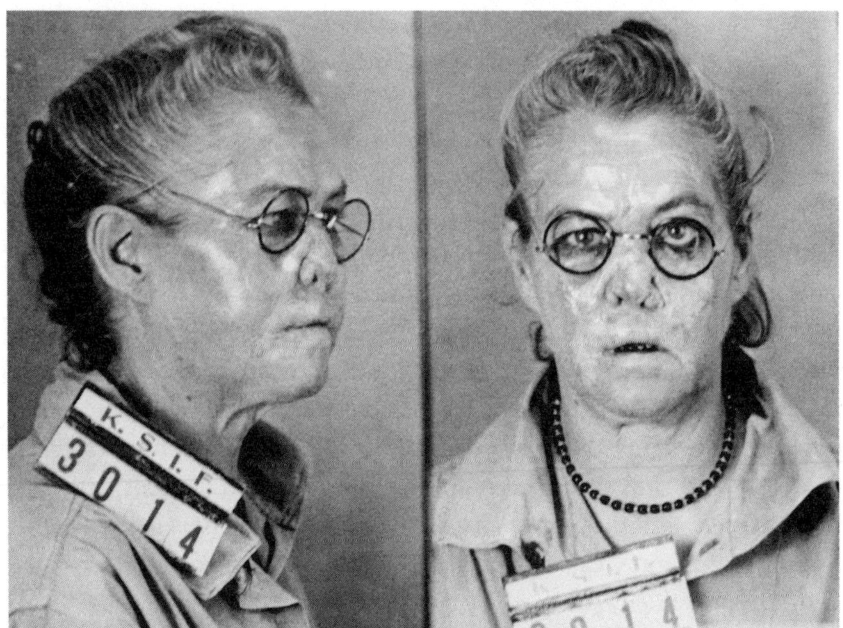

A photograph of inmate Edna Vance, who had advanced-stage syphilis by the time she arrived at the Farm for treatment. Kansas State Industrial Farm for Women, Glass Plate Negative, #3014, KSHS.

> For three months there was very little change in her condition and very little hope for her recovery. Much of this time she was not moved from her bed; could not turn over without intense pain and assistance. She was unconscious much of the time, and was as helpless as a child. She was given nourishment with feeding tube for weeks. She recovered, walked out of the hospital, well and happy and very grateful to us all. We hear from her, and she is in good health.[62]

This inmate had some very serious health problems and clearly benefited from the care she received at the KSIFW.

Several of the inmates who volunteered described severe health problems in their interviews. Edna Vance got married in 1899 at the age of nineteen; she went on to have seven children by her first husband, whom she divorced in 1912. Marrying again in 1924, Edna settled down with her second husband in White Cloud, Kansas. She volunteered to go to the Farm in 1926 at the age of forty-five after beginning treatment with another doctor. Edna reported: "Volunteered to come here for syphilis for treatment for my face. Took seven-606 and face is healing and eye is better. Have no idea where I became diseased." Edna's comment about 606 refers to the drug arsphenamine, or Salvarsan, which was commonly used to treat syphilis. As evidenced by her photo, Edna had advanced-stage syphilis with severe facial deformities.[63]

Another woman's story illustrates both the seriousness of syphilis during this time and the inefficiencies of the Kansas system in adequately caring for patients. Opal Simmons was a twenty-one-year-old Black maid who volunteered to go to the Farm after hearing about it from a friend. She reported: "Was suffering. terribly. Heard of Lansing and begged to come here." Opal's interview form included a stenographer's note at the bottom of the report that read: "Opal came to the institution in a terrible condition—Having corrupted syphiletic sores all over her body, face and hands. One limb a mass of raw, running sores. Too odorous to be in room with other patients." Clearly, this inmate was in dire need of medical care and the Farm filled that need for her. Yet Opal also reported that it took law enforcement officials five days to bring her to the Farm.[64] For other patients, the medical care received at the Farm came too late. Elizabeth Case was a thirty-year-old Black woman who volunteered to come to the Farm. The stenographer's note at the bottom of her interview reported: "Elizabeth Case was received at the institution in a very bad condition. In fact had to drive car very slowly. Said she had tumors on liver and womb. Died two days after being received."[65] Though this inmate's tumors were not necessarily related to gonorrhea (the disease she was committed to the institution under), her story illustrates her dire need for medical treatment and her desperation to find it. The fact that both of these inmates were Black was not accidental. The Farm became a last resort for those seeking medical treatment for venereal disease, and existing social hierarchies shaped who had other recourse for getting treatment.

Physician Incompetence and Access to Care

Given the potential seriousness of venereal diseases during this period, it is understandable that many women would go to great lengths to get treatment. The women who volunteered to go to the Farm tell a story of complicated relationships with the medical profession, one that involved a genuine desire for treatment that was often frustrated by poor treatment options and lack of training. Many women reported that they volunteered to come to the Farm because a doctor recommended that they could get better care there. Winona Allen had married at age fifteen, but she divorced her husband after two years because he "run around with other women." She reported: "He gave me this disease and I went to the doctor at Smith center and he doctored me for awhile and then said I had better come here for treatment."[66] Similarly, Mabel Jones reported that her doctor recommended she go to the Farm to get better treatment. She had also married young (at age sixteen) and was separated from her husband when she volunteered to go to the Farm in 1932. At age twenty-two Mabel was raising her two small children (ages two and four) and trying to get treatment for her family: "I had been taking treatments of a doctor in Winfield, Kansas, but he suggested that I bring myself, 2 children and come here for treatment as they were also diseased."[67] Given the poor or nonexistent training that most doctors received in treating venereal disease, it is not surprising that they felt unprepared to effectively treat these women's diseases. Some doctors explicitly stated that they refused to treat venereal disease cases. Lula Sanders, a twenty-three-year-old white/French-Indian woman, reported:

> After I divorced my husband I went with first one and then another and I got this disease three years ago; I began taking treatments right away and took treatments, and a year later I took another course, but I did not seem to get much better. I came to Wichita, Kansas as I learned they had a free clinic there. The next morning after I got to Wichita I felt so bad that the lady at the hotel called a doctor and when he found I had a disease he said he did not doctor such cases. So he turned me over to Doctor Hobbs and he sent me here for treatment.[68]

Lula's account shows several attempts to get treatment for her disease, ultimately ending up at the Farm. Having a medical workforce that was poorly trained in venereal disease treatment fed into the implementation of Chapter 205: doctors were pushed to send their patients to the Farm when they could not provide the treatment themselves, prompting unnecessary imprisonment for patients who otherwise would have complied with treatment regimens outside an institution.

Unlike the "Targeted Arrest" quotes above where inmates reported that a doctor turned them in to law enforcement to have them arrested after the inmate failed to show up for treatment, many women's accounts showed their doctors as helping them navigate the treatment options available to them. Emily Robertson was a twenty-three-year-old white married woman who volunteered to go to the Farm in 1925. She reported: "I treated with Dr. Everharty for several days. Then he told me I had Shankers and told me of this place and arranged with Dr. Axford so I could come here."[69] This inmate portrayed her doctor as an ally who tried to help her find the best way to access treatment for her disease. Similarly, Eleanor Stonefield narrated her path to the Farm in a way that highlighted her agency and her doctor's role in helping her. This twenty-one-year-old white/Irish-English woman reported that she had "been using dope for almost two years off and on." Eleanor sought her doctor's help when she began having health problems:

> About a month ago I went to our family doctor and told him I had been having such fevers every night and I thought my blood was bad; So he took a blood test and it came back 4-plus; I asked him if I might come down here for treatment, and he said for me to go to the Sherriff and ask him to make out a committment for me to enter the institution.[70]

These accounts show doctors trying to help their patients get the best care available within a health-care system that offered few options.

Many inmates were familiar with navigating this health-care system. Darlene Doubleday Newby's 1918 undercover report of the Farm included the following observation:

> The girls were interested at all times in getting information concerning the process of medical treatment; the examinations; the reports on positives and negatives. The new girls plied the old ones with questions until they had become entirely familiar with the vernacular, if indeed they had not already known it before they came to the Farm. As time passed I was convinced that nearly every girl had had treatments at some previous time.[71]

The inmate interviews confirmed the idea that many inmates had previously received treatment. Thelma Woods was a twenty-seven-year-old white woman who reported that she had contracted a venereal disease from her husband. She reported a long history of treatment for her disease: "I was taking treatments from Dr. Post at Lawrence for about a week and they sent me up here for treatment. I had taken treatments 3 years for same trouble."[72] Though going to the Farm would have been a considerable disruption to her life (her four children stayed with her husband and his mother in her absence), Thelma was probably able to access much better health care at the Farm. Erma Marshall also had a history of treatment before coming to the Farm. A thirty-five-year-old white/Cherokee-Irish mother of three, Erma reported that her husband was "mentally deranged from Syphilis." She stated: "Volunteered to come up for treatment after I heard of this place and knew I was diseased. . . . Dr. Moore of Eureka doctored me, 7 mercury and 7,600, Dr. McDonald wanted me to come."[73]

Hazel Adams also used language that showed familiarity with venereal disease treatment. An eighteen-year-old Italian immigrant, Hazel reported that she had received treatments at the Geneva training school in Illinois prior to coming to Kansas, and she was clearly familiar with treatment: "I took 54 shots of 606 and my blood is now 4 plus."[74] Given the expense and difficulty of carrying out the fully recommended treatment for venereal diseases at this time, this is not surprising that women may have taken some treatments without following through on the full course of treatment. Even if they had, the women still would have had the disease since the treatments mitigated the effects of the diseases rather than curing them. The fact that so many women had previously taken treatments shows that, for many women, the problem with their medical care was not necessarily women's failure to take responsibility for their health, but rather the ineffective and cumbersome treatment options that were available at the time.

While some women surely did not comply with the treatments recommended to them by their doctors, other inmates reported that their doctors misdiagnosed their condition or that they were unhappy with the treatment they received. Helen Faulkner was a twenty-six-year-old mother of two whose husband had died in the flu epidemic of 1919. Helen reported that she "doctored with Dr. Moore of Eureka, Kansas since February 1925 and was not satisfied with my condition so I slipped away and came to Lansing."[75] Similarly, Martha Johnston sought out another doctor when she sensed she was not getting the best care. Martha was a twenty-three-year-old white/Dutch woman who was applying for a divorce when she volunteered to go to the Farm in 1932. She reported: "I had been taking treatment for four months before I came here and the doctor gave a slip or certificate saying I was free from venereal disease, but I went to another doctor and he said I needed treatments, but I did not have the money so I came here for treatment as had been here before."[76] Martha had been to the Farm twice before under Chapter 205, making her more aware of the treatment options; this may have led to greater skepticism of her first doctor, but the fact remains that a doctor told her she was cured of a disease when she was not. Several women reported that a doctor had erroneously said that they did not have a venereal disease when they really did.[77] Jean McConnell's account illustrates how a doctor's misdiagnosis might lead to the spreading of disease. Jean had married at the age of fifteen, only to have her husband leave after fourteen months to go look for work in California. Suspecting that she might have a disease, Jean sought out medical care: "I went to a doctor but he said I was alright. I have been out with several men since my husband and I separated but have never been intimate with them."[78] Women like Jean were trying to get medical care, but were told by a doctor that they did not have a disease.

Other women had ongoing health problems that their doctors did not recognize as being symptoms of venereal disease. Edith Nelson had been married three times by the time she came to the Farm in 1924 to get treatment for syphilis. She reported that a doctor had pronounced one of her husbands "cured" before they were married, possibly leading to her getting the disease in the first place. A stenographer's note on the bottom of her interview sheet noted: "Edith is badly scared and broken out but her doctor said it was kidney and her face poisoned from cold cream."[79] For this inmate, two doctors' misunderstanding of syphilis led to her deteriorating health. Maggie Kennedy also reported a series of doctors who failed to diagnose her with syphilis. This fifty-two-year-old woman had been married twice (once divorced and once widowed), and had trouble getting an accurate diagnosis as to why a wound would not heal:

> Was hurt in a cyclone at Helena Arkansas. we made a run to a storm cellar when something with nails in it struck me in the head. It never healed fast and last summer I made it bleed with a comb and then it seemed to be festered. I went to Dr. Coffey at Independence and he thought it was T.B. I went to several Doctors after that but they all thought the same finally Dr. Wickersham took a blood test and I found out what was the trouble.

A stenographer's note at the bottom of Maggie's interview noted: "Sells crams and lotions never was a bad woman and dont know where she got disease. Slipped on sidewalk in April and broke leg in two places if that hadn't happened she would not have known what was the matter with her head."[80] This note, which showed obvious sympathy for Maggie, highlighted this inmate's struggle to get her condition accurately diagnosed. These cases illustrate the dangers of having a medical profession uneducated in recognizing and treating venereal diseases: not only were these women at risk for spreading the disease for extended periods of time, but they suffered unnecessarily from their conditions. What the state board of health and many female reformers took to be these women's failure to take responsibility for their health care was, in some cases, an example of them trying to do so and being thwarted by incompetent doctors.

Poverty and Access to Care

Patients interacting with the medical system faced another challenge besides physician incompetence: money. With an average year of treatment for syphilis being outside the price range of 80 percent of the US population, most Kansas women would have been unable to pay for treatment on their own.[81] The limited availability of free health-care clinics that would treat venereal disease in Kansas meant that finances played an important role in many women's decision to volunteer to go to the Farm. At age twenty-one Lorraine Holmes was living with her parents after a recent divorce and had just been laid off from her job at Mrs. Stone's Bungalow Candy factory in Kansas City. She reported: "I went to the Bell Memorial Hospital and had a blood test made and it was four plus. So I started to take treatments and had taken three when the police matron came out to the house and talked to me and said it would be for the best to come here for treatment as I was'nt working."[82] Though Lorraine was taking care of her treatment outside of the institution, she was advised to come to the Farm because of her financial situation. Several women indicated that a doctor turned them in once they disclosed that they would not be able to afford private treatment. Haley Boyd was an eighteen-year-old white waitress who reported contracting a disease from another man after separating from her husband. She reported: "I went to a Doctor and he turned me over to the officers. He aske me if I had enough money to pay for a treatment and when I told him I had not he turned me in."[83] Similarly, Sadie Hines reported that her inability to pay for treatment led her doctor to turn her in to authorities. This twenty-year-old white/Irish-Dutch woman discovered she had a disease after she failed to heal properly following an operation. Sadie reported that the doctor "asked if I had the money to take treatments here, but I did not have so he turned my case over to the health authorities and they sent me here."[84] Although these doctors' actions were fitting with the spirit of the law (i.e., these women would not have been able to get treatment on their own), they were also punishing women who were not in a position to pay for their very expensive services. Chapter 205 afforded them added power over their patients.

Other women narrated their story as if they had more agency, saying that they volunteered to go to the KSIFW after realizing they could not afford private treatment for their disease. Margaret Lee had been married just three months before coming to the Farm in 1929. Age eighteen, she reported: "I got the disease from my husband, I turned myself in because we didn't have the money to pay doctor bills to be cured."[85] While Margaret did not work for pay outside the home, other women reported that they had jobs and were still unable to afford treatment. Jacqueline Smith was a twenty-two-year-old white woman who worked as a maid for an officer at Fort Riley; she reported that she contracted a disease from her husband. Jacqueline spoke of her choice to volunteer to come to the Farm as a calculated decision: "I volunteered to come for treatment when I found I couldnt earn enough for treatment."[86] Similarly, Pearl Crowley stated that she volunteered to go to the Farm when she realized she could not pay for treatment on her own. A twenty-one-year-old Black woman, Pearl had been married for a year before volunteering to go to the Farm. She reported:

> For almost a year I had worked as an apprentice for Mrs. Lottie White, who has an exclusive beauty shop, learning beauty culture. In order for me to be a beauty operator it was necessary for me to pass an examination by the State Board of Health, when my tests came back it was positive. I did not have the money to pay for the treatment, so I found out I could volunteer and come here for treatment.[87]

Without the financial resources to pay for private medical care, these women saw the KSIFW as their only chance for getting treatment and volunteered to come to the institution. The interviews in this sample indicate that the Depression accelerated this pattern of poor women needing to submit themselves to imprisonment in order to access medical treatment. While the other full years in the sample averaged 5.75 women volunteering to go to the Farm per year, fourteen women in the sample volunteered in 1932. Whether it was due to a desire for better health care or an inability to afford care on their own, the fact that 20 percent of the women in the sample actually submitted themselves to imprisonment in order to receive treatment provides a very different portrait of the typical inmate than what the biennial reports of the Farm present.

Chapter 205 in Practice

These various ways that women came to be detained under Chapter 205 led to some confusion on the part of inmates about the charge under which they were officially detained. Under the "History of offense" section of the interview form, several women's comments indicate that they were under the impression that authorities sentenced them to the Farm for something other than the Chapter 205 charge noted on their record. Fern Ellis, a thirty-five-year-old Black woman who was detained under Chapter 205 due to a gonorrhea diagnosis, reported: "About ½ pint of liquor was found in the house. I was sent up for it."[88] Claire Densmore, a twenty-four-year-old white/Irish woman, was under the impression that she was sent to the Farm for writing bad checks.[89] Given that women were often initially detained under one charge before they were quarantined under Chapter 205, it is not surprising that some women would be confused about the reason for their imprisonment. The dual nature of the KSIFW as both a prison and a medical treatment facility also led to confusion. Lizzie Cole, age forty-six, had been arrested for soliciting several times in California, and was again picked up for prostitution after she solicited a man in Wichita. This man failed to appear in court to testify against her, but she was quarantined under Chapter 205 for gonorrhea. Lizzie reported: "Did not know they were in favor of sending me to Lansing. Thought it a state hospital."[90] Whether it was due to the nature of the charge or the institution itself, the fact that some inmates were unaware of the actual charge under which they were imprisoned was highly problematic.

As Lizzie Cole's case above illustrates, prosecutors often used Chapter 205 to imprison women that they could not charge with a more serious crime. Some interviews indicate that police used Chapter 205 to detain women whom they considered to be a public nuisance. Francine Martin, a twenty-six-year-old Black woman, had been interned at the KSIFW twice before and reported that she'd previously been addicted to drugs. She was arrested again in 1923: "Sadie Hixon and a bunch had been at my house and put on a wild party. I was not using drugs but the police thought if they sent me up here they could keep me from using them."[91] Francine's previous history at the KSIFW might have resulted in police being aware of her disease, opening up this avenue for imprisoning her. Another inmate, a twenty-four-year-old white/Irish-Indian woman named Clarese Hill, reported repeated encounters with police:

> I have always drank quite a lot and have been arrested for speeding, and being drunk several times, but always made Bond, and was released. I have been running a rooming house, and I had 4 girls and several, men that rooms at my place, and one day the law came down and was looking for a girl, and thought she roomed at my place but she did not. I got into an argument with the officers, and talked smart to them. So they said "Clarese you come along with us" So they sent me up here.[92]

Clarese, who had been arrested several times and was hostile with police officers, was clearly a nuisance to the police. Chapter 205 became a mechanism for local police to rid themselves of this nuisance, even without enough evidence to convict her of another offense.[93]

Overall, these women came to the KSIFW under a variety of circumstances, some voluntarily but most against their will. Many lamented their fate, as did a young woman that Darlene Doubleday Newby observed during her undercover stint at the Farm. Only married six weeks before being detained, this woman "didn't' believe that any man would be faithful to an absent wife, and she begged to be allowed to return to her 'little man,' saying her home would be wrecked unless she were permitted to go back to him."[94] Being forcibly removed from one's home for months at a time could cause serious disruptions in women's lives, from marital relationships to employment to childcare. At the same time as the policy was disruptive and unjust, however, it also provided some concrete benefits to women.[95] Particularly for the women who volunteered to go to the Farm, the medical treatment provided was very much appreciated. Daisy Hunt, a nineteen-year-old mother of three, stated: "I am glad to get cured and more than glad to be in Lansing."[96] Similarly, Beatrice Cook, a twenty-two-year-old woman who reported that she contracted a disease from her husband, reported: "I certainly appreciate what is being done for me here, and I will do anything I can in the way of work."[97] Newby's report described the inmates' feelings toward the Farm: "The majority of the women, while restless under restraint and eager to get out as soon as possible, seem grateful for the medical treatment given them at the Farm."[98] These stories push us to understand the Farm not only as an institution of social control but also as a resource that poor women could utilize to gain access to needed health-care services. While this is most clearly apparent in the case of the women who volunteered to go to the Farm, many inmates likely appreciated the access to medical treatment and regular food and shelter, particularly as the Depression took hold of Dust Bowl–stricken Kansas.

Conclusion

The inmate interviews from the Kansas State Industrial Farm for Women provide a very different picture of the inmates than is presented in other state documents. Many accounts offer a glaring indictment of men's sexual behaviors and show how Chapter 205 enforced the sexual double standard. Time and again, women reported that Chapter 205 brought them into the crosshairs of the law while letting the men who gave them a disease go free. These women's stories illustrate the ways that existing social hierarchies informed the implementation of Chapter 205. Gender hierarchies were upheld when a husband turned in his wife for venereal disease. Black women faced a greater chance of being caught up in a raid and quarantined for disease than their white counterparts. Class differences became more stark when some women had to volunteer to go to the Farm while others could afford private treatment. Looking at Chapter 205 from the perspective of the inmates, the influence of inequality in the implementation of this law becomes apparent in ways that are both obvious and more subtle.

What is clear from these interviews is the seriousness of venereal disease as a health concern and the complete inadequacy of Chapter 205 as an effective means of addressing this public health challenge. With all of the discussion about the need for the inmates to be morally reformed, it is easy to forget that there was a genuine social problem at hand in Kansas. In this age before antibiotics, syphilis and gonorrhea had no cure, and social stigma and high cost prevented many women from accessing what treatments were available. The fact that a full 20 percent of the inmates in the sample actually volunteered to go to the Farm to access health care speaks volumes to the inadequacy of Chapter 205 as the primary means of addressing this public health issue. The inmates' stories illustrate the difficulties of accessing affordable treatment for their disease and their genuine desire to take care of their health. Hidden among the rhetoric of “loose women” and changing morals, there were real people getting infected with venereal disease who were in dire need of state policies and services to help them. While men were left out of the purview of state policies and certain groups of women became the scapegoat, a public health issue in Kansas went largely unaddressed. Rather than a genuine engagement with the social problem at hand, the implementation of Chapter 205 was guided by ideas of gender, race, and class, leading to an ineffective system that left many women suffering.

CHAPTER 6
STAKING A CLAIM TO RESPECTABILITY
INMATE ACCOUNTS OF THEIR SEXUAL PASTS

Loretta Mark was twenty years old when she found herself at the Farm after being detained under Chapter 205. Just like other inmates, KSIFW staff interviewed Loretta on her arrival. Loretta's interview form does not provide many specifics about her sexual history or how she came to be arrested under Chapter 205. She had been married a few years earlier, but she left her husband after only three months. However, Loretta's interview form does provide a glimpse into one woman's attempt to stake a claim to respectability. Loretta stated, "I lived just as near right as I know how to live. I taught Sunday School."[1] Regardless of what her internment under Chapter 205 might have meant for her reputation, Loretta Mark was there to assure her interviewer that she was a respectable woman.

Just like Loretta, the inmates of the KSIFW found themselves in a highly charged situation when they arrived at the Farm: they were detained under an indefinite sentence, so they had every incentive to present themselves as respectable women and make a good impression on the person interviewing them. Yet they were also asked very personal questions about who they had sex with and why. In their answers, the inmates constructed narratives about themselves and their sexual histories that portrayed their choices in the best possible light.[2] An exploration of the inmate interviews reveals two narratives of the women's sexual pasts: (1) inmates emphasized how they had not broken dominant sexual norms; and (2) inmates emphasized that they had been led astray by others and were thus not responsible for breaking sexual norms. While these narratives positioned some women to be viewed as respectable, they often failed to articulate ideas of love that might have legitimated their sexual pasts. Through the interviews, the inmates detained under Chapter 205 sought to account for their stigmatized diseases in a situation where

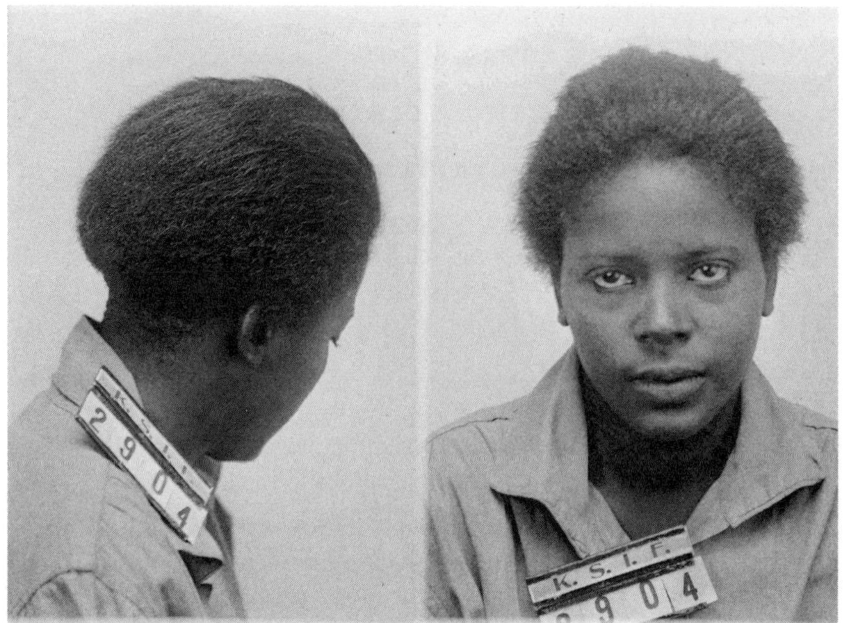

Mugshot of Loretta Mark, sent to the KSIFW under Chapter 205 in 1926. Photo has been cropped. Lansing Historical Museum, "KSIF Prisoners 2904 & 2905," http://lansingmuseum.omeka.net/items/show/32.

their respectability was highly questioned. Similar to the accounts of how women came to be arrested, these narratives of inmates' sexual histories reveal the complex interplay of gender, sexuality, and power through the implementation of Chapter 205.

Inmate accounts of their sexual pasts tell a very different story of the function and implications of Chapter 205 from what is presented in official state reports. The women incarcerated under Chapter 205 were a varied group, coming from different backgrounds and bringing with them various engagement with what might have been termed "lascivious conduct" at the time. Some of the women fit the portrait painted of them by official state documents as sexually promiscuous and of questionable moral character. Others were clearly the victim of men's vices, caught up in a legal system that punished women for venereal disease but not men. Most inmates were likely somewhere in between, women with moral strengths and weaknesses, trying to navigate life but finding it interrupted by Chapter 205. Regardless of who they were, Chapter 205 brought them to the KSIFW as inmates.

Money and Sex in the Inmate Interviews

Before discussing how women narrated their sexual histories, it is important to explore one barrier to perceptions of inmates' respectability: the underlying assumption that many of the women were prostitutes. The different categorizations of sexual behavior used by professional social workers and working-class women themselves during this period in history complicates any simple answers about whether or not the inmates of the Farm engaged in prostitution. Similar to the professionals in Clement's study of sexuality in New York City, professional social workers in Kansas often did not distinguish between prostitution (exchanging sex for money) and treating (exchanging sex for small gifts or a night on the town). Social worker Alice Hill's 1920 investigation into the backgrounds of inmates from the KSIFW published in *Public Health Reports* stated: "Of the 58 girls for whom the information was secured, 49 were reported as having been paid either in money or gifts, and 9 were definitely reported as having never been immoral for gain."[3] Hill glossed over the distinction between receiving money (prostitution) and receiving gifts (treating), yet this was likely an important difference for the inmates. Treating girls, also known as "charity girls," distinguished themselves from prostitutes in that they did not generally accept money, only "treats." They developed their own moral codes about the morality and respectability of treating, positioning themselves as modern women just out for a good time.[4]

The inmate interviews reveal the importance of monetary exchanges in Kansas inmates' understanding of the morality of their sexual pasts. One woman who referenced the practice of treating was Minnie Taylor, a Black fifteen-year-old girl interviewed in 1924: "Have lived an immoral life about a year. All I ever got was a pair of hose (silk) from Joe Parker at Plattsburg, Missouri. Have been intimate with Joe only. He is 19 years old."[5] Through the phrase "all I ever got," Minnie positioned herself against women who accepted money in exchange for sex. This articulation of the category of treating was not common in the interviews, however, indicating that this either was not as common of a moral category in Kansas as it was in places like New York City, or that the interviewer simply failed to record these types of comments because she did not see them as being significant.

Another complicating factor in understanding the commercial nature of these sexual relationships is that many of the women likely engaged in sexual activities on the side, occasionally receiving money or gifts but not making their living from having sex. A statement from Darlene Doubleday Newby's 1918 undercover report indicated that many inmates did not think of themselves as prostitutes. Describing one inmate of the Farm who was troublesome and bossy, Newby reported that the other inmates did not like her and "declared that she was 'lots worse than any of them—a regular prostitute, crooked in her mode of living and dishonest in all her relations.'"[6] The fact that these women did not see themselves as "regular prostitutes" shows the different categorizations of sexual behaviors used by working-class women during this time that were sometimes overlooked by moral reformers and professional social workers.

While the commercial nature of sexual exchanges was unclear for some inmates, other women admitted to prostitution in their interviews. Next to "Cause of downfall" on the interview form, seven women replied "Needed money." A few women explicitly stated that they received money for having sex. Mae Elliot was thirty-three when arrested in 1924. Following her third marriage (twice divorced, once a war widow), Mae was running a boardinghouse in Wichita when arrested. She reported: "Have not always lived a straight life but havent been too bad. Got money when I did have a friend."[7] Similarly, Charlotte Bell reported receiving money in exchange for sex. This twenty-year-old white/Irish-English woman was serving her second sentence under Chapter 205 when she reported: "Lived an immoral life about 3 years when I was out for the money I never got less than $3.00."[8] Pauline Murphy, a thirty-eight-year-old married mother of two, discussed the financial pressures pushing her into prostitution: "My husband took the children and went to Ill. There was not money enough for me to go. So I stayed behind and was to work and go too. But could not get work of any kind and had to resort to what ever I could do. I'll never do it again."[9] These accounts confirm that at least some of the women sentenced under Chapter 205 were prostitutes. Given the situation under which these interviews were conducted, it is not surprising that few women admitted to prostitution, since this would have amounted to confessing to a different crime than the one for which they were sentenced.

Though we cannot know the exact percentage of women detained under Chapter 205 who were prostitutes, it is safe to say that a portion of the women engaged in some sort of commercial sexual exchange. However, it is also safe to say that many of the women were not prostitutes and in fact had never had sex outside of marriage. Regardless of their histories, though, the state detained these women under the assumption that they were in need of moral reform. The KSIFW and the interview form itself were set up under the premise that women detained under Chapter 205 were immoral and needed the reforming influences of the Farm to set them on the right path. It is within this context that prison staff interviewed the inmates.

Abiding by Dominant Rules of Sexuality

Through the inmate interviews, women had an opportunity to stake a claim to respectability by explaining their contraction of venereal disease in a way that fit with dominant norms of sexuality. One form this took was inmates asserting that they had not broken any moral norms. In stark contrast to the tales told about them, these women claimed that they ended up with a venereal disease despite their adherence to middle-class norms for sexual behavior. Though they varied on how they narrated the contraction of their disease, all of the women in this group asserted their own respectability through recognizing the validity of dominant sexual mores and claiming that they abided by those rules. Their stories give a glaring indictment of the men in their lives and shift the responsibility for the women's disease onto men.

The Victims of Husbands' Vice

The most common form that this argument took was through women claiming that they contracted a venereal disease through their husbands. Engaging with wider cultural narratives of the transmission of venereal disease from prostitutes to wives through their husbands, many of the women at the KSIFW claimed that they were the innocent wives in this scenario, not the prostitutes.[10] Indeed, despite their young age, 56 percent of the women in the interview sample had been married at some point before being interned at the KSIFW.[11] According to social worker Alice Hill's analysis at the time, inmates' marriage rate was much higher than the general population for women in this age group in Kansas; only 38 percent of the general female population was married, widowed, or divorced by age twenty in 1910, compared to 63 percent of the KSIFW inmates that Hill studied in 1918.[12]

A comparison of age by marital status reveals the rapidly shifting family dynamics of many of these young women. Of the fifteen-year-olds in the sample, 72 percent had never married at the time of their interview, 8 percent were married, and 19 percent were separated or divorced. Of the twenty-year-old women in the sample, 40 percent had never married, 10 percent were married, and 50 percent were either divorced or separated. This compares to a national divorce rate of eight divorces per thousand marriages in 1920, placing the inmates of the Farm well above national averages.[13] Indeed, by the age of twenty, many of these women were already on their second marriage. The population of women that was sent to the Farm was thus much more likely to have experienced a divorce. During the 1920s, when societal fears about the fragility of new love-based marriages and the implications of a freer sexual culture for family relations were running high, this population of recent *divorcées* made a ripe target for government control.[14] The fact that the majority of the women at the KSIFW had at some point been married has important implications for their respectability: it was quite possible that they had contracted a venereal disease through no moral "lapse" of their own, but rather through their husbands' sexual misdeeds.[15]

In their interviews, many women made exactly this claim. Maude Parker was a white/Scotch-Welsh-Irish woman who reported that she "had never lived an immoral life." She married her first husband at age sixteen, but after a year and half she "told him to leave because he was trifling on" her. Maude married for a second time in 1924, but after only a few months she found herself at the Farm. She reported: "Husband turned me in to the Health Officers. He is more diseased than I am. I got my disease from him."[16] Like Maude, Cora Hammond reported that she had not been promiscuous. Cora had married at the age of sixteen, had two children, and then divorced. Now twenty-two, she reported: "My husband is to balme. . . . husband not good to me, drank so much I couldnt live with him. I've learned that my daughters will not marry as young as I."[17] Many women asserted their own sexual propriety while stating that they got a disease from their husbands. Anna Wright was a twenty-one-year-old Black woman who had married at the age of thirteen. She reported: "I have always been a good girl never had anything to do with any man but my husband."[18] Velma Turner, a twenty-year-old white woman, made a similar claim, stating: "I got this disease from my Husband. I have gone to dances and different place with a crowd since my husband and I separated but I have never led an immoral life."[19] The inmates repeatedly spoke of their husbands giving them a disease. Of the 128 women in the

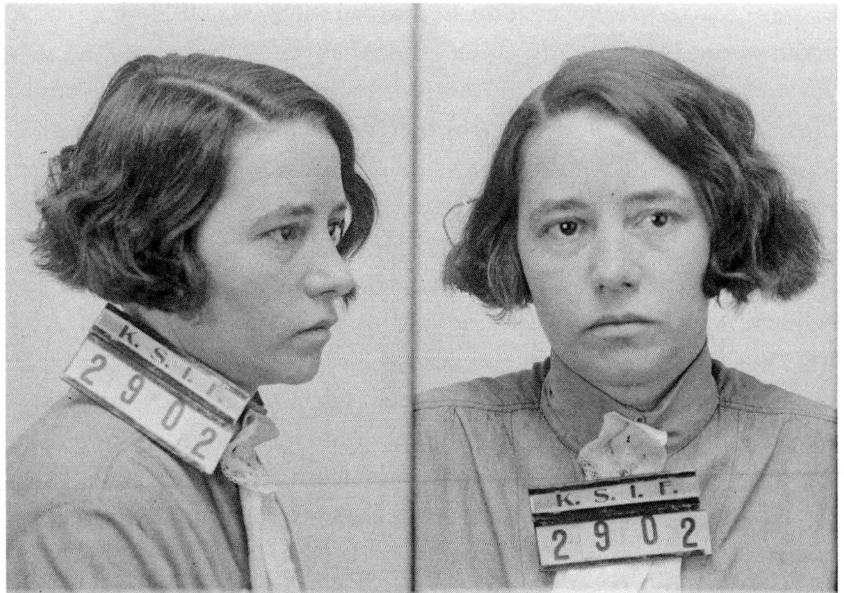

Photo of inmate Maude Parker, who reported that her husband turned her in to authorities for having venereal disease. Photo has been cropped. Lansing Historical Museum, "KSIF Prisoners 2902 & 2903," http://lansingmuseum.omeka.net/items/show/35.

sample who reported where they contracted their disease (about one-third of the women), 51 percent claimed that they contracted venereal disease through their husbands. Thus, many of those who were willing to specify from whom they contracted the disease did so in order to position themselves as abiding by dominant norms of sexuality.

In claiming that they contracted their disease from their husbands, these women were drawing on cultural discourses about the transmission of venereal disease from "fallen" prostitutes to philandering husbands, and finally to the innocent wives and children of these supposedly upstanding men. For prostitutes and unfaithful husbands, venereal disease was commonly understood as a just punishment for their sexual indiscretions. An innocent wife getting infected through no fault of her own, however, was cause for major social concern. Physicians across the country in the first few decades of the twentieth century worried about "venereal *insontium*," or the innocent getting infected, and publicly lamented men's sexual excesses that led to this condition. At times, the Kansas State Board of Health promoted this interpretation of wives' contraction of venereal disease. A 1922 pamphlet addressed to "all Mothers and Mothers-to-be" about women's health-care needs stated that venereal diseases "are usually contracted, directly or indirectly, through sexual intercourse with a prostitute." The text went on to say that "gonorrhea is very often transmitted from the husband to the new wife."[20] When inmates such as Lilian Hart, a white/German-Indian woman who was the mother of a four-year-old child, made such statements as "Husband brought disease home to me," they explicitly connected to this cultural narrative.[21]

However, the forced detention and treatment of the inmates at the KSIFW shows that the state did not always view these women as the innocent wives in this scenario. The conflicting messages sent through the state (i.e., the board of health promoting the idea that wives might get the disease through their husbands and the criminal justice system then imprisoning those same women and subjecting them to moral reform) is partially indicative of the uncoordinated and poorly designed efforts to control venereal disease in the state. Yet it also speaks to state authorities' tendency to classify women as either "good" or "bad," and their assumption that the inmates, by virtue of their being at the Farm, fell into the latter category. Thus, the inmates' claim that they were the innocent wives in this narrative of venereal disease transmission was counter to many of the assumptions made about them. Regardless of where the venereal disease originated, the fact that so many of the women were married only amplified the ineffectiveness of the overall approach of detaining only women under Chapter 205. Even if a woman were to be morally reformed and made noninfectious (a goal the Farm rarely achieved due to ineffective treatment options), her husband would likely immediately reinfect her on leaving the Farm.

Asexual Contraction of Venereal Disease

Another way in which women narrated the contraction of venereal disease in such a way that reinforced dominant cultural norms about sexuality was through claiming that they contracted the disease asexually. Though it was not commonly articulated, several women in the sample claimed that they contracted venereal disease through nonsexual means. Of the third of the sample who specified where they contracted the disease, seventeen women, or about 13 percent, claimed that they contracted the disease through nonsexual contact.[22] Some of these stories involved the transfer of bodily fluid, making nonsexual contraction of venereal disease a distinct possibility. Blanche Howard was a nineteen-year-old white woman who gave such an account: "Lucy Baker was sick and I was taking care of her. I didnt know what was the matter with her. One day I had cramps so she told me to use her syringe which I did. I later found out she was diseased. I was told to go see Dr. Carter and I went and was examined and was sent here. Have never lived an immoral life." Though it is entirely possible that this woman contracted a disease through sharing a syringe, she just as easily could have contracted the disease from her estranged husband.[23] The attribution of her disease to nonsexual means was a way to distance herself from the kind of disreputable sexuality that was so commonly blamed for venereal disease. Other women claimed that they contracted a disease from roommates. Frances Pearson was only twelve years old when she was interned at the Farm in 1926. She reported: "If I am diseased I got it from sister Kathern as we slept together."[24] Similarly, Norma Stewart, a twenty-one-year-old white woman, reported: "I do not know how I got this disease as I have never done any thing wrong. I think I may have gotten it at the place where I worked. I also roomed at a house where there had been girls who was wrong and I think I got it from them in the room."[25] Claims to nonsexual contraction were particularly common for young women (such as the twelve-year-old girl quoted above) and among women who reported "never" when asked about the age that they "first broke the law of chastity."

Other statements indicate that doctors and husbands employed narratives of nonsexual contraction as they discussed these diseases with women. Doris Green, a twenty-eight-year-old woman who was interned at the KSIFW along with her baby in 1924, reported: "Husband told me got disease from toilet seats."[26] Whether Doris believed her husband's story about how he contracted venereal disease or not, the narrative of nonsexual contraction allowed her to keep her own respectability, and that of her husband's, intact. Another young woman, age fifteen when interned in 1930, illustrated how this narrative might have surfaced in doctor/ patient interactions: "Dr. Beach said he thought that I got this disease from drinking out of some body cup."[27] By telling his patient that she probably contracted the disease through nonsexual means, this doctor gave backing to her claim that she had "never broken the laws of chastity" and offered her a way to present her disease to others in a respectable way. When these inmates claimed that they contracted venereal disease through nonsexual means, they distanced themselves from sexuality. They were also able to explain their presence at the KSIFW through no admission of moral fault on their own part, all while upholding dominant cultural norms about respectable sexual behavior.

Similar to national discourses about innocent wives contracting venereal disease, inmates claiming that they contracted a venereal disease asexually drew on larger cultural narratives. In the first few decades of the twentieth century, doctors claimed that public drinking cups, towels, public restrooms, and toothbrushes were common means of transmitting venereal infections. By asserting that people could contract venereal disease nonsexually, these public health officials and doctors offered people with venereal disease a respectable narrative by which they could account for their contraction of the disease. These professionals hoped that this would not only make people more likely to seek treatment for venereal disease but also bolster their own public image, since people often blamed doctors who treated venereal disease for condoning immoral behavior. In 1922 a Kansas State Board of Health bulletin repeated these national claims that venereal diseases could be spread nonsexually, claiming that these diseases could "be innocently contracted through kissing or drinking after infected persons, from public toilets, toilet paper, chains or handles of the various types of toilet flush, public towels, etc." Noting that this rarely occurs, the publication still warned readers to "be extremely careful to avoid touching anything which may have recently been contaminated."[28] While claims of nonsexual contraction served to bolster the respectability of those infected with venereal disease, they also reflected a growing anxiety among middle-class residents of urban areas about increased rates of interactions with immigrants and poor people. By claiming that diseases could be spread asexually, the danger of venereal disease became a danger to everyone, not only those people who failed to subscribe to middle-class standards of respectable sexual behavior.[29]

These national narratives about the asexual contraction of venereal disease can be seen in a speech that Superintendent Julia Perry gave to the Woman's Christian Temperance Union and then printed in the 1924 biennial report of the KSIFW:

> I am just now trying to shut out of my mind a girl of fifteen with a diseased spine, a face and neck disfigured with horrible sores. Another picture that bothers me is a rather vigorous young woman standing by her bedside with an ugly sore on her lip—the result of a sweetheart's

> kiss. In the same ward I see a young girl that drank out of the same glass that had been used by some one else, and infection set in. The most pitiful sight was that of a gray-haired, gentle, old lady whose face was swathed in bandages, who had contracted the disease from her son.
>
> A great majority of cases are congenital. But each person or case I have mentioned was a victim of infection and each sufferer was a silent argument in favor of a widespread knowledge of danger of infection to innocent victims. The public at large do not realize the danger abroad in the land and when venereal diseases are mentioned too many have the idea that the health officer is an alarmist and would be out of a job if he failed to emphasize the need of care being exercised in the spread of these two diseases that are doing more toward undermining the health of our young people than all other contagious, infectious or communicable diseases.[30]

In these statements, Perry made a case for not only the pressing social danger of venereal disease but also many of the inmates' respectability. By asserting that many cases were acquired innocently, Perry downplayed many of the inmates' sexual experiences. Though these statements were part of a larger argument to raise alarm about venereal disease and justify the existence of the KSIFW, they also indicate a certain level of buy-in for the inmates' claims that they contracted venereal disease asexually.

Inheritance of Venereal Disease

In a similar vein, several women and girls at the KSIFW claimed that they inherited a venereal disease. The claim that the disease was passed down from parents was most frequently seen among the twenty inmates in the sample aged thirteen or younger (though some of these girls reported sexual abuse; see below). For example, Elsie Roberts was an eleven-year-old girl who went to live on a farm near Grenola, Kansas, with her grandparents after her parents separated. She did various chores around the farm, reporting: "I help mow hay and put it away. I work in the field too. We have about 100 acres of land. I do some housework too." Elsie ended up at the KSIFW in Lansing in 1924 after seeking medical care. She recalled: "I inherited bad blood from my mother. Grandmother didnt have money to pay Doctor bill so she sent me here. My eyes were bad so I went to the Doctor and was examined and was found syphilitic."[31] Given their age, the claim from girls like Elsie that the bacteria that caused syphilis or gonorrhea was passed down from their mother was fairly likely. The fact that children's presence at the KSIFW was one of the most publicly debated aspects of the KSIFW indicates that many people viewed them as innocent victims of the disease.[32] As children, their sexuality was not as much in question. However, several older women with sexual experience also claimed that they inherited a disease. For example, Marion Phillips, a white-Indian woman who was married with two children, reported: "To my knowledge I inherited this disease."[33] By attributing her disease to her parents rather than her sexual relationship with her husband (her only reported sexual partner), Marion distanced her own sexual behavior from the contraction of a venereal disease. Claiming that they inherited syphilis or gonorrhea allowed these inmates to account for their disease without questioning dominant cultural norms about appropriate sexual behavior.

Rape and Sexual Abuse

The most disturbing narrative of contracting a venereal disease involved women claiming to have been raped or sexually abused as children. Though the stigma of being a victim of rape certainly would have affected their respectability, this narrative also allowed women to explain their contraction of a venereal disease while recognizing the legitimacy of moral norms that limited sexual behavior to marriage. While not particularly common among this sample (only around 2 percent of the total sample reported rape or sexual abuse), these women's stories illustrate some of the fears that policy makers and social activists harbored about the effects of changing family structures and sexual culture on the safety and sexual purity of young women. Of the women who claimed to have been raped or sexually abused, almost all of them were under the age of twenty. Older women did not mention sexual abuse or rape; this may be connected to shifting legal and cultural understandings of rape (for example, marital rape was not a widely understood concept at the time), or perhaps the women just attributed their contraction of the disease to other causes.[34]

The most disturbing of these stories are those told by young girls about sexual abuse by family members or guardians. These accounts described the broken homes and unsteady family relationships about which so many social commentators worried. Julia and Sarah Park were two sisters who found themselves at the KSIFW in 1927. Julia, age nine, reported on the events that led to them being there:

> My mother whipped me and made me do wrong with men. Had dates with 5 men, made by mother. When they gave me money I gave it to mother to get something to eat with. Been doing this way since early last summer. Mother & Stepfather separated about 15 times. Sometimes we would all go into a room, other times down around a creek. Just any place.[35]

Sarah, who was fifteen years old, corroborated this account in her interview, stating: "Joe Coleman, Columbus Jail, 43 years old was in bed with Julia when arrested." Sarah reported that her mother had also made arrangements for her to have sex with men in exchange for money, commenting that she "would rather be here than with my Mother."[36] Though the girls' comments indicate that the man who was with Julia was arrested, it is unclear whether their mother was punished in any way other than having her children taken away from her. Similarly, there seemed to be few repercussions for the perpetrators of sexual violence against Leona Reed, who was fourteen when interned at the Farm for gonorrhea. Her mother had died when she was just nine days old, and her father had married several different times before the courts removed her from his care at the age of eight; she was then placed with various aunts to care for her. She reported:

> My father forced me one time at 8 years of age and then my uncle Bill Walters forced me on July 1925. These two times are the only two times. I have ever been bothered. Don't know where I got diseased unless from Father or Uncle. My Uncle told me that I had let boys and said that he could tell if I would show him. I did because he said he would not keep me any longer. He then misused me.[37]

Though it is not entirely clear, it seems that Leona was taken from her father after he raped her at age eight. No mention is made of criminal charges against either her father or her uncle. Georgia Clarke, age fifteen when sent to the Farm in 1927, did see some legal action as a result of her case. She reported: "Father is cause of my downfall. First time I had intercourse with anyone was with him. Four times one night. When I was 13 years of age. Case was brought to court, but for some unknown reason was dismissed. All jurors were friends of my father and were Catholics as was my father."[38] Though charges were pressed against this inmate's father, there did not appear to be any long-term consequences for him.

While Georgia left the house after this incident, she reported that she had five siblings still living with her parents. Together, these accounts show the vulnerabilities of children and the lack of accountability for perpetrators of sexual abuse.

These girls' disturbing stories have mixed meanings in terms of their claims to respectability. Their accounts certainly illustrate their lack of choice about having sex, allowing them to subscribe to dominant moral codes about sexuality. However, their stories also reveal sexual conduct in their families that deeply violated social norms. Given the prevalence of beliefs about the heritability of sexual immorality and the sexually deviant patterns of "undesirable" genetic pools in the United States during this time (see chapter 3), their stories condemned them as members of a group at the same time that they exonerated them as individuals. As evidenced by the fact that the interview form prompted the interviewer to ask women about other family members who had been imprisoned, the respectability of a person's family had direct implications for that person's own respectability in the age of eugenics.

Among the women in their teens who reported being raped, what is particularly striking is the prevalence of the automobile in their accounts. Indeed, the growing mobility and freedom that personal cars afforded American youth was a cause of concern for parents and social commentators across the country. With girls no longer restricted to supervised visits on the family's front porch, parents worried about the safety and sexual purity of their daughters as they negotiated a new sexual culture.[39] In many ways the stories of the young women in this sample who reported that they were raped confirmed this generation of worried parents' worst fears. One example comes from the accounts of Carrie Morris and Laura Gray. These two friends, ages seventeen and nineteen, were hitchhiking from Oklahoma City to Saint Joseph, Missouri. Carrie reported: "Just outside of Independence, two men came along in a car. They stopped and made us get in the car. Laura jumped out of the car. They Raped us before she got away."[40] Laura gave a similar account, adding that one man "hit [her] with his fist." At some point during this attack, Laura got away from the perpetrators, "went to a filling station and called the law"; she reported that "both men were caught—one is in jail now in Fredonia, the other out on bond."[41] Though the men involved in this case faced some legal repercussions, so did their victims. Another account of rape comes from

Stella Baker, a seventeen-year-old who volunteered to go to the Farm. The automobile was also a prominent feature in her account:

> George Blackwell of Wichita, Kansas, North Washington is responsible for my condition. He forced me. He is only man I was ever intimate with. He tried to force me to be registered in at a Hutchinson Hotel. I refused to comply with his request. He then drove me miles from the city and after several hours of quarreling, pleading and struggling he over povered [*sic*] me after I had got away from him and ran about ¾ of a mile.[42]

Stella's account echoes some themes from Carrie and Laura's experience: there was direct physical violence (being punched or overpowered), and cars allowed men to take women to isolated spaces.

Other accounts of rape lacked the physical violence described above. Mamie Cooper was a nineteen-year-old white/Irish woman sentenced to the Farm under a gonorrhea diagnosis. She reported: "I became diseased through Sam Parkinson; I was intimate with him just one time. He took me out 53 miles from home and would have made me walk home if I did not give up to him."[43] Irene Bailey, age sixteen, reported a very similar situation. After attending a dance in Elk Falls, Kansas, with one female friend and two male companions, she reported: "On our way back we were forced to do wrong or walk. I did not know waht to do."[44] While these are certainly cases of rape, the language used in the interviews indicates that the lack of direct physical force led to some confusion about the experience on the part of inmates. The three women quoted in the previous paragraph all listed "raped" next to the prompt, "Cause of downfall." These two women, however, had "Influenced" (Mamie Cooper) and "Walk or 'else'---" (Irene Bailey) recorded next to this prompt. The inmates also used language indicating that they felt like they had at least partially participated in a decision to have sex, such as when Mamie said that she had to "give up to him" or when Irene said that she "did not know waht to do." Then and now, the lack of physical force in cases of rape led to some confusion about how to understand the event, particularly in a time before date rape was a culturally understood category.[45]

Whether physically violent or not, these cases of rape were one way that inmates narrated their sexual pasts in a way that denied their active choice to have sex outside of marriage. These inmates' accounts not only speak to their claims to respectability; they also present an important element of the history of sexual violence that is not currently well recorded in the literature. The scenario of a man driving a woman out to a remote location and refusing to take her home unless she had sex with him showed up in several different women's stories. This pattern of sexual coercion may be something specific to rural locations during this period. Indeed, it may be that while urban parents worried about places such as dances and skating rinks as sources of immorality, it was the act of getting to those places across long distances that posed the real sexual danger for young women in rural areas.

Whether they claimed to have contracted a disease through their husbands, asexually, or through sexual abuse, many girls and women in this sample narrated their personal histories in such a way that accepted dominant moral codes about respectable sexual behavior. These women told the stories of their lives in a way that distanced their venereal disease from immoral sexual behavior. Husbands, parents, and male acquaintances were guilty of sexual misconduct, not the women themselves. Because these women claimed to have contracted their disease in a situation where they were not violating dominant rules about proper sexuality, the fact that they had a venereal disease made them victims of others' misconduct rather than the perpetrators of their own fate. They staked a claim to respectability by claiming innocence.

Led Astray by Others

A second common type of narrative given by the women in this sample was that they were led astray or influenced by someone else to break sexual norms. Like the previous group of narratives, these women accepted dominant moral codes for sexual behavior. Unlike the previous group, however, these women admitted that they had broken dominant sexual mores and accounted for their error by saying that they were negatively influenced by others. They recognized that their behavior violated dominant moral codes about sexuality without taking full responsibility for their actions.

The Dangers of Bad Company

Many women in the sample mentioned that they were negatively influenced by someone else, be that a wild friend or a romantic interest who led them astray. Next to the prompt on the interview form that read "Cause of downfall," a full 77 percent of the women who answered this question reported that either bad company, a lover, or other environmental influences were to blame. Bad company was such a common response to this prompt that at times it feels like the interviewer wrote it down for every inmate.[46] Many inmates at the Farm did not view their "downfall" as entirely their fault.

For some women, this bad influence took the form of an eager boyfriend or fiancé. Katherine Collins was a seventeen-year-old white/Irish woman who claimed: "Was intimate with 1 man several times. The first time I went with him he made me drink."[47] Another inmate, fifteen-year-old Lucille Stout, reported: "I got the disease from a boy I was engaged to. . . . I have found it does not pay to keep bad company, and am going to remember that."[48] By emphasizing how they were talked into having sex, these women positioned themselves as being basically respectable people who were negatively influenced by an ill-intentioned lover.

While some inmates, such as those above, specified who it was that gave them the disease and talked about specific men who led them astray, it was more common for women to discuss a general group of friends or a lifestyle as being the cause of their "downfall." For example, Bernice Richardson was a sixteen-year-old white woman who blamed bad company for her presence at the Farm: "Running around with bad company but my sister got me into it. . . . Learned that bad company hasn't gotten me anywhere, but into trouble."[49] These women gave accounts of their sexual histories in such a way as to give more responsibility for their actions to their companions than to their own personal choices. Another example comes from Florence Hayes, a sixteen-year-old interned in 1931:

> My folks are poor, and I had no one to chum with but the Bellview girls. and one evening I went out with them and some boys. The boy I was with took advantage of me and gave me this disease. . . . I will obey all rules and when I go home I am going to school and I certainly will be careful of the company I keep.[50]

As the age of these respondents indicates, the young average age of women imprisoned at the KSIFW is part of the reason that this explanation was so common: the inexperience of youth made them susceptible to the negative influence of others. However, as the statements of Violet Patterson, age thirty-five, reveal, older women also made claims to being influenced by others: "I got in with a girl who was wrong, about six weeks before coming here. I always lived the right kind of life. . . . I would not gone wrong if this other women had not talked me into it. But I was old enough to have known better. I am going to try and do better."[51] While this inmate took some responsibility for her actions, the general pattern of blaming bad company for being at the Farm showed up repeatedly in the interviews.

This narrative of being led astray helped these women divert attention away from their own sexuality and onto their companions. For example, one of the few women who admitted to receiving money in exchange for sex told her story as being almost completely driven by her persuasive friend. Josephine Ross was a seventeen-year-old white/Indian-Irish woman who was separated from her husband:

> I got to running around with Betsy and she led me astray. I got to going to dances & running back and forth from Iola to Chanute in cars at night & Betsy forced me to be intimate with a stranger for $5.00, I did not want to and was in his company for about 7 hours before I could make myself give up to him. . . . Have been living immorally about 6 weeks. Needed money and Betsy convinced me to get it "easy."[52]

Josephine's account downplayed her own agency and blamed Betsy for her situation. Talking about their acquisition of venereal disease in terms of hanging out with bad company allowed these women to answer the interviewer's question without directly talking about their own sexual experiences. For example, Bertha Watson, a sixteen-year-old white woman, reported: "I had been running around with people that were wrong and became infected."[53] This statement skirts the issue of sexuality altogether. Speaking about their disease in terms of the people they associated with allowed the inmates to acknowledge their wrongdoing as choosing bad companions, not actively choosing to have sex.

The Dangers of Youth Culture

Another common way that inmates claimed they were led astray was by talking about skating rinks, dances, and car riding as being the cause of their downfall. Similar to how they talked about being influenced by bad company, these women talked about these activities as being intimately bound up in their sexual choices. For example, in response to the prompt "Cause of downfall," several women responded with phrases such as

"Ignorance and dances," "Going to dances with bad company," "Wanted car rides," or "Not going to school and going car riding."[54] Inmates spoke of car riding, dances, and sexual misconduct in the same breath, reflecting wider cultural associations between these new forms of recreation and disreputable sexuality.[55] Even when women were denying that they had had sex outside of a marital relationship, their denials reflected a close association of dances with illicit sexuality. Fannie Price, a nineteen-year-old who was separated from her husband, stated, "Before I was married I was intimate with two or three. I went to dances or shows but always came home early."[56] Similarly, Virginia Bennett, a twenty-year-old white woman, said, "I got this disease from my Husband. I have gone to dances and different place with a crowd since my husband and I seperated but I have never led an immoral life."[57] These statements reveal the close associations that many of these women made between participating in the youth culture of dances, car rides, and skating rinks and extramarital sexuality. Confirming their participation in this youth culture offered an explanation for the inmates' sexual past without actually requiring the women to openly discuss sexuality.

These associations between illicit sexuality and commercial spaces were consistent with the concerns of anti-vice activists and state health officials in Kansas at the time. In times where the state was allocating more money to the Division of Venereal Diseases in the early 1920s, the division employed social workers to investigate the origins of vice within communities. One such social worker charged with investigating the sources of venereal disease around Wichita in 1919 inspected sixteen public dances as part of her investigation. In discussing the various sources of prostitution, another agent of the board of health listed hotels, rooming houses, and dance halls in a 1920 report. He lamented the lack of supervision of dances in some smaller communities in Kansas, where dance halls were used "as a meeting place for immoral women and men. There was no supervision whatsoever in some communities, and little girls with short dresses and braids down their backs were allowed to frequent these places until a late hour."[58] This agent's description of the "little girls" at the dances stresses the innocence and vulnerability of the young women in attendance. In this sense, the inmates' accounts of their sexual misdeeds as being caused by commercial spaces drew on common cultural understandings of the causes of immorality. The degree to which the inmates' respectability was salvaged by them appealing to this association between commercial spaces and sexual immorality hinged on the degree to which the listener viewed the inmates as the innocent victims of these places of vice or the wild ones who were causing these places to be immoral. This tension can be seen in comments from Mildred Reed, a reporter who visited the Farm in 1920 and observed inmates at a dance held for their entertainment: "I noticed that the dancing was exceptionally graceful and that nearly all of the girls danced, which was not surprising when one remembers that many of them were habitués of dance halls before their sentence to the farm."[59] While dance halls were connected with immorality in the popular imagination, so too were the inmates of the KSIFW.

The overall narrative strategy of talking about the negative influences of other people or places had mixed meanings in terms of the inmates' claims to respectability. It allowed women to acknowledge that they had violated mainstream notions of proper sexual behavior while claiming that they were not fully at fault. They became the victims of bad company and dance halls, not fully responsible for their actions. However, by associating oneself with the types of people and places that were culturally understood as being the sources of vice, the inmates risked their respectability as well. While the listener could have interpreted these women as the victims of these circumstances, they just as easily could have interpreted them as being just the type of woman in need of the Farm's corrective moral training.

The Missing Narrative of Love

While inmates used the strategies above to try to assert their own respectability, one narrative is conspicuously missing from the inmate interviews: discussions of love. As sexual behaviors changed over the first few decades of the twentieth century, the way that a woman talked about her sexual history became increasingly important to her respectability. Sexual morality came to be based less on the idea of physical chastity—whether or not someone was a virgin when married—and more on the context and emotions in which someone had sex. In this context, how people narrated their sexual pasts was a key determinant in whether their actions would be perceived as respectable or not. Advice columnists during this period gave women more leniency if they accounted for their sexual histories as being motivated by love rather than physical pleasure. Dating advice writer Juliet Farnham urged women to learn the distinction between "promiscuity (that is, petting for petting's sake) and slight romantic lapses."[60] The status of the relationship still mattered: marital sexuality was still the ideal, and certain communities still condoned the longtime practice of engaged couples having sex before marriage. However, love gained cultural importance as the thing that distinguished casual sex from more respectable expressions of emotional connection with a partner. It was key to a respectable narration of one's sexual past.[61]

Within this context, talking about love might have served as a legitimizing discourse for the inmates, allowing them to talk about their contraction of a venereal disease as a result of a "slight romantic lapse" rather than an indication of their own moral character. Yet the interviews rarely mention love. Of the 488 interviews in the sample, only ten listed "love" next to the prompt "Cause of downfall." Very few interviews included the word "love" in the text or talked about emotional connections between the woman and her partner.

While they rarely mentioned love directly, inmates did emphasize two connected ideas: that they did not have very many sexual partners and that they were in a committed relationship. Only fifty-nine women in the sample indicated how many sexual partners they had; of those, twenty-two (37 percent) said that they only had one partner and thirteen (22 percent) said that they only had two partners. Thus, the women who did indicate how many partners they had often did so in order to emphasize that they had not had sex with very many people. Many women used language that also emphasized this point, saying things such as "Have been intimate with only 1 man" or "He is the only man that I have been with."[62] Other women mentioned that they were in a long-term or committed relationship when they had sex. For example, Ada Evans stated that she was "engaged to marry," Esther Barker reported having sex with a man "with whom [she] had been going for some time," and Lillie Jenkins reported that she "got this disease from a boy that [she] had gone with for about four or five months."[63] Rosa Flores was a twenty-three-year-old Mexican woman who was staying with an uncle in Wichita while her family worked in the sugar beet fields as migrant laborers. She reported: "I had been going with a young [man] for about six month, with whom I was intimate and I became pregnant and he left me."[64] Though these interviews did not discuss the emotional connections between the women and their partners, emphasizing that they had few partners and that they were in long-term relationships was consistent with larger cultural narratives of romantic love.[65]

However, other inmates talked about these elements of romantic love in ways that were at odds with mainstream notions of the relationship between love and sex. For example, the interview for eighteen-year-old Ella Whitmore had "Do not know (Love)" recorded next to "Cause of downfall," yet it also stated that she "led an immoral life last few years. Got discouraged when first sweetheart turned me down."[66] Ella claimed that a broken heart led her to go down an immoral path, a considerably different scenario than simply saying that her feelings led her to go too far with someone she loved. Similar to Ella, other inmates attempted to invoke the ideals of romantic love with limited success. Some women emphasized that they had not had very many sexual partners in relation to casual sex, utilizing this element of the narrative in a way that was very much at odds with the ideal of romantic love. Ruby Foster was fourteen when she went to the Farm in 1926. She reported her only sexual encounter from the previous year: "Was intimate with 1 man 1 time, Lloyd Carpenter of a Carnival that stopped near our home."[67] Lucy Bryant recounted her only sexual encounter as a similarly casual affair. This twenty-one-year-old waitress reported: "was with one man, one time. Know nothing about him now."[68] While these women articulated some elements of romantic love, they failed to use it in a way that might have resonated with mainstream notions of appropriate sexual behavior.

Other women more starkly violated sexual norms in their narratives. For example, Emma Long was an eighteen-year-old white/Indian woman who reported: "Have been intimate with about 12 men. I usually had steadies. Was intimate with other men while I lived with my husband."[69] This inmate's report that she "usually had steadies" could be read as an attempt to claim respectability because sex was within the context of a relationship, yet the higher number of sexual partners and the fact that she had sex outside of her marriage would have violated social norms. A few women reported that they had casual sex, not making any attempts to disguise the fact that they were not in a committed relationship with their sexual partner. Bonnie Peterson was working as a domestic in Kansas City before she was sent to the Farm in 1926. Eighteen at the time of arrest, Bonnie reported next to the spot on the interview form marked "Cause of downfall": "Came straight from Catholic School into Kansas City; never saw a boy before and just run wild."[70] Viola Kelly, a fourteen-year-old girl who was turned in to authorities by her sister, reported: "I got this disease from a man that I went with once but I do not know his name."[71] Admitting to

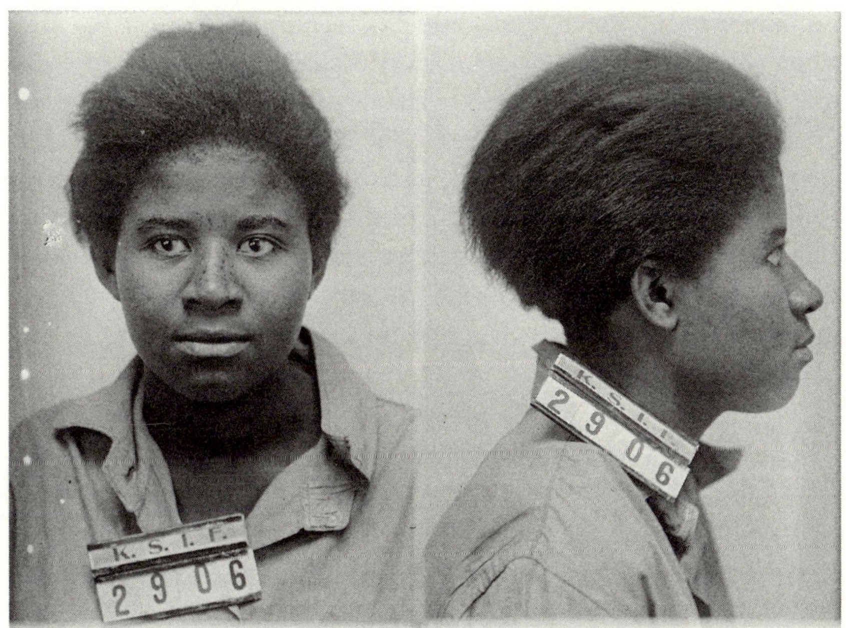

Mugshot of inmate Bonnie Peterson, who reported that she "went wild" after she left Catholic school. Photo has been cropped. Lansing Historical Museum, "KSIF Prisoners 2906 & 2908," http://lansingmuseum.omeka.net/items/show/33.

"running wild" and not knowing the name of one's sexual partner were in stark contrast to the ideal of romantic love. Mildred James, age sixteen when interned in 1926, reported: "Lived an immoral life since 14 years. . . . I ran with any & everyone until I was arrested. Been intimate with about 10 or 12. Just out for a good time."[72] Gertrude Henderson also talked about her personal desires in discussing her past. This nineteen-year-old white woman detained in 1927 stated: "Living wrong 2 months, last summer. Knew better. Just wanted to have a 'fling.'"[73] Though sexual pleasure was not often explicitly mentioned in the interviews, phrases such as being "out for a good time" or "wanting to have a fling" hint at it. Indeed, social commentators at the time frequently associated working-class women and women of color with being motivated by sexual pleasure, not love. It was partially through the juxtaposition of the perceived baselessness and immorality of other women that the middle-class notion of respectable sexual experiences based on love gained its power.[74]

Though the inmate interviews hinted at elements of the ideal of romantic love, such as having few sexual partners and limiting sex to within committed relationships, overall love was not a strong theme in the interviews. Given that the idea of love was a critical component to a respectable narration of one's sexual past, this inability to draw on the legitimizing discourse of love placed the women of the Farm outside the bounds of respectability.[75] Given how central ideas of respectability were to the process of deciding who needed to be sent to the KSIFW, it was likely that this inability to articulate their sexual histories in a respectable way contributed to them being classified as "disreputable" and in need of incarceration in the first place.

Conclusion

The inmates of the KSIFW had mixed success in staking a claim to respectability through the inmate interviews. As historian Pamela Haag points out, the consequences of a woman's ability to narrate her sexual past in a respectable way became more serious as the state increased its interventions in the sex lives of everyday Americans during this period in history. Women's narratives became important in court cases, just as their accounts were important in health officers' decisions about committing the women under Chapter 205 in Kansas.[76] Some of the narratives of venereal disease contraction presented in the inmate interviews, such as the claim that a woman had only had sex with her husband and had gotten the disease from him, clearly provide a claim to respectability. However, other claims to respectability were less clear-cut in their implications: a woman claiming to have been negatively influenced by the youth culture of car riding and dances could just as easily be interpreted as the source of the problem. What they did not say is also important, as the interviews as a whole fail to clearly articulate mainstream discourses of romantic love. These mixed results in terms of inmates' ability to narrate their sexual pasts in a respectable way hint at the critical role of cultural capital in achieving respectability. The inmates lacked the cultural resources to narrate their sexual pasts according to middle-class norms. Indeed, it is likely this lack of ability to narrate their sexual pasts in a legitimizing way that led to their incarceration in the first place.

Regardless of the degree to which the inmates' narratives helped them appear respectable, what becomes apparent when reading the interviews is that the women did not fit one single mold. Women contracted venereal diseases in various ways, whether it was through a philandering husband, from sexual violence, or the result of too many evenings spent with "bad company." Some of the women, such as those who admitted to prostitution or who talked about casual sex, fit the stereotype that state documents gave of the type of woman being detained under Chapter 205: sexually active, few connections to a stable home, and in violation of middle-class norms for female behavior. Other women's stories illustrate their adherence to dominant norms for sexual behavior. Though women were the ones placed under quarantine, the inmate interviews offer a glaring indictment of the men in their lives. Chapter 205 imprisoned some women who fit the image of the target population, yet it also ensnared women who came to have a disease through no moral lapse of their own.

CONCLUSION

World War II changed venereal disease control efforts in the United States as a new treatment, penicillin, turned syphilis and gonorrhea into easily curable diseases. With the unanimous passage of the May Act in the summer of 1941, the government's approach to controlling venereal disease paralleled its actions during World War I: they cracked down on prostitution around military bases, warned troops to stay away from "loose women," and encouraged states and cities to revive their American Plan laws that were still on the books. Eliot Ness, the famed Prohibition agent who had pegged Al Capone, took the lead at the Social Protection Division, which was charged with shutting down prostitution around military bases nationwide. The federal government set up rapid treatment centers across the country to house the influx of quarantined women. Similar to World War I, these facilities blurred the line between hospitals and prisons, providing medical treatment but also attempting to morally reform women. The emphasis shifted from prostitutes during World War I to the "victory girls" of World War II who misplaced their patriotism by having sex with soldiers, yet the blame for the spread of venereal disease remained largely on the shoulders of women.[1]

Female social reformers had mixed responses to the renewed enforcement of the American Plan during World War II. Some were supportive. The General Federation of Women's Clubs passed a resolution endorsing the American Plan in 1942. The organization urged its two million members to get involved by advocating for state laws to repress prostitution, promoting vigorous enforcement of laws by local and federal officials, and supporting efforts to incarcerate and rehabilitate recalcitrant women. On June 9, 1943, federal officials hosted a meeting titled "Woman's Role in Social Protection" for representatives of some of the leading women's organizations in the country. First Lady Eleanor Roosevelt was in attendance and voiced support for the positive elements (education, social work, etc.) of the campaign against venereal disease while being more reticent about the repressive elements. Despite some reservations, the women in attendance unanimously passed resolutions in support of the American Plan. Other activist women during World War II were vocal in publicly opposing the sexual double standard that was enforced through the American Plan. Reformer Jessie Binford argued that women would comply with treatment regimens without incarceration if the government would invest in good social work. Washington, DC, policewoman Rhoda Milliken told a group of male police officials that they should be detaining men as well as women and urged them to shorten the length of detention for women, but to little avail. The American Plan had returned in full force.[2]

There were significant differences in how the government approached venereal disease between the world wars, however. The government relented on its expectation that troops remain chaste during World War II, distributing as many as fifty million condoms per month during the war and repealing its policy that men would lose pay if missing service for treatment of venereal disease. The scare tactics employed to dissuade soldiers from having sex during World War I were even less effective during World War II, particularly after the US Public Health Service began distributing penicillin in 1943. This new drug was remarkably effective in treating both syphilis and gonorrhea, with cure rates as high as 90 to 97 percent. Though it was not widely available at first, penicillin quickly became the standard of care for syphilis and gonorrhea and was being used across the armed services by the end of 1944. With such an easy and effective treatment available, the health dangers of illicit sexuality decreased dramatically. One military study estimated that between 53 and 63 percent of soldiers had sex during the war.[3]

In Kansas the venereal disease control policies of the 1930s continued into wartime. Attempting to keep the same "nonpolitical, nondictatorial and business-like and scientific" tone of federal campaigns against venereal disease during the 1930s, the board of health stepped up efforts to enforce Chapter 205 and increased the availability of free clinics across the state during the war.[4] Most of the funding for clinics (in 1942, there were fifteen such clinics in Kansas) and venereal disease education came from the federal government, with state officials being in charge of local implementation of venereal disease control policies. By 1942 the federal government provided $100,100 annually for venereal disease control and the state offered just $15,160. While the Kansas State Board of Health worried about the initial rates of venereal infection among incoming soldiers, which among the first 14,311 drafted in Kansas averaged 27.1 out of every thousand men, rates of venereal disease among Kansans was consistent with national averages of forty-eight infections out of every thousand men.[5]

The total number of women detained under Chapter 205 rose slightly during the war, with 188 women interned at the Farm between 1938 and 1940 and 205 women between 1940 and 1942. More of these women came from areas surrounding military bases; the number of women sent to the Farm from Geary County by Fort Riley increased from nineteen between 1938 and 1940 to sixty-seven women between 1940 and 1942.[6] However, the availability of penicillin drastically changed the landscape of public health work related to venereal disease; the quick, inexpensive, and effective treatment of administering antibiotics to treat venereal disease was preferable to the expense of detaining women for extended periods of time at the KSIFW.

There are records of women being quarantined under Chapter 205 in Kansas as late as 1955, but the number of women detained decreased steadily following World War II. Nationally, the women's reformatory model lost prominence, and women's institutions became more like regular prisons. The Kansas State Industrial Farm for Women itself remained in operation as a women's correctional facility until 1980, when it became co-correctional. Chapter 205 itself was never repealed and remains on the books in Kansas in amended form today. In 2005 the Kansas legislature passed regulations that gave additional guidance to county health officers in enforcing quarantine orders. In contrast to the women who tried to challenge their imprisonment in the 1920s and 1930s and were told that quarantine orders were outside the jurisdiction of the legal system, the 2005 legislation explicitly gave individuals the right to contest their quarantine in court. As legal scholar Scott Wasserman Stern points out, the American Plan laws that states across the country passed as the United States entered World War I have proven remarkably resilient. Though the federal government stopped recommending that syphilis and gonorrhea be subject to quarantine in the early 1980s, and state quarantine laws against these diseases are no longer enforced, every state in the country still has a law similar to Chapter 205 on the books.[7]

The ultimate consequences of imprisonment for the women who were interned under Chapter 205 are not entirely clear. The lack of parole work for women who left the institution leaves a thin paper trail. What accounts we do have suggest that the women who left the Farm carried on lives as varied as the ones they had led before they entered the institution. Historian Christopher Lovett identified one woman who came to Kansas to have a baby out of wedlock, was sent to the Farm under Chapter 205, and then went back to Iowa to become a nun after giving her baby up for adoption.[8] The biennial reports of the KSIFW contain a few letters from former inmates indicating that the Farm turned their life around, providing them with an opportunity to start their life anew.

Social worker Darlene Doubleday Newby attempted to follow up with women who had left the Farm a couple years after she had gone undercover. One young woman whom she was able to locate had been addicted to morphine when sent to the Farm and wished to stay clean after her release. Welfare workers connected her with a job as a telephone operator, but she was only able to keep the position for two weeks before slipping back into her old ways. When Newby visited her, she was using drugs again, and shortly after that Newby learned that the woman had moved to a nearby city and was running a house of prostitution. Another inmate had repeatedly been sent to the Farm. At fourteen this girl had married a soldier, only to be arrested in a raid a few weeks later and sent to the KSIFW. She escaped from the Farm but returned voluntarily five days later. On her release, she moved frequently and took up friends that her mother termed the "worst associates." The girl was arrested a second time in a rooming house raid; a wealthy married man who had been supporting her for over a year, despite his wife's repeated appeals to authorities to intervene, escaped out a back window. She was released and, at the age of seventeen, was sent to the Farm for a third time after another encounter with police. Other women followed a path after leaving the Farm that was more in keeping with reformers' hopes. One nineteen-year-old woman was arrested outside a military base during the war on a vagrancy charge. At the time of her arrest, she was dressed in men's clothes and had only nine cents, a package of cigarettes, and a book of poetry in her pockets. She had followed a soldier to Kansas from another state, only to separate from him once she found out he was already married. She stayed at the Farm for six months then returned to her family home. Newby reported that "there was no mistaking the awakening of this reckless girl during her quarantine." Some two years after the girl had left the Farm, the mother wrote in a thankful letter that "the little tramp is changed into a dutiful daughter."[9]

While some inmates were transformed into "dutiful daughters" by their experience at the Farm, others slipped back into their former ways of living. Some women returned to the Farm, either voluntarily or against their will, to get another round of treatment for their diseases. Regardless of where they went after leaving the Farm, these women all found their lives interrupted by Chapter 205.

Lessons from the Kansas State Industrial Farm for Women

Altogether, the state of Kansas detained 5,331 women and girls under Chapter 205 between the years of 1918 and 1942. The incarceration of such a large number of women for venereal disease involved a range of people: female activists who lobbied to create the Farm, professional women who ran its day-to-day operations, male legislators and government officials who oversaw and funded the operation, and a complacent citizenry who let it all happen. Through the gendered enforcement of Chapter 205, the state of Kansas officially sanctioned the sexual double standard, imprisoning women for having venereal disease while letting their sexual partners go free. As an example of the social control of sexuality and government-sanctioned gender inequality, Chapter 205 is an important piece of the history of Kansas and our overall understanding of women's sexuality in the United States.

The implementation of Chapter 205 in Kansas reveals key aspects of regional and national history. First, it illustrates the long-term effects of government interventions in sexuality that were originally implemented during World War I. While it is fairly well documented in the historical literature that state and federal governments cracked down on prostitution and venereal disease during World War I, it is less well known how these policies carried over into peacetime.[10] In Kansas and in other states across the country, the policies that were developed during the crisis of wartime became the new normal as women continued to be quarantined for venereal diseases into the 1920s. However, without federal financial backing, the campaign against venereal disease in Kansas was poorly coordinated and underfunded. The public health element of the original campaign against venereal disease became increasingly distant, and the punitive element of Chapter 205 became more prominent. For most of the period of this study, the women detained under Chapter 205 were prisoners first and patients second. Chapter 205 was part of a broader growth in government intrusion into citizens' sex lives in the United States, particularly for women, racial minorities, and the poor.

Second, this research deepens our understanding of the implications of white female activists' involvement in social issues for their own respectability and social position during this period in history. Involvement with the KSIFW gave the activists who created it and the professional women who worked there a cause to lobby for and a way to position themselves as the ideal of proper femininity. The history of Chapter 205 exemplifies historian Peggy Pascoe's term "relations of rescue." Just as the women in her research benefited from their involvement with social causes to help other women, Lucy Johnston and Julia Perry benefited from their connection with the Farm. The KSIFW was a site where different social groups met, each taking distinct paths to get there and each having unique implications of their involvement with the Farm for their own respectability. The differences between the activist and professional women in this book illustrate the transition from female public authority based on ideas of women's innate moral superiority to an authority based on women's roles as professionals within state-run organizations. However, there was overlap and intermingling between the two groups, such as when activist women drew on ideas of social science to argue for the Farm and when professional women used their social connections with the clubwomen to lobby for changes. Understanding these groups of women in relation to each other deepens our understanding of the power dynamics taking place within various social hierarchies through institutions like the KSIFW.[11]

Finally, the inmate interviews provide a rich source for understanding the implementation of policies like Chapter 205 and give us glimpses into the sexual lives of ordinary women. The paths that women took to the Farm illustrate the variety of ways that growing government intrusion into Americans' sex lives during this period materialized. Some women were detained directly by state officials, whereas others were turned in by someone they knew. State intervention into women's sex lives was not simply a top-down endeavor: it involved participation from citizens who utilized the legal mechanism provided through Chapter 205 to report women. The 20 percent of the sample who volunteered to go to the Farm highlight that individual actors have some level of agency, even within social systems that are extremely unjust. Inmate accounts of their sexual histories also add an important piece to our historical understanding, particularly accounts of rape in rural settings. Stories like those of inmates who reported that men drove them out to remote locations and threatened to leave them there unless they had sex are not well documented, suggesting patterns of sexual violence unique to rural locations that merit further study. These accounts of women's arrest and sexual histories provide a rare opportunity in the historical record to understand how a policy like Chapter 205 was actually implemented, as well as giving us glimpses into the everyday sexual lives of Kansas women.

Respectability and the Women of the Farm

As a public health policy, Chapter 205 was both unjust and ineffective. It was a policy guided by ideas of gender, race, class, sexuality, and respectability, not a well-reasoned response to a social problem. Amid all the hype about immoral women and the absurdity of detaining women but not men, it is easy to forget that venereal disease was a pressing social problem at the time. There was no cure for these serious medical conditions, and what treatment was available was prohibitively expensive for most Americans. The fact that 20 percent of inmates actually volunteered to go to the Farm in order to access health care is one indication of the human suffering that resulted from this failed social policy. It is important to remember that Chapter 205 was not the only course of action that could have been taken. Military leaders during World War I could have dispersed condoms to soldiers. Federal and state officials could have invested in public health clinics that provided ongoing access to health care without disrupting people's lives. Indeed, federal efforts to offer free venereal disease testing and treatment in the city of Chicago in the 1930s did just this, with dramatic reductions in venereal disease rates.[12] With even some thought and reflection, the whole premise of detaining women, but not men, for venereal disease was clearly misguided. The question thus becomes: why did anyone think this was a good idea?

To answer this question, we must dive into the messy details of history. While it would make for a cleaner narrative to have one central government figure who was bent on controlling poor women's sexuality through Chapter 205, the historical record reveals a much messier, far-reaching, and reactive chain of events. Individuals and institutions operated within changing circumstances, inconsistent funding, incomplete information, and a lack of time to reflect on or integrate what information they did have. The activist women who lobbied for the Farm did not plan on it becoming an institution to house venereal disease patients, but World War I changed the purpose of the Farm nonetheless. State and federal health officials devised a plan to address venereal disease during the war when men were receiving treatment for venereal diseases in the armed forces, but they failed to adjust this strategy in peacetime. Rather than one person behind the curtain implementing this program to control women's sexuality, Chapter 205 required multiple individuals to continue to implement this policy from their various positions within the state bureaucracy.

Rather than asking, "Why did anyone think this was a good idea?," our question must thus become, "How did hundreds of people think this was a good idea and continue to implement this policy for over two decades?" This second question pushes us to consider how wider discourses about gender, race, class, and sexuality informed Chapter 205, and how the implementation of this policy in turn reinforced those stereotypes and beliefs. In order to make sense of the decisions made by the many people associated with the implementation of Chapter 205, we must look at the underlying logic and consistencies among people's behaviors and decisions. This leads us to the central argument of this book: that perceptions of respectability, which are informed by these larger social currents of race, class, and gender, are a key mechanism through which people create and reinforce symbolic and social boundaries. Discussions of respectability, both of their own and that of the women imprisoned under Chapter 205, were the primary mechanisms through which the activist and professional women drew symbolic boundaries through the KSIFW. Perceptions of respectability were also part of institutional practices: doctors used social criteria to diagnose who had a venereal disease, health officers relied on perceptions of women's respectability when determining whether they needed to be sent to the Farm for treatment, and prison administrators decided when a woman was morally "cured" enough to be released back into society. From claims to one's own respectability to the production of symbolic boundaries to the institutional practices that determined how Chapter 205 was enforced, respectability was central to the story of Chapter 205 in Kansas.

Assumptions about the respectability of certain groups of people led to the complete disconnect between Chapter 205 and the social problem, widespread venereal disease, which it was allegedly trying to address. Central to these conceptions of respectability were ideas about the sexual behaviors of different groups of people. The idea that poor or racial minority women were sexually out of control played into those hundreds of decisions made by health officers when they decided who needed to go to the Farm, just as the idea that a woman's moral worth was intimately bound up with her sexual behaviors influenced the overall strategy of incarcerating women but not men. The inmate interviews reveal a very different story of the morality of the women incarcerated under Chapter 205 than that presented in the official rationale behind the policy. Wives reported getting diseases from cheating husbands, victims of rape reported that they were sent to the Farm while their assailants went free, and women desperate for medical care volunteered to be imprisoned in order to access treatment. Many of these women were not the "disreputable" prostitutes portrayed in official state documents. While there are differences between how groups are constructed and how they actually are within all social hierarchies, the privacy of sexuality heightens the potential for ideas about the sexuality of certain groups to be widely divergent from reality. Strong social stigmas and norms exist surrounding sexuality, yet at the same time sex is something that happens in private. This aspect of sexuality, its privacy, makes it a powerful force in the construction of boundaries between groups precisely because ideas about sexuality are so susceptible to being completely divorced from reality. As has been shown in several instances across history, sexuality has been a particularly useful tool for drawing boundaries around race and class.[13] In the case of Chapter 205, these ideas about sexuality and respectability informed who would be sent to the Farm and were also reinforced through public discussions of the inmates' need for moral reform.[14]

The various women involved with the KSIFW experienced privileges and disadvantages based on their positions along different social hierarchies. Through their involvement with the KSIFW, the activist and professional women utilized their social advantages of race and class to carve out a space for women's involvement in the public sphere. Women's activism to create the Farm played on cultural ideas of the superiority of the white race and the immorality of the lower classes that both justified a public role for female activists and highlighted their racial and class privileges. The professional women who ran the Farm gained status as female professionals where their "expertise" in femininity and morality could be used to "help" other women in need of moral reform. Through discussing the types of women who needed to be sent to the KSIFW and the plan of moral reform that they needed, the activist and professional women involved with the Farm were shaping ideas of proper femininity, sexuality, and relations between different social classes and racial groups. Implementing Chapter 205 was simultaneously an effort to combat disease and a larger project to shore up symbolic boundaries around key areas of social organization.

At the same time that these women experienced and reinforced privileges, though, they were caught in cultural discourses about gender that held them back. While the activist and professional women were in the position to construct working-class women's sexuality, they had limited influence on boundaries between men and women, particularly those boundaries that directly challenged men's privileges. The activist women in Kansas had fought for equal political rights for women, successfully challenging the ideas that associated women with the home and the laws that denied them the ballot. Yet their efforts to establish the KSIFW illustrate their limited social power: they had to convince male legislators to pass the legislation and allocate funding for the institution, and they had little influence on the Farm once it was established. By responding to activists' pleas to establish the Farm and putting a woman in charge of the institution, male legislators gave activist and professional women the symbolic power to define poor women's sexuality and shape their fate. Yet this power was ultimately men's to give within the gendered structure of power in 1910s and 1920s Kansas, and it was limited to areas that contained little challenge to male privilege. Julia Perry and the other superintendents might have been able to exercise control over the Farm, but they had no authority to question the fact that only women were detained under Chapter 205 and were ultimately reporting to men and dependent on them for their jobs. At the level of symbolic boundaries between men and women, Chapter 205 reinforced the idea that women should be chaste and "boys will be boys." These ideas translated into concrete actions as the state detained victims of rape and wives who contracted diseases from their husbands, leaving men's sexual behaviors, intentions, and diseased bodies outside the purview of state control. Thus, while the activist and professional women enjoyed many benefits of their class and racial privileges, all three groups of women operated within a gender system that limited their ability to challenge male privilege.

Women's Imprisonment and Respectability Today

While the state of Kansas no longer detains women under Chapter 205, modern examples of the abuse of female prisoners are not difficult to find. The explosion of the prison population in the United States since the period of this research has amplified the reach of the prison system in the lives of everyday Americans. The US prison population in the 1970s was one-fifth what it is today. The United States now imprisons 25 percent of the world's prisoners, though it has only 4 percent of the world's population, and far outpaces other countries—democracies and repressive regimes alike—in the incarceration rate of its citizens.[15] The war on drugs, decreased investment in social services, and mandatory minimum sentencing laws have all contributed to this massive increase in the number of Americans in federal prisons, local jails, and on parole. As scholars going back to Foucault have pointed out, the state's decision to imprison its citizens does not happen in isolation from the rest of society. The prison system is conceived of and enacted in relationship to other social systems, like health care and the economy, as well as to the larger cultural discourses that shape our everyday actions. Similar to the way that enforcement of Chapter 205 reinforced social boundaries in 1920s Kansas, scholars of our current moment point to the clear racial disparities in the growth of the prison population as a symptom of and causal force behind deep-seeded ideas about race in the United States.[16] Female reformers' impulse to imprison young women for minor offenses in order to reform them during the first few decades of the twentieth century was a precursor to the intrusive role that the prison system would take on in relation to a variety of social problems. The moral casting of the inmates of the KSIFW as irresponsible and in need of reform previewed how people with mental illness and drug addiction would be seen later in the century. At the intersection of the prison and health-care systems, notions of respectability are a powerful force to rationalize people's imprisonment.

Women have been swept up in the growth of the prison population in the United States. As of July 2015 the United States imprisoned more women than any other country in the world; with over two hundred thousand female inmates, women constitute 9.3 percent of the total prison population (up from 3.1 percent in 1970). Most female inmates are convicted for nonviolent offenses, reflecting the state's increasing willingness to imprison women for crimes like drug possession. Due in part to a change in state probation laws that limited judge's discretion, the women's prison population in Kansas grew 60 percent between 2000 and 2019, outpacing growth in the state men's population (14 percent) and national trends for women's prisons. As was true during the time of the KSIFW, female prisoners are disproportionately poor and marginalized. Black and Latina women are more likely to be imprisoned, and the poor and unemployed are more likely to be imprisoned than those that are better off. The growth of the prison population has happened along lines of gender, race, and class.[17]

Among this general rise in incarceration in the United States, two examples in particular highlight parallels between historical patterns and modern-day conditions for female prisoners. The first example comes from the California prison system, where nearly 150 female inmates were sterilized without proper authorization between 2006 and 2010. The attitude toward their sexuality and fertility echo the eugenicist arguments that informed concerns about poor women's sexuality in the era of the KSIFW. California inmates reported being coerced to have a tubal ligation, sometimes repeatedly being offered the procedure or urged to have one while in labor. While some inmates willingly agreed, others reported feeling pressured to have the procedure, and none of the surgeries went before the California state committee that was responsible for approving the surgeries according to state laws. It seems that administrative systems simply failed, with several officials failing to realize that the practice was morally problematic. Dr. Ricki Barnett, who led the Health Care Review Committee that should have been notified of the intent to perform these operations, commented that he had felt "slightly queasy" when he heard about the operations. He went on: "It wasn't so much that people were conspiratorial or coercive or sloppy. It concerns me that people never took a step back to project what they would feel if they were in the inmate's shoes and what the inmate's future might hold should they do this." Just as the implementation of Chapter 205 relied on widespread acceptance of the limited rights of women who were not deemed "respectable," the sterilization of inmates in California relied on an inability of multiple people to fully consider them as human beings. The doctors and administrators at the two prisons where the surgeries were performed failed to see the problem with asking inmates repeatedly to have a tubal ligation. James Heinrich, the doctor who performed the operations, justified the nearly $150,000 that the state paid for the surgeries by saying: "Over a 10-year period, that isn't a huge amount of money . . . compared to what you save in welfare paying for these unwanted children—as they procreated more." Echoing the sentiments of the activist women who lobbied to create the KSIFW, these prison officials framed their concern about the fertility of prisoners in terms of economic efficiency for the state.[18]

The California case illustrates some continued themes that, as a society, we would like to think that we have moved past since the time of eugenics. Though the regulation of poor women's sexuality is not always as direct as in the California case, the sexuality of the poorest women in society is under constant scrutiny. Pregnant teenagers, welfare moms, and fertile immigrants all populate the speeches of politicians eager to justify slashing social services by portraying working-class women and women of color as hypersexual and irresponsible. These women and their children are routinely denied basic social services, such as a living wage or health care, due in part to the moral distinctions drawn by debates over their sexuality. After all, only the "respectable" working class deserves government assistance, and discourses about sexuality make respectability a scarce resource for the nation's poor. The ease with which California officials disregarded inmates' right to have children is rooted in larger concerns about the sexuality and reproductive potential of poor women and women of color. Perceptions of respectability continue to shape and provide justification for our prison system today.[19]

The second example comes from the institution that has replaced the KSIFW as the sole prison for women in Kansas since 2001, the Topeka Correctional Facility (TCF). In 2009 the *Topeka Capital-Journal* ran a series of articles documenting accusations of sexual abuse at the prison, both between inmates and between prison staff and inmates. The accounts illustrate the concerns of the original female reformers who advocated for separate women's prisons in the early 1900s. In 2014 TCF prison official Bryon Dixon was charged with unlawful sexual relations after forcing an inmate to perform oral sex on him in a closet in the prison; the inmate was serving a twenty-two-month sentence for a drug-related charge. Another inmate became pregnant after being raped by TCF plumbing instructor Ananstacio Gallardo, who was later convicted for the crime. In a disturbing parallel to inmate accounts of rape in rural settings from the

1920s and 1930s, another TCF employee, Nathan Vandyke, was accused of driving female inmates to remote locations to rape them. Though the pattern of sexual violence was the same, it was now an agent of the state, not a civilian, who was the perpetrator. One of Vandyke's victims received a $30,000 settlement from the state. The pattern of sexual abuse at TCF led to several investigations, resulting in a 2012 US Department of Justice report that condemned the widespread culture of sexual violence at the prison and the state's inadequate response to the situation. In January 2015 the Department of Justice and the state of Kansas announced an agreement to address some of the issues at TCF, including independent monitoring, increased staffing, use of video monitoring, more training about sexual assault, and clear reporting mechanisms, to bring the facility into accord with the federally mandated Prison Rape Elimination National Standards. Among the recommendations was to increase the number of female officials at the prison.[20]

Comparing the Kansas State Industrial Farm for Women to its modern-day equivalent raises important questions about what has changed, and what has stayed the same, about female incarceration in the state of Kansas. The conditions at TCF are exactly the type of scenario about which female reformers of the early 1900s worried. These sexual abuses illustrate Kristin Luker's argument that the original social critique offered by women's organizations was lost as male-dominated government bureaucracies took over their causes during the Progressive Era.[21] Many women's prison reformers from the early twentieth century espoused a critique of male sexual violence and the sexual double standard, as well as a belief in the inherent dignity of the inmate and her ability to be reformed. Recent events at TCF raise questions about the degree to which these values continue to be paramount in the state's approach to imprisoning female offenders.

The ways in which activist and professional women's actions led to the suffering of inmates in Kansas should not be overlooked: the Farm unnecessarily imprisoned women for venereal disease, imposed visions of moral reform on women who did not necessarily view themselves as in need of change, and, at its worst, sterilized inmates. Yet next to those bars on the windows, there were also doilies on couches. There were baseball teams, dances, discussions of ways to bring out inmates' "better natures," and offers of employment to former inmates. A basic recognition of inmates' humanity and their potential to lead a meaningful life underpinned many of the elements of everyday life at the KSIFW. To varying degrees, women such as Julia Perry and Lucy Johnston espoused this belief in the dignity of inmates, seeing inmates' fate as part of all women's responsibility within the state. The activist and professional women involved with the KSIFW constructed and reinforced social boundaries in many ways, but there were also moments where they reached across boundaries to recognize the similarities between themselves and inmates as human beings and as women.

The story of Chapter 205 in Kansas makes clear the pivotal role that respectability plays in our own historical moment and the social hierarchies that inform our current prison and health-care systems. Perceptions of respectability continue to influence who is, and is not, imprisoned in the state of Kansas. Understandings of a social problem like drug addiction lead to decisions about whether the issue is best addressed through the health-care or penal systems, just as understandings of young women's sexuality led officials to decide that it was "reform," not just health care, that those quarantined under Chapter 205 truly needed. The boundary work accomplished through discussions of respectability is critical to the assessments that people make as they decide which social system is best suited to address a problem. Social problems that occupy the blurred jurisdiction between the prison and health-care systems—venereal disease in Kansas in the 1920s, the deinstitutionalization of mental asylums in the 1960s, drug addiction today—provide key sites to explore how deviance and illness are constructed, how perceptions of the "other" rationalize inequality, and how respectability informs our pursuit of a more just society.

NOTES

ABBREVIATIONS

Inmate Interviews All inmate interviews accessed at the Kansas State Historical Society, Topeka, Kansas, call nos. 35-07-08-01 to 35-07-08-02

Administration [Year] Report These refer to the *Kansas State Board of Administration Biennial Reports* (Topeka: Kansas State Printing Plant), accessed at the Kansas State Historical Society, Topeka

Health [Year] Report These refer to the *Kansas State Board of Health Biennial Reports* (Topeka: Kansas State Printing Plant), accessed at the Kansas State Historical Society, Topeka

KSHS Kansas State Historical Society, Topeka

KSIFW [Year] Report These refer to the *Kansas State Industrial Farm for Women Biennial Reports* (Topeka: Kansas State Printing Plant), accessed at the Kansas State Historical Society, Topeka.

PREFACE

1. "Pandemic, Creating a Usable Past: Epidemic History, COVID-19, and the Future of Health," American Association for the History of Medicine, May 8–9, 2020, http://www.histmed.org/epidemic-history; Eric Adler, "A Coronavirus Lesson? How KC's Response to 1918 Flu Pandemic Caused Needless Death," *Kansas City (MO) Star*, March 15, 2020, https://www.kansascity.com/news/business/health-care/article241058181.html; Nancy Bristow, "Loosening Public-Health Restrictions Too Early Can Cost Lives. Just Look What Happened During the 1918 Flu Pandemic," *Time*, May 1, 2020, https://time.com/5830265/1918-flu-reopening-coronavirus/.

2. Jeff Yang, "Breaking the Cycle of Discrimination against Asian Americans," CNN, May 8, 2020, https://www.cnn.com/2020/05/08/opinions/coronavirus-apahm-anti-asian-american-discrimination-yang/index.html; Chance Swaim, "Kansas Has Largest Racial Disparity in COVID-19 Death Rates, Study Finds," *Wichita Eagle*, May 13, 2020, https://www.kansas.com/news/rebuild/article242680156.html; Linda So and Grant Smith, "In Four U.S. State Prisons, Nearly 3,300 Inmates Test Positive for Coronavirus--96% without Symptoms," Reuters, April 25, 2020, https://www.reuters.com/article/us-health-coronavirus-prisons-testing-in/in-four-u-s-state-prisons-nearly-3300-inmates-test-positive-for-coronavirus-96-without-symptoms-idUSKCN2270RX.

3. The laws that are built off of the original 1917 Chapter 205 legislation include "65-128. Rules and Regulations of Secretary to Prevent Spread and Dissemination of Diseases; Testing and Quarantine; Protection of Providers and Recipients of Services," Kansas Office of Revisor of Statutes, https://www.ksrevisor.org/statutes/chapters/ch65/065_001_0028.html; "65-129. Penalties for Unlawful Acts," Kansas Office of Revisor of Statutes, https://www.ksrevisor.org/statutes/chapters/ch65/065_001_0029.html. For updated 2005 legislation, see "65-129b. Infections or Contagious Diseases; Authority of Local Health Officer or Secretary; Evaluation or Treatment Orders, Isolation or Quarantine Orders; Enforcement," Kansas Office of Revisor of Statutes, https://www.ksrevisor.org/statutes/chapters/ch65/065_001_0029b.html. See also Jonathan Shorman and Lisa Gutierrez, "In Coronavirus Fight, Kansas and Missouri Hold 'Awesome' Powers to Isolate You," *Kansas City (MO) Star*, March 15, 2020, https://www.kansascity.com/news/politics-government/article241176436.html.

INTRODUCTION

1. Inmate Interviews, 1925; 2568.

2. Elizabeth Alice Clement, *Love for Sale: Courting, Treating, and Prostitution in New York City, 1900–1945* (Chapel Hill: University of North Carolina Press, 2006), 115–117; Kristin Luker, "Sex, Social Hygiene, and the State: The Double-Edged Sword of Social Reform," *Theory and Society* 27, no. 5 (1998): 622.

3. As part of the $427,000 that the federal government spent nationally, the hospital at the KSIFW was built in 1920 with matching funds from the state and federal government. Harriet C. Frazier, "The State Industrial School for Girls at Beloit, Kansas: The First 50 Years, 1889–1939," paper presented at the American Society of Criminology conference, Chicago, November 1988, 5.

4. *Health 1920 Report*, 343.

5. All data about the inmates of the Farm come from KSIFW biennial reports between 1918 and 1942.

6. Christopher Lovett, "Bad Girls: Sex, Shame, Public Health, and the Forgotten Legacy of Samuel J. Crumbine in Kansas, 1917–1955," *Kansas History* 41, no. 1 (Spring 2018): 20.

7. The most in-depth discussion of Chapter 205 in Kansas comes from Lovett, "Bad Girls." For a discussion of Chapter 205 as an example of a comprehensive approach to public health, see K. Allen Greiner, "Samuel J. Crumbine: Individualizing the Standard for Twentieth-Century Public Health," in *John Brown to Bob Dole: Movers and Shakers in Kansas History*, ed. Virgil W. Dean (Lawrence: University Press of Kansas, 2006). For an example of Chapter 205 discussed as part of the history of prostitution in Kansas, see Kansas Historical Society, "Sinners and Saints, Part 6: Vice and Reform in Kansas," http://www.kshs.org/p/online-exhibits-sinners-and-saints-part-6/10723.

8. This book uses the term "prostitute" for women who were engaged in sex work in order to stay consistent with the language used during this time period.

9. American reformers were critical of European approaches to control venereal disease, often called regulationist, because they thought that they effectively sanctioned illicit sexual behavior. Scott Wasserman Stern, "The Long American Plan: The U.S. Government's Campaign against Venereal Disease and Its Carriers," *Harvard Journal of Law and Gender* 38 (2015): 373–436; Scott W. Stern, *The Trials of Nina McCall: Sex, Surveillance, and the Decades-Long Government Plan to Imprison Promiscuous Women* (Boston: Beacon Press, 2018), 121.

10. For a discussion of sexuality during the first few decades of the twentieth century, see Mary E. Odem, *Delinquent Daughters: Protecting and Policing Adolescent Female Sexuality in the United States, 1885–1920* (Chapel Hill: University of North Carolina Press, 1995); Clement, *Love for Sale*; John D'Emilio and Estelle B. Freedman, *Intimate Matters: A History of Sexuality in America*, 2nd ed. (Chicago: University of Chicago Press, 1997); Cynthia M Blair, *I've Got to Make My Livin': Black Women's Sex Work in Turn-of-the-Century Chicago* (Chicago: University of Chicago Press, 2010); Ruth Rosen, *The Lost Sisterhood: Prostitution in America, 1900–1918* (Baltimore: Johns Hopkins University Press, 1983); Carolyn Strange, *Toronto's Girl Problem: The Perils and Pleasures of the City, 1880–1930* (Toronto: University of Toronto Press, 1995). For a discussion of the value of studying sexuality in the Midwest, see Beth L. Bailey, *Sex in the Heartland* (Cambridge, MA: Harvard University Press, 1999). For discussions of the practice of putting young women in reformatories for minor sexual offenses, see Nicole Hahn Rafter, *Partial Justice: Women in State Prisons, 1800–1935* (Boston: Northeastern University Press, 1985); Estelle Freedman, *Their Sisters' Keepers: Women's Prison Reform in America, 1830–1930* (Ann Arbor: University of Michigan Press, 1981); Odem, *Delinquent Daughters*, 95–127.

11. Anne E. Parsons, *From Asylum to Prison: Deinstitutionalization and the Rise of Mass Incarceration after 1945* (Chapel Hill: University of North Carolina Press, 2018). See also William G. Staples, *Castles of Our Conscience: Social Control and the American State, 1800–1985* (Cambridge: Polity Press, 1990).

12. Michelle Alexander, *The New Jim Crow: Mass Incarceration in the Age of Colorblindness* (New York: New Press, 2010).

13. Kelly Lytle Hernández, Khalil Gibran Muhammad, and Heather Ann Thompson, "Introduction: Constructing the Carceral State," *Journal of American History* 102, no. 1 (2015): 18–24.

14. For scholarly work on the development of the prison system, see Brett Story, *Prison Land: Mapping Carceral Power across Neoliberal America* (Minneapolis: University of Minnesota Press, 2019); John Pfaff, *Locked In: The True Causes of Mass Incarceration and How to Achieve Real Reform* (New York: Basic Books, 2017); Alexander, *New Jim Crow*; Dan Berger, *Captive Nation: Black Prison Organizing*

in the Civil Rights Era (Chapel Hill: University of North Carolina Press, 2014); Max Felker-Kantor, *Policing Los Angeles: Race, Resistance, and the Rise of the LAPD* (Chapel Hill: University of North Carolina Press, 2018); Michel Foucault, *Discipline and Punish: The Birth of the Prison*, 2nd ed., trans. Alan Sheridan (New York: Vintage Books, 1995).

15. Foucault, *Discipline and Punish*; Micol Seigel, *Violence Work: State Power and the Limits of Police* (Durham, NC: Duke University Press, 2018).

16. See Alexander, *New Jim Crow*; Berger, *Captive Nation*; Story, *Prison Land.*

17. Michèle Lamont and Virág Molnár, "The Study of Boundaries in the Social Sciences," *Annual Review of Sociology* (August 2002): 168.

18. Scholars have analyzed the relationship between symbolic and social boundaries in order to shed light on the formation and maintenance of various social hierarchies. For examples of research exploring ethnoracial boundaries, see Michèle Lamont, Graziella Moraes Silva, Jessica Welburn et al., *Getting Respect: Responding to Stigma and Discrimination in the United States, Brazil, and Israel* (Princeton, NJ: Princeton University Press, 2016); Alford A. Young Jr., *The Minds of Marginalized Black Men: Making Sense of Mobility, Opportunity, and Future Life Chances* (Princeton, NJ: Princeton University Press, 2004). For influential work on boundaries and social class, see Pierre Bourdieu, *Distinction: A Social Critique of the Judgement of Taste* (Cambridge, MA: Harvard University Press, 1984); Michèle Lamont, *The Dignity of Working Men: Morality and the Boundaries of Race, Class, and Immigration* (New York: Russell Sage Foundation, 2000). For research that examines how different social hierarchies reinforce or potentially disrupt each other, see Annette Lareau, *Unequal Childhoods: Class, Race, and Family Life*, 2nd ed. (Berkeley: University of California Press, 2011); Crystal M. Fleming and Lorraine E. Roses, "Black Cultural Capitalists: African-American Elites and the Organization of the Arts in Early Twentieth Century Boston," *Poetics* 35, no. 6 (December 2007): 368–387. For discussions of the importance of morality in drawing symbolic boundaries, see Michèle Lamont, *Money, Morals, and Manners: The Culture of the French and the American Upper-Middle Class* (Chicago: University of Chicago Press, 1992); Michèle Lamont, *The Dignity of Working Men: Morality and the Boundaries of Race, Class, and Immigration* (Cambridge, MA: Harvard University Press, 2002); Vegard Jarness, "Cultural vs. Economic Capital: Symbolic Boundaries within the Middle Class," *Sociology* 51, no. 2 (2017): 360; Nicola Kay Beisel, *Imperiled Innocents: Anthony Comstock and Family Reproduction in Victorian America* (Princeton, NJ: Princeton University Press, 1997).

19. For discussions of respectability as something produced in interactions, see Mitchell Duneier, *Slim's Table: Race, Respectability, and Masculinity* (Chicago: University of Chicago Press, 1994), 65; Donald W. Ball, "The Problematics of Respectability," in *Deviance and Respectability: The Social Construction of Moral Meanings*, ed. Jack D. Douglas (New York: Basic Books, 1970), 336–339.

20. For discussions of the need for concepts that allow for the analysis of multiple social hierarchies at once, see Yvette Taylor, "Complexities and Complications: Intersections of Class and Sexuality," in *Theorizing Intersectionality and Sexuality*, ed. Yvette Taylor, Sally Hines, and Mark E. Casey (New York: Palgrave Macmillan, 2011); Elizabeth McDermott, "The World Some Have Won: Sexuality, Class and Inequality," *Sexualities* 14, no. 1 (February 1, 2011): 66. For further reading on intersectionality, see Kimberlé Crenshaw, "Demarginalizing the Intersection of Race and Sex: A Black Feminist Critique of Antidiscrimination Doctrine, Feminist Theory and Antiracist Politics," *University of Chicago Legal Forum* 140 (1989): 139–167; Patricia Hill Collins, *Black Feminist Thought: Knowledge, Consciousness, and the Politics of Empowerment* (London: Routledge, 1990); Leslie McCall, "The Complexity of Intersectionality," *Signs: Journal of Women in Culture and Society* 30, no. 3 (2005): 1771–1800.

21. Brian Donovan, *Respectability on Trial: Sex Crimes in New York City, 1900–1918* (Albany: State University of New York Press, 2016), 8–9; McDermott, "World Some Have Won," 66; Yvette Taylor, "Complexities and Complications: Intersections of Class and Sexuality," *Journal of Lesbian Studies* 13, no. 2 (2009): 189–203.

22. Pachucki et al. call for concepts that can help scholars explore "multiple, interacting boundaries" simultaneously. See Mark A. Pachucki, Sabrina Pendergrass, and Michèle Lamont, "Boundary Processes: Recent Theoretical Developments and New Contributions," *Poetics* 35, no. 6 (2007): 344. Though respectability has this potential to be used as a shorthand, scholars will need to be careful to be sure that they actually include various social hierarchies seriously in their analysis. With a shorthand also comes the potential to claim that you are studying multiple elements of oppression and then glossing over certain elements in your analysis.

23. For associations between respectability, social class, and masculinity, see Duneier, *Slim's Table*; Lamont, *Dignity of Working Men*. For a discussion of the association between working-class women and out-of-control sexuality, see Steph Lawler, "Mobs and Monsters: Independent Man Meets Paulsgrove Woman," *Feminist Theory* 3, no. 1 (April 1, 2002): 103–113; Beverley Skeggs, *Formations of Class and Gender: Becoming Respectable* (London: Sage, 1997). For parallel discourses linking middle-class women with heterosexuality, chastity, and self-restraint, see Alexandra Allan, "The Importance of Being a 'Lady': Hyper-Femininity and Heterosexuality in the Private, Single-Sex Primary School," *Gender and Education* 21, no. 2 (2009): 145–158; Julian B. Carter, *The Heart of Whiteness: Normal Sexuality and Race in America, 1880–1940* (Durham, NC: Duke University Press, 2007); Pamela S. Haag, "In Search of 'the Real Thing': Ideologies of Love, Modern Romance, and Women's Sexual Subjectivity in the United States, 1920–40," *Journal of the History of Sexuality* 2, no. 4 (1992): 547–577; Laura Hamilton and Elizabeth A. Armstrong, "Gendered Sexuality in Young Adulthood: Double Binds and Flawed Options," *Gender and Society* 23, no. 5 (2009): 611.

24. Kate Huppatz, "Respectability and the Paid Caring Occupations: An Empirical Investigation of Normality, Morality, Impression Management, Esteem in Nursing and Social Work," *Health Sociology Review* 19, no. 1 (2010): 73–85.

25. See David Goodhew, "Working-Class Respectability: The Example of the Western Areas of Johannesburg, 1930–55," *Journal of African History* 41, no. 2 (2000): 241–266; Evelyn Brooks Higginbotham, *Righteous Discontent: The Women's Movement in the Black Baptist Church, 1880–1920* (Cambridge, MA: Harvard University Press, 1993); Victoria W. Wolcott, *Remaking Respectability: African American Women in Interwar Detroit* (Chapel Hill: University of North Carolina Press, 2001).

26. Pachucki et al. have called for more research into how boundary work is accomplished through institutions and social policies and the exact mechanisms through which this occurs; see Pachucki et al., "Boundary Processes." For examples of research that explores this relationship between boundaries and institutions, see Natalia Molina, *Fit to Be Citizens? Public Health and Race in Los Angeles, 1879–1939* (Berkeley: University of California Press, 2006); Brian Steensland, "Cultural Categories and the American Welfare State: The Case of Guaranteed Income Policy," *American Journal of Sociology* 111, no. 5 (2006): 1273–1326.

27. For a discussion of the class and gender implications of the term "lady," see Allan, "Importance of Being a 'Lady,'" 146–147.

28. Peggy Pascoe, *Relations of Rescue: The Search for Female Moral Authority in the American West, 1874–1939* (New York: Oxford University Press, 1990), xvi; Karen J. Blair, *The Clubwoman as Feminist: True Womanhood Redefined, 1868–1914* (New York: Holmes & Meier, 1980); Regina G. Kunzel, "The Professionalization of Benevolence: Evangelicals and Social Workers in the Florence Crittenton Homes, 1915 to 1945," *Journal of Social History* 22, no. 1 (1988): 21–43; Luker, "Sex, Social Hygiene, and the State"; Barbara Meil Hobson, *Uneasy Virtue: The Politics of Prostitution and the American Reform Tradition* (Chicago: University of Chicago Press, 1990).

29. Huppatz, "Respectability."

30. Kunzel, "Professionalization of Benevolence"; Daniel J. Walkowitz, "The Making of a Feminine Professional Identity: Social Workers in the 1920s," *American Historical Review* 95, no. 4 (1990): 1051–1075; Odem, *Delinquent Daughters*.

31. Clement, *Love for Sale*; Luker, "Sex, Social Hygiene, and the State."

CHAPTER 1. WORLD WAR I, SEXUALITY, AND VENEREAL DISEASE CONTROL IN KANSAS

1. Pseudonyms are used for both the soldier and his fiancée to protect their anonymity. X to Arthur Capper, April 18, 1918, box 21, folder 20, Arthur Capper Governor's Records, KSHS.

2. John D'Emilio and Estelle B. Freedman, *Intimate Matters: A History of Sexuality in America*, 2nd ed. (Chicago: University of Chicago Press, 1997), 173; Mary E. Odem, *Delinquent Daughters: Protecting and Policing Adolescent Female Sexuality in the United States, 1885–1920* (Chapel Hill: University of North Carolina Press, 1995), 2; Elizabeth Alice Clement, *Love for Sale: Courting, Treating, and Prostitution in New York City, 1900–1945* (Chapel Hill: University of North Carolina Press, 2006), 15; Beth L. Bailey, *From Front Porch to Back Seat: Courtship in Twentieth-Century America* (Baltimore: Johns Hopkins University Press, 1989).

3. Daniel Scott Smith, "The Dating of the American Sexual Revolution: Evidence and Interpretation," in *The American Family in Social-Historical Perspective*, ed. Michael Gordon (New York: St. Martin's, 1978); Clement, *Love for Sale*, 17.

4. Barry Reay, "Promiscuous Intimacies: Rethinking the History of American Casual Sex," *Journal of Historical Sociology* 27, no. 1 (2014): 1–24; Clement, *Love for Sale*, 14.

5. Scott W. Stern, *The Trials of Nina McCall: Sex, Surveillance, and the Decades-Long Government Plan to Imprison Promiscuous Women* (Boston: Beacon Press, 2018), 31; Allan M. Brandt, *No Magic Bullet: A Social History of Venereal Disease in the United States since 1880* (New York: Oxford University Press, 1985), 38; D'Emilio and Freedman, *Intimate Matters*, 204; Kristin Luker, "Sex, Social Hygiene, and the State: The Double-Edged Sword of Social Reform," *Theory and Society* 27, no. 5 (1998): 601–634; John Parascandola, *Sex, Sin, and Science: A History of Syphilis in America* (Westport, CT: Praeger, 2008), 44–45.

6. D'Emilio and Freedman, *Intimate Matters*, 207.

7. Brandt, *No Magic Bullet*, 30–31, 23, 43, 46.

8. Brandt, *No Magic Bullet*, 13, 40; Clement, *Love for Sale*, 121.

9. Clement, *Love for Sale*, 117–124.

10. Quoted in Brandt, *No Magic Bullet*, 112.

11. Brandt, *No Magic Bullet*, 112; Luker, "Sex, Social Hygiene, and the State," 618–621.

12. Effie W. Gellow to Arthur Capper, December 21, 1917, box 17, folder 18, Arthur Capper Governor's Records, KSHS.

13. "To Protect Soldier Boys," *Hays (KS) Free Press*, September 1, 1917, 2.

14. Arthur Capper to Woodrow Wilson, May 23, 1917, box 15, folder 9A, Arthur Capper Governor's Records, KSHS; "Camp Funston," last modified October 2018, https://www.kshs.org/kansapedia/camp-funston/16692; Clement, *Love for Sale*, 117.

15. Brandt, *No Magic Bullet*, 59–66; Clement, *Love for Sale*, 117; Stern, *Trials of Nina McCall*, 50.

16. Parascandola, *Sex, Sin, and Science*, 62.

17. Quoted in Brandt, *No Magic Bullet*, 67.

18. Frank W. Blackmar, ed., *History of the Kansas State Council of Defense* (Topeka: Kansas State Printing Plant, 1920), 77.

19. Parascandola, *Sex, Sin, and Science*, 64–65; Nancy K. Bristow, *Making Men Moral: Social Engineering during the Great War* (New York: New York University Press, 1996), 65.

20. Arthur Capper to John J. Pershing, January 10, 1918, box 15, folder 13, Arthur Capper Governor's Records, KSHS.

21. Quoted in "Army Chaplain Credited with Inventing Basketball," US Department of Defense, 2015, https://dod.defense.gov/News/Article/Article/604354/army-chaplain-credited-with-inventing-basketball/; M. D. Exner, "Social Hygiene and the War," *Social Hygiene* 5 (1919): 277–297; Parascandola, *Sex, Sin, and Science*, 50–51.

22. Luker, "Sex, Social Hygiene, and the State," 618; Clement, *Love for Sale*.

23. Quoted in Luker, "Sex, Social Hygiene, and the State," 614; Brandt, *No Magic Bullet*, 77; Thomas MacKey, *Red Lights Out: A Legal History of Prostitution, Disorderly Houses, and Vice Districts, 1870–1917* (New York: Garland, 1987).

24. K. Allen Greiner, "Samuel J. Crumbine: Individualizing the Standard for Twentieth-Century Public Health," in *John Brown to Bob Dole: Movers and Shakers in Kansas History*, ed. Virgil W. Dean (Lawrence: University Press of Kansas, 2006); "Samuel J. Crumbine," Kansapedia, Kansas Historical Society, last modified January 2016, https://www.kshs.org/kansapedia/samuel-j-crumbine/12025.

25. Samuel J. Crumbine, *Frontier Doctor* (Philadelphia: Dorancy, 1948), 234–237; *Health 1920 Report*, 16, 336.

26. Quoted in Brandt, *No Magic Bullet*, 81.

27. Kathy Peiss, *Cheap Amusements: Working Women and Leisure in Turn-of-the-Century New York* (Philadelphia: Temple University Press, 1986); Clement, *Love for Sale*; Joanne J. Meyerowitz, *Women Adrift: Independent Wage Earners in Chicago, 1880–1930* (Chicago: University of Chicago Press, 1988).

28. Brandt, *No Magic Bullet*, 81; Clement, *Love for Sale*, 170; Stern, *Trials of Nina McCall*, 51.

29. "Board of Health Quarantine Bill Goes thru House," *Topeka Capital*, February 20, 1917, 1.

30. "House Passes Senate Board of Health Bill," *Topeka Capital*, February 21, 1917, 5.

31. *Session Laws*, 1917 (Topeka: Kansas State Printing Plant, 1917), May 26, 1917.

32. Emmet D. George, *Senate Journal, State of Kansas* (Topeka: Kansas State Printing Plant, 1917), 145, 419; Clarence W. Miller, *House Journal, State of Kansas* (Topeka: Kansas State Printing Plant, 1917), 471.

33. Capper to Pershing, January 10, 1918.

34. Charles E. Hill, "Progressive Legislation in Kansas," in *Collections of the Kansas State Historical Society, 1911–1912* (Topeka: Kansas State Historical Society, 1912), 69.

35. Robert Smith Bader, *Prohibition in Kansas: A History* (Lawrence: University Press of Kansas, 1986), 160–161; D'Emilio and Freedman, *Intimate Matters,* 203–204; Parascandola, *Sex, Sin, and Science,* 40–41; Daniel Rogers, "In Search of Progressivism," *Reviews in American History* 10 (1982): 113–132.

36. Stern, *Trials of Nina McCall,* 63–64, 73–74, 105; Luker, "Sex, Social Hygiene, and the State," 623; Brandt, *No Magic Bullet,* 85–86; Karin L. Zipf, "In Defense of the Nation: Syphilis, North Carolina's 'Girl Problem,' and World War I," *North Carolina Historical Review* 89, no. 3 (2012): 281; Scott Wasserman Stern, "The Long American Plan: The U.S. Government's Campaign against Venereal Disease and Its Carriers," *Harvard Journal of Law and Gender* 38 (2015): 373–436; Odem, *Delinquent Daughters,* 124.

37. *Health 1920 Report,* 336.

38. Odem, *Delinquent Daughters,* 124; *Health 1918 Report,* 77; Crumbine, *Frontier Doctor,* 222.

39. *Health 1920 Report,* 343.

40. Crumbine, *Frontier Doctor,* 224.

41. Quoted in Stern, *Trials of Nina McCall,* 54–55.

42. Blackmar, *History of the Kansas State Council of Defense,* 76.

43. Brandt, *No Magic Bullet,* 88–90; Estelle Freedman, *Their Sisters' Keepers: Women's Prison Reform in America, 1830–1930* (Ann Arbor: University of Michigan Press, 1981), 147; Odem, *Delinquent Daughters,* 126.

44. George, *Senate Journal,* 609; Miller, *House Journal,* 804, 865; Freedman, *Their Sisters' Keepers,* 144–145; Paul W. Garrett and Austin H. MacCormick, *Handbook of American Prisons and Reformatories* (New York: National Society of Penal Information, 1929); Dr. Florence Brown Sherbon, "State Womens' Farm Is Place for Rebuilding," *Topeka Capital,* March 29, 1931.

45. *Administration 1918 Report,* 24.

46. President Wilson earmarked funds for women's reformatories throughout the country, ultimately electing to fund some state efforts to detain women after deciding that federally funded and operated women's reformatories would be too expensive. Zipf, "In Defense of the Nation," 281.

47. Garrett and MacCormick, *Handbook of American Prisons,* 365; Eugenia C. Lekkerkerker, *Reformatories for Women in the United States* (Groningen: J. B. Wolters, 1931), 118–119; *Health 1920 Report,* 336; *Administration 1918 Report,* 24–25; "Locate Detention Farm for Women," *Topeka Capital,* August 11, 1917; Darlene Doubleday Newby, "A Study of the Causes of Delinquency of Women Quarantined for Disease at the State Industrial Farm for Women," *Bulletin of the Kansas*

State Board of Health, February 1921, 20; Mildred Reed, "A Prison without Walls Is Women's Industrial Farm!" *Topeka State Journal*, August 21, 1920.

CHAPTER 2. PRISONERS FIRST, PATIENTS SECOND

1. Scott W. Stern, *The Trials of Nina McCall: Sex, Surveillance, and the Decades-Long Government Plan to Imprison Promiscuous Women* (Boston: Beacon Press, 2018), 127–128. For a discussion of ways that World War I influenced domestic policy, see Robert P. Saldin, *War, the American State, and Politics since 1898* (New York: Cambridge University Press, 2010), 65–99.

2. *Health 1920 Report*, 10.

3. See, for example, "Ordinance No. 208," *Baxter Springs (KS) News*, August 23, 1918, 29, 8; "Ordinance No. 862," *Hays (KS) Free Press*, October 16, 1919, 5.

4. "The Venereal Disease Problem," *Baxter Springs (KS) News*, January 10, 1919.

5. *Health 1920 Report*, 349; see also Alice M. Hill, "Psychiatric Studies of Delinquents: Part III. Social and Environmental Factors in the Moral Delinquency of Girls Committed to the Kansas State Industrial Farm," *Public Health Reports* 35, no. 26 (1920): 1505.

6. Stern, *Trials of Nina McCall*, 180–185; Scott Wasserman Stern, "The Long American Plan: The U.S. Government's Campaign against Venereal Disease and Its Carriers," *Harvard Journal of Law and Gender* 38 (2015): 407.

7. Women's reformatories in Nebraska and Wisconsin also focused on venereal disease patients, but the number of women sent to the KSIFW was much higher than at these smaller institutions. See Nicole Hahn Rafter, *Partial Justice: Women in State Prisons, 1800–1935* (Boston: Northeastern University Press, 1985), 62, 67; Eugenia C. Lekkerkerker, *Reformatories for Women in the United States* (Groningen: J. B. Wolters, 1931), 123, 191, 382, 557.

8. *Health 1922 Report*, 156.

9. Stern's examination of court cases reveals instances of American Plan laws being implemented in cities and states across the country following World War I. Yet the 1933 *Handbook of American Prisons and Reformatories* noted in reference to Chapter 205 in Kansas: "There appears to be only one other state, Nebraska, where such a law is found." This discrepancy may simply be the result of a lack of awareness of American Plan laws at the time, or it may indicate that, in other states, enforcement of venereal disease ordinances did not result in such large numbers of detained women that it came to define the women's reformatory in the same way that it did in Kansas. Paul W. Garrett and Austin H. MacCormick, *Handbook of American Prisons and Reformatories* (New York: National Society of Penal Information, 1929), 366.

10. The low percentage in 1918 is partially attributed to the fact that many of the women who otherwise would have been detained under Chapter 205 were

instead sentenced under a vagrancy charge: of the 211 total inmates, 107 were there under Chapter 205, and sixty-six were there for vagrancy.

11. The board of administration itself was established in 1917, the same year as the KSIFW and Chapter 205, under House bill no. 517. Newspapers initially praised this highly concentrated form of administration as a cost-saving measure and a model for modern, efficient government. Mary Scott Rowland, "Social Services in Kansas, 1916–1930," *Kansas History* 7, no. 3 (1984): 212–225; "Runs State as Business: Kansas Board of Administration an Efficient Machine: A Creation of the Last Legislature Is Saving Thousands of Dollars by Eliminating Wastes in Managing the Institutions," *Kansas City Star,* February 17, 1918; "Business Sense Pays the State: Methods of 'Big Business' as Applies to State's Affairs Isn't So Bad after All, Two Years' Experience Shows," *Topeka Capital,* June 8, 1919; "Work for Caton: All State Institutions Put on a Business Basis: Legislature Doubled State Accountant's Appropriation," *Topeka Journal,* April 17, 1919; *Administration 1918 Report,* 1–8.

12. *Administration 1920 Report,* xxvi.

13. *Administration 1924 Report,* 6.

14. *Health 1920 Report,* 46.

15. *Health 1916 Report,* 315; *Health 1920 Report,* 46–49, 345; *Health 1922 Report,* 153.

16. *Health 1920 Report,* 48–50.

17. *Health 1920 Report,* 337.

18. *Health 1940 Report,* 125.

19. *Health 1920 Report,* 340.

20. Hill, "Psychiatric Studies of Delinquents," 1515.

21. *Health 1920 Report,* 339.

22. Hill, "Psychiatric Studies of Delinquents," 1502.

23. *Health 1920 Report,* 343.

24. *Health 1920 Report,* 50.

25. Public Welfare Temporary Commission, *Report of the Public Welfare Temporary Commission to the State of Kansas* (1933), 232, https://catalog.hathitrust.org/Record/001742592/Home.

26. Stern, *Trials of Nina McCall,* 97–98.

27. James N. Leiker, "Race Relations in the Sunflower State," *Kansas History: A Journal of the Central Plains* 25, no. 3 (2002): 214–236; John Parascandola, *Sex, Sin, and Science: A History of Syphilis in America* (Westport, CT: Praeger, 2008), 67.

28. Reported racial categories reflect those used in official government documents at the time. Percentages about racial and class makeup of the institution are for the general population of the KSIFW, including women sent to the Farm for other offenses. Given that women imprisoned under Chapter 205 made up

the majority of the population at the KSIFW, this is somewhat representative of the population sent there under quarantine law. Any suspected differences between this general data and information about the population quarantined under Chapter 205 is noted in the text. Rowland, "Social Services in Kansas," 218; "Kansas Contents: 1940 Census," National Archives, 14, https://1940census.archives.gov/; *KSIFW 1918 Report*, 12; *KSIFW 1920 Report*, 24; *KSIFW 1922 Report*, 15; *KSIFW 1924 Report*, 30; *KSIFW 1926 Report*, 20; *KSIFW 1928 Report*, 19; *KSIFW 1930 Report*, 20; *KSIFW 1932 Report*, 19; *KSIFW 1934 Report*, 17; *KSIFW 1936 Report*, 16; *KSIFW 1938 Report*, 20; *KSIFW 1940 Report*, 30; *KSIFW 1942 Report*, 27.

29. Though the division between northern and southern/eastern Europeans was socially significant at this time, the interview form did not report very many women as being of southern or eastern European descent (only five were listed as such; these are included in the "other" category).

30. Julian B. Carter, *The Heart of Whiteness: Normal Sexuality and Race in America, 1880–1940* (Durham, NC: Duke University Press, 2007), 33; Matthew Frye Jacobson, *Whiteness of a Different Color: European Immigrants and the Alchemy of Race* (Cambridge, MA: Harvard University Press, 1998); Noel Ignatiev, *How the Irish Became White* (New York: Routledge, 1995).

31. Though scholars disagree about the best measures of social class, particularly for women, common measures include income, education level, and occupation.

32. The higher percentage of racial minority women at the KSIFW also influences this figure. In 1920, 31.2 percent of Black women in the state reported working for wages. Kansas Contents: 1940 Census, 34–37.

33. Lekkerkerker, *Reformatories for Women*, 207.

34. Hill, "Psychiatric Studies of Delinquents," 1517.

35. *Report of the Public Welfare Temporary Commission*, 230. Of the women imprisoned at the KSIFW between 1917 and 1942, an average of 75.8 percent reported that they had ten years of schooling or less, while 24.3 percent reported that they had ten years or more of education, with a few having attended college or a business school. The 1940 census reports that the median years of school attended by women in Kansas was 8.9. *KSIFW 1918 Report*, 12; *KSIFW 1920 Report*, 23; *KSIFW 1922 Report*, 14; *KSIFW 1924 Report*, 29; *KSIFW 1926 Report*, 19; *KSIFW 1928 Report*, 17; *KSIFW 1930 Report*, 19; *KSIFW 1932 Report*, 18; *KSIFW 1934 Report*, 14; *KSIFW 1936 Report*, 19; *KSIFW 1938 Report*, 19; *KSIFW 1940 Report*, 29; *KSIFW 1942 Report*, *26*; 1940 Census, 29.

36. Allan M. Brandt, *No Magic Bullet: A Social History of Venereal Disease in the United States since 1880* (New York: Oxford University Press, 1985), 90–91. See also Rowland, "Social Services in Kansas," 218.

37. *Health 1928 Report*, 129.

38. Brandt, *No Magic Bullet*, 131.

39. *Health 1924 Report*, 76–77; see also *Health 1922 Report*, 153–154.

40. *Health 1918 Report*, 5; *Health 1922 Report*, 153.

41. Stern, *Trials of Nina McCall*, 170; Brandt, *No Magic Bullet*, 123–125; Henry Allen to Arthur Capper, January 14, 1921, box 19, folder 18, Henry Allen Governor's Records, KSHS; Henry Allen to Charles Curtis, January 14, 1921, box 19, folder 18, Henry Allen Governor's Records, KSHS.

42. *Health 1920 Report*, 347–348; S. J. Crumbine, "Three Letters Important to Clubs—How Our Board of Health Functions," *Federation News*, May 1922, 3; *Health 1922 Report*, 21–22, 154; *Health 1934 Report*.

43. Brandt, *No Magic Bullet*, 131.

44. *Report of the Public Welfare Temporary Commission*, 232.

45. Stern, *Trials of Nina McCall*, 194–198; Brandt, *No Magic Bullet*, 138–158; Parascandola, *Sex, Sin, and Science*, 72–73, 90–97.

46. *Health 1940 Report*, 117–118; "Topekan Will Present Social Disease Course to Doctors of Kansas," *Topeka Capital*, March 13, 1938.

47. *Health 1936 Report*, 79.

48. *Health 1938 Report*, 139; *KSIFW 1938 Report*.

49. Stern, "Long American Plan"; Stern, *Trials of Nina McCall*, 142–143.

50. "In Re Walter McGee, George Andrews, and George Buckner, Petitioners, Kansas Supreme Court Case No. 22,691," July 1919, Kansas Historical Society, https://www.kshs.org/km/items/view/446143.

51. "Right to Quarantine Upheld in Kansas," *Social Hygiene Bulletin*, February 1920.

52. Stern, *Trials of Nina McCall*, 191–192; Stern, "Long American Plan," 388–401; Brandt, *No Magic Bullet*, 85–86; Estelle Freedman, *Their Sisters' Keepers: Women's Prison Reform in America, 1830–1930* (Ann Arbor: University of Michigan Press, 1981), 130.

53. Kansas Supreme Court and Oscar Leopold Moore, *Reports of Cases Argued and Determined in the Supreme Court of the State of Kansas* (Topeka: Kansas State Printing Plant, 1919), 146–147.

54. Freedman, *Their Sisters' Keepers*, 148; Patricia O'Brien, *Making It in the "Free World": Women in Transition from Prison* (Albany: State University of New York Press, 2001), 4–5; Kristin Luker, "Sex, Social Hygiene, and the State: The Double-Edged Sword of Social Reform," *Theory and Society* 27, no. 5 (1998): 601–634.

55. Barbara Meil Hobson, *Uneasy Virtue: The Politics of Prostitution and the American Reform Tradition* (Chicago: University of Chicago Press, 1990), 167.

56. "News Items from All Over Kansas," *Hays (KS) Free Press*, April 18, 1918, 6.

57. Mildred Reed, "A Prison without Walls Is Women's Industrial Farm!" *Topeka State Journal*, August 21, 1920, 4.

58. "Printers' Ink-Prophylactic," *Emporia (KS) Gazette*, April 28, 1919, 2.

59. Walter L. Treadway, L. O. Weldon, and Alice M. Hill, "Psychiatric Studies of Delinquents. Part V. Conclusions and Recommendations," *Public Health Reports* 35, no. 27 (1920): 1595.

60. Lekkerkerker, *Reformatories for Women*, 26.

61. Darlene Doubleday Newby, "A Study of the Causes of Delinquency of Women Quarantined for Disease at the State Industrial Farm for Women," *Bulletin of the Kansas State Board of Health*, February 1921, 21.

62. Prison Industries Reorganization Administration (PIRA), *The Prison Labor Problem in Kansas* (1938), 8, https://kgi.contentdm.oclc.org/digital/collection/p16884coll8/id/737/.

63. Garrett and MacCormick, *Handbook of American Prisons and Reformatories*, 366.

64. *Report of the Public Welfare Temporary Commission*, 229–231.

65. "Right to Quarantine Upheld in Kansas"; "In Re Walter McGee," 10.

66. *KSIFW 1920 Report*, 17.

67. *KSIFW 1942 Report*, 9.

68. Brandt, *No Magic Bullet*, 154.

69. Brandt, *No Magic Bullet*, 152; Stern, *Trials of Nina McCall*, 94.

70. Comparable data from 1918 is not available. *KSIFW 1920 Report*, 17; *KSIFW 1922 Report*, 21; *KSIFW 1924 Report*, 16; *KSIFW 1926 Report*, 21; *KSIFW 1928 Report*, 10; *KSIFW 1930 Report*, 12; *KSIFW 1932 Report*, 11; *KSIFW 1934 Report*, 6; *KSIFW 1936 Report*, 7; *KSIFW 1938 Report*, 13; *KSIFW 1940 Report*, 22; *KSIFW 1942 Report*, 11.

71. The grouping of women sent to Lansing under Chapter 205 and the general inmate population in the data make it hard to determine the exact percentage of women sentenced under Chapter 205 who had negative test results, although several statements about the high rate of venereal disease among the population serving different sentences indicates that the numbers between the two groups may not have been that different (see, for example, *KSIFW 1922 Report*, 20). The data from 1920 only include those sentenced under Chapter 205, however, and the similarity of this data to other years, combined with the fact that quarantine patients averaged 71 percent of the inmate population, gives us some degree of confidence that a portion of those sentenced under Chapter 205 did not test positive for syphilis.

72. *Report of the Public Welfare Temporary Commission*, 232.

73. *KSIFW 1936 Report*, 7.

74. Stern, *Trials of Nina McCall*, 102; Brandt, *No Magic Bullet*, 12; John Duffy, *The Sanitarians: A History of American Public Health* (Urbana: University of Illinois Press, 1992), 281.

75. Brandt, *No Magic Bullet*, 10–12, 40–41; Rafter, *Partial Justice*, 218; Karin L. Zipf, "In Defense of the Nation: Syphilis, North Carolina's 'Girl Problem,' and World War I," *North Carolina Historical Review* 89, no. 3 (2012): 296; Stern, *Trials of Nina McCall*, 95–96; Parascandola, *Sex, Sin, and Science*, 22, 78. For a discussion of the Tuskegee syphilis study, in which the US Public Health Service failed to give adequate health care to poor Black men over a forty-year period, see James H. Jones, *Bad Blood: The Tuskegee Syphilis Experiment* (New York: Simon & Schuster, 1993).

76. Brandt, *No Magic Bullet*, 130–133.

77. *KSIFW 1928 Report*, 10.

78. For comparison, Brandt reports that the average term for women detained under American Plan laws during World War I was 10 weeks (*No Magic Bullet*, 88–90).

79. *KSIFW 1924 Report*, 15.

80. *KSIFW 1938 Report*, 12.

81. PIRA, *Prison Labor Problem in Kansas*, 8.

82. *Report of the Public Welfare Temporary Commission*, 232; PIRA, *Prison Labor Problem in Kansas*, 9.

83. "Samuel J. Crumbine," Kansapedia, Kansas Historical Society, last modified January 2016, https://www.kshs.org/kansapedia/samuel-j-crumbine/12025.

CHAPTER 3. "ANYTHING TO PLEASE THE LADIES"

1. Lucy B. Johnston, 1917, "Legislation," box 6, folder 8, Lucy B. Johnston Papers, KSHS, 5–6.

2. Louise Michele Newman, *White Women's Rights: The Racial Origins of Feminism in the United States* (New York: Oxford University Press, 1999), 29.

3. "Lucy Brown as a Young Woman," January 29, 1930, box 6, folder 11, Lucy B. Johnston Papers, KSHS; Marilyn S. Blackwell and Kristen Tegtmeier Oertel, *Frontier Feminist: Clarina Howard Nichols and the Politics of Motherhood* (Lawrence: University Press of Kansas, 2010); Kansas Historical Society, "William A. Johnston Papers," https://www.kshs.org/p/william-a-johnston-papers/14053; Kansas Historical Society, "Lucy Browne Johnston Papers," http://www.kshs.org/p/lucy-browne-johnston-papers/14052; June Underwood, "Civilizing Kansas: Women's Organizations, 1880–1920," *Kansas Historical Quarterly* 7, no. 4 (1984): 303.

4. Robert Smith Bader, *Prohibition in Kansas: A History* (Lawrence: University Press of Kansas, 1986), 176.

5. Bader, *Prohibition in Kansas*, 175–176; Martha B. Caldwell, "The Woman Suffrage Campaign of 1912," *Kansas Historical Quarterly* 12, no. 3 (1943): 300–301; Michael L. Goldberg, "Non-Partisan and All-Partisan: Rethinking Woman Suffrage and Party Politics in Gilded Age Kansas," *Western Historical Quarterly* 25,

no. 1 (1994): 21–44; Christine Stansell, *The Feminist Promise: 1792 to the Present* (New York: Modern Library, 2010), 87.

6. Matthew Frye Jacobson, *Whiteness of a Different Color: European Immigrants and the Alchemy of Race* (Cambridge, MA: Harvard University Press, 1998); Noel Ignatiev, *How the Irish Became White* (New York: Routledge, 1995).

7. Julian B. Carter, *The Heart of Whiteness: Normal Sexuality and Race in America, 1880–1940* (Durham, NC: Duke University Press, 2007), 78; Gail Bederman, *Manliness and Civilization: A Cultural History of Gender and Race in the United States, 1880–1917* (Chicago: University of Chicago Press, 1995).

8. Quoted in Newman, *White Women's Rights*, 5.

9. Paula Baker, "The Domestication of Politics: Women and American Political Society, 1780–1920," *American Historical Review* 89, no. 3 (1984): 642; Newman, *White Women's Rights*, 5, 56; Paula Giddings, *When and Where I Enter* (New York: Bantam Books, 1985). For an example of earlier research about racism in the suffrage movement, see Aileen Kraditor, *Up from the Pedestal: Selected Writings in the History of American Feminism* (Chicago: Quadrangle Books, 1968); for more recent scholarship, see Nancy F. Cott, *The Grounding of Modern Feminism* (New Haven, CT: Yale University Press, 1987), 7; Newman, *White Women's Rights*, 19; Allison L. Sneider, *Suffragists in an Imperial Age: U.S. Expansion and the Woman Question, 1870–1929* (New York: Oxford University Press, 2008), 13.

10. Blackwell and Oertel, *Frontier Feminist*, 233–235; Stansell, *Feminist Promise*, 87.

11. Henrietta Briggs-Wall, "American Woman and Her Political Peers," Kansas Memory, Kansas State Historical Society, https://www.kansasmemory.org/item/208011.

12. Quoted in Goldberg, "Non-Partisan," 33.

13. Quoted in Bader, *Prohibition in Kansas*, 174.

14. Lucy B. Johnston to Mamie Axline Fay, July 3, 1926, box 2, folder 11, Lucy B. Johnston Papers, KSHS.

15. Alberta L. Corbin, "Mrs. Lucy B. Johnston, Her Years of Achievement," January 28, 1930, box 6, folder 11, Lucy B. Johnston Papers, KSHS, 1.

16. Corbin, "Mrs. Lucy B. Johnston," 8; "Women's Bills to Legislature Today," *Topeka Capital*, January 31, 1917.

17. "To Ask for Reformatory and Girls' Dormitories," *Topeka Capital*, June 30, 1915; Bader, *Prohibition in Kansas*, 172; "Women's Bills to Legislature Today," 124; "Mrs. Goddard Heads Club Representing 100,000 Women," *Leavenworth (KS) Times*, June 10, 1928, 180.

18. Underwood, "Civilizing Kansas," 296; Anne Firor Scott, *Natural Allies: Women's Associations in American History* (Urbana: University of Illinois Press, 1991), 113, 146; Baker, "Domestication of Politics," 640; Karen J. Blair, *The Club-*

woman as Feminist: True Womanhood Redefined, 1868–1914 (New York: Holmes & Meier, 1980), 117.

19. None of the records found for the Kansas Council of Women mentioned Black women's organizations or the membership of women of color in any of the member organizations. Rules about membership in these organizations were often unstated, however, so there were also not any documents that officially banned Black women from these clubs. While the customs of women's organizations during the time indicate that these were all white women's organizations in the council, there is certainly the possibility that a few of them could have been racially integrated. See Marilyn Dell Brady, "Kansas Federation of Colored Women's Clubs, 1900–1930," *Kansas History: A Journal of the Central Plains* 9 (1986), 19–30.

20. Quoted in Brady, "Kansas Federation of Colored Women's Clubs," 23.

21. Brady, "Kansas Federation of Colored Women's Clubs," 23; Giddings, *When and Where I Enter*; Blair, *Clubwoman as Feminist*; Glenda Elizabeth Gilmore, *Gender and Jim Crow: Women and the Politics of White Supremacy in North Carolina, 1896–1920* (Chapel Hill: University of North Carolina Press, 2019).

22. "Mrs. Goddard Heads Club Representing 100,000 Women," 181.

23. Bader, *Prohibition in Kansas*, 173; Estelle Freedman, *Their Sisters' Keepers: Women's Prison Reform in America, 1830–1930* (Ann Arbor: University of Michigan Press, 1981); Nicole Hahn Rafter, *Partial Justice: Women in State Prisons, 1800–1935* (Boston: Northeastern University Press, 1985), 41–59; Eugenia C. Lekkerkerker, *Reformatories for Women in the United States* (Groningen: J. B. Wolters, 1931), 112.

24. Simmons shared this report about the KSIFW as an enclosure in a letter to Governor Arthur Capper in January 1915; see Mrs. J. S. Simmons to Arthur Capper, January 18, 1915, box 2, folder 106, Arthur Capper Governor's Records, KSHS.

25. Mrs. J. S. Simmons to Capper, January 18, 1915.

26. Arthur Capper to Emily Haelcel, December 19, 1914, box 23, folder 8, Arthur Capper Governor's Records, KSHS.

27. Julia Perry to Arthur Capper, December 23, 1914, box 23, folder 8, Arthur Capper Governor's Records, KSHS.

28. Magdalen B. Munson to Arthur Capper, December 24, 1914, box 23, folder 8, Arthur Capper Governor's Records, KSHS.

29. Munson to Capper, December 24, 1914.

30. Mrs. C. W. Smith to Arthur Capper, January 6, 1915, box 23, folder 8, Arthur Capper Governor's Records, KSHS.

31. Corbin, "Mrs. Lucy B. Johnston," 9.

32. Frank W. Blackmar to Lucy B. Johnston, January 12, 1917, box 2, folder 12, Lucy B. Johnston Papers, KSHS; "Schools of Crime, Blackmar Calls," *Topeka Capital*, December 27, 1916.

33. "Mrs. Goddard Heads Club Representing 100,000 Women," 182–184; Effie Graham, "Women Explain Purpose of the Kansas Women's Industrial Farm," *Topeka Capital*, May 20, 1917; "To Ask for Reformatory and Girls' Dormitories," 68–70; Lucy B. Johnston, "Legislation," 1917, box 6, folder 8, Lucy B. Johnston Papers, KSHS; Lucy B. Johnston, n.d., "Should Kansas Have a Woman's Reformatory?," box 6, folder 8, Lucy B. Johnston Papers, KSHS.

34. Freedman, *Their Sisters' Keepers*.

35. Graham, "Women Explain Purpose."

36. The other initiatives advanced by the KGFWC in this year were regulations regarding mothers' pensions, movie censorship, cigarettes, and kindergartens. Johnston, "Legislation," 2–3.

37. Johnston, "Legislation"; "Chapter 298," in Clippings: Kansas State Industrial Farm for Women, 1917, KSHS, 436; Emmet D. George, *Senate Journal, State of Kansas* (Topeka: Kansas State Printing Plant, 1917), 571; Clarence W. Miller, *House Journal, State of Kansas* (Topeka: Kansas State Printing Plant, 1917), 806.

38. "Women Outline Demands on the Next Legislature," in Clippings: Kansas State Industrial Farm for Women, KSHS, January 29, 1916.

39. Johnston, "Should Kansas Have a Woman's Reformatory?," 3, 10.

40. See, for example, "Reformatory for Women Prisoners," *Topeka Capital*, January 16, 1917; "Women's Reformatory Is Approved in Senate," *Topeka Capital*, February 28, 1917; "Care of Women Becomes Real Problem for State," *Topeka Capital*, November 1, 1917; Dr. Florence Brown Sherbon, "State Womens' Farm Is Place for Rebuilding," *Topeka Capital*, March 29, 1931.

41. Mildred Reed, "A Prison without Walls Is Women's Industrial Farm!" *Topeka State Journal*, August 21, 1920.

42. Johnston, "Legislation," 5.

43. "Industrial Farm for Women," *Emporia (KS) Gazette*, March 1, 1917, 1, 3.

44. "Women Outline Demands on the Next Legislature."

45. Graham, "Women Explain Purpose."

46. Wendy Kline, *Building a Better Race: Gender, Sexuality, and Eugenics from the Turn of the Century to the Baby Boom* (University of California Press, 2001), 3.

47. Quoted in Kline, *Building a Better Race*, 19.

48. Alexandra Minna Stern, *Eugenic Nation: Faults and Frontiers of Better Breeding in Modern America* (Berkeley: University of California Press, 2015), 20–21; Newman, *White Women's Rights*, 31.

49. Lucy B. Johnston to Walter R. Stubbs, January 7, 1913, box 2, folder 12, Lucy B. Johnston Papers, KSHS, 1.

50. Graham, "Women Explain Purpose."

51. Karin L. Zipf, "In Defense of the Nation: Syphilis, North Carolina's 'Girl Problem,' and World War I," *North Carolina Historical Review* 89, no. 3 (2012):

278. For further discussion of the association between whiteness and female chastity, see also Susan K. Cahn, *Sexual Reckonings: Southern Girls in a Troubling Age* (Cambridge, MA: Harvard University Press, 2007).

52. Julia Perry to Henry Allen, March 19, 1919, box 22, folder 10, Henry Allen Governor's Records, KSHS.

53. Reed, "Prison without Walls," 5; Sherbon, "State Womens' Farm"; "Women Prisoners Like College Work," *Liberal (KS) Democrat*, December 29, 1916, 32, 9.

54. Graham, "Women Explain Purpose."

55. *Health 1920 Report*, 356; *KSIFW 1940 Report.*

56. Paul W. Garrett and Austin H. MacCormick, *Handbook of American Prisons and Reformatories* (New York: National Society of Penal Information, 1929), xxxiv.

57. Blair, *Clubwoman as Feminist*; Kristin Luker, "Sex, Social Hygiene, and the State: The Double-Edged Sword of Social Reform," *Theory and Society* 27, no. 5 (1998): 601–634; Underwood, "Civilizing Kansas," 305.

58. Quoted in Scott W. Stern, *The Trials of Nina McCall: Sex, Surveillance, and the Decades-Long Government Plan to Imprison Promiscuous Women* (Boston: Beacon Press, 2018), 100–101.

59. Annie C. Porritt, "Trumpet Call to Action: From the Social Hygiene Committee of the National League of Women Voters," *Woman Citizen*, 1920, 1264; Stern, *Trials of Nina McCall*, 187–189.

60. For a discussion of activist women's opposition to American Plan laws, see Stern, *Trials of Nina McCall*, 51–53, 69–71, 100–101, 117, 145–147, 179–180, 187–189. See also Luker, "Sex, Social Hygiene, and the State"; John Parascandola, *Sex, Sin, and Science: A History of Syphilis in America* (Westport, CT: Praeger, 2008), 60; Mary E. Odem, *Delinquent Daughters: Protecting and Policing Adolescent Female Sexuality in the United States, 1885–1920* (Chapel Hill: University of North Carolina Press, 1995), 124.

61. Quoted in Stern, *Trials of Nina McCall*, 147.

62. Quoted in Parascandola, *Sex, Sin, and Science*, 74; Alexandra M. Lord, "'Naturally Clean and Wholesome': Women, Sex Education, and the United States Public Health Service, 1918–1928," *Social History of Medicine* 17, no. 3 (2004): 423–441.

63. There are records of the superintendent of the KSIFW, Julia Perry, critiquing this practice of detaining only women under Chapter 205; see chapter 4 for discussion.

64. Darlene Doubleday Newby, "Health Work in Kansas," *Federation News*, vol. 3, no. 8, May 1925, 5.

65. See, for example, Samuel J. Crumbine to Lucy B. Johnston, June 26, 1913, box 2, folder 12, Lucy B. Johnston Papers, KSHS; Samuel J. Crumbine, *Frontier Doctor* (Philadelphia: Dorancy, 1948).

66. Frederic J. Haskin, n.d., "Women's Club Work: VI.—In Conserving Health," vol. 1, Women's Clubs Clippings, KSHS.

67. S. J. Crumbine, "Three Letters Important to Clubs—How Our Board of Health Functions," *Federation News*, vol. 1, no. 4, May 1922, 3.

68. *Health 1926 Report*, 4.

69. *Health 1922 Report*, 156.

70. *Health 1924 Report*, 78.

71. Darlene Doubleday Newby, "Division of Health," *Federation News*, vol. 2, no. 7, March 1924, 2.

72. Newby, "Health Work in Kansas."

73. This was not the first board of health publication aimed specifically at clubwomen. In 1914 the Kansas State Board of Health worked with the American Medical Association and a representative from the General Federation of Women's Clubs to develop a "Study Course on Public Health" that included information about venereal disease. They distributed more than fifteen hundred copies by 1916. See *Health 1918 Report*, 14.

74. *Health 1924 Report*, 76.

75. John D'Emilio and Estelle B. Freedman, *Intimate Matters: A History of Sexuality in America*, 2nd ed. (Chicago: University of Chicago Press, 1997), 215.

76. Quoted in Allan M. Brandt, *No Magic Bullet: A Social History of Venereal Disease in the United States since 1880* (New York: Oxford University Press, 1985), 23.

77. *Health 1920 Report*, 10.

78. Carter, *Heart of Whiteness*, 128.

79. Brandt, *No Magic Bullet*, 16, 215; Kline, *Building a Better Race*, 11.

80. Carter, *Heart of Whiteness*, 35.

81. Quoted in Molly Ladd-Taylor, *Fixing the Poor: Eugenic Sterilization and Child Welfare in the Twentieth Century* (Baltimore: Johns Hopkins University Press, 2017), 4.

82. Laura L. Lovett, "'Fitter Families for Future Firesides': Florence Sherbon and Popular Eugenics," *Public Historian* 29, no. 3 (Summer 2007): 76.

83. Ladd-Taylor, *Fixing the Poor*, 1.

84. Dr. Florence Sherbon, one of the organizers of the Fitter Families contests in Kansas, later went on to visit and write an approving article about the KSIFW; see Sherbon, "State Womens' Farm." See also Lovett, "Fitter Families."

85. Scott W. Stern, *Trials of Nina McCall*, 90; Alexandra Minna Stern, *Eugenic Nation*; Kline, *Building a Better Race*.

86. Scott Wasserman Stern, "The Long American Plan: The U.S. Government's Campaign against Venereal Disease and Its Carriers," *Harvard Journal of Law and Gender* 38 (2015): 404n224.

87. Porritt, "Trumpet Call to Action," 1264.

88. Kline, *Building a Better Race*, 5, 59; Parascandola, *Sex, Sin, and Science*, 37; Michael A. Rembis, *Defining Deviance: Sex, Science, and Delinquent Girls, 1890–1960* (Urbana: University of Illinois Press, 2011), 3–4.

89. Lucy B. Johnston to Walter R. Stubbs, April 1, 1912, and May 11, 1911, box 2, folder 10, Lucy B. Johnston Papers, KSHS, 1–2.

90. Johnston mentioned marriage laws in her reports on the State Home for the Blind, the Home for the Feeble-Minded, the State's Orphan's Home, the Home for the Insane, the Home for Epileptics, and the Girls' Industrial School. She did not mention eugenics-related legislation in her letter concerning the Boys' Industrial School.

91. Lucy B. Johnston to Walter R. Stubbs, January 7, 1913, box 2, folder 12, Lucy B. Johnston Papers, KSHS, 4.

92. "Mrs. C. C. Goddard Heads Kansas Women's Council," *Topeka Capital*, January 29, 1924, 151.

93. Buena Burr, *Program of Work: Division of Venereal Diseases* (Topeka: Kansas State Printing Plant, 1924), 3.

94. *Federation News*, vol. 5, no. 12, September 1927, 10.

95. Kline, *Building a Better Race*, 27–28; Mary Ziegler, "Eugenic Feminism: Mental Hygiene, the Women's Movement, and the Campaign for Eugenic Legal Reform, 1900–1935," *Harvard Journal of Law and Gender* 31 (2008): 211–235.

96. Kline, *Building a Better Race*, 29, 46.

97. Mrs. A. J. Kull, "Kansas Council of Women Minutes of Meeting" (January 30, 1935), 2–3, KSHS.

98. Darlene Doubleday Newby, "A Study of the Causes of Delinquency of Women Quarantined for Disease at the State Industrial Farm for Women," *Bulletin of the Kansas State Board of Health*, February 1921, 22.

99. Kline, *Building a Better Race*, 20, 32; Odem, *Delinquent Daughters*, 98.

100. Newby, "A Study of the Causes of Delinquency," 23, 34.

101. *Administration 1920 Report*, xvi.

102. Kansas Board of Administration, *Procedure to Be Followed in Sterilization Cases* (Topeka, July 14, 1928), 3, KSHS.

103. Kansas Board of Administration, *Procedure to Be Followed in Sterilization Cases*, 14.

104. Kansas Municipal Judges Association, "A Step Back in Time," *The Verdict* 51 (Spring 2010): 3, http://www.kmja.org/wp-content/uploads/2010/09/Verdict Spring2010.pdf; Mary Scott Rowland, "Social Services in Kansas, 1916–1930," *Kansas History* 7, no. 3 (1984): 224; Michael L. Wehmeyer, "Eugenics and Sterilization in the Heartland," *Mental Retardation* 41, no. 1 (2003): 58–59.

105. Ladd-Taylor, *Fixing the Poor*, 7; *KSIFW 1936 Report*, 7; Stern, *Trials of Nina McCall*, 198–199; Harriet C. Frazier, "The State Industrial School for Girls at Beloit, Kansas: The First 50 Years, 1889–1939," paper presented at the American

Society of Criminology conference, Chicago, November 9–12, 1988; Heather Hollingsworth, "Shuttered Girls Reformatory Recalls Horror, Haven," Associated Press, October 24, 2009, https://www.nevadaappeal.com/news/local/shuttered-girls-reformatory-recalls-horror-haven/; Dan T. Kelliher, "Sterilization: The Unholy Horror of Lost Motherhood," *Front Page Detective*, July 1938; "Crime: Finishing Schools," *Time*, November 18, 1937.

106. Stern, *Trials of Nina McCall*, 198–199.

107. *KSIFW 1922 Report*, 21.

108. For a discussion of salpingectomies, see Kline, *Building a Better Race*, 69, 75; Stern, *Trials of Nina McCall*, 90. See also *KSIFW 1936 Report*, 8.

109. *KSIFW 1938 Report*, 13; *KSIFW 1940 Report*, 23.

110. Rowland, "Social Services in Kansas," 225.

111. See Baker, "Domestication of Politics." As Michael Goldberg argues in his research about populism and the suffrage movement in Kansas in the 1890s, this public/private distinction also ignores divisions along the lines of social class and rural versus urban settings. While distinct public and private spheres may have been prevalent for the urban middle class in Kansas, most of the population resided in rural areas with more heterosocial leisure, religious, and work patterns than existed in the cities. See Goldberg, "Non-Partisan," 30–31.

112. Newman, *White Women's Rights*.

113. Rafter, *Partial Justice*, 51.

CHAPTER 4. TRAINING INMATES FOR RESPECTABILITY

1. *Health 1920 Report*, 355, 356, 357, 360.

2. Nicole Hahn Rafter, *Partial Justice: Women in State Prisons, 1800–1935* (Boston: Northeastern University Press, 1985), xxiii.

3. "He Wants a Debate," *Wichita Daily Eagle*, July 8, 1901, 3, http://chroniclingamerica.loc.gov/lccn/sn82014635/1901-07-08/ed-1/seq-3; Mary Scott Rowland, "Social Services in Kansas, 1916–1930," *Kansas History* 7, no. 3 (1984): 214; William E. Connelley, *History of Kansas: State and People*, vol. 4 (American Historical Society, 1928), 1957–1958.

4. *Health 1920 Report*, 358.

5. Eugenia C. Lekkerkerker, *Reformatories for Women in the United States* (Groningen: J. B. Wolters, 1931), 269.

6. Peggy Pascoe, *Relations of Rescue: The Search for Female Moral Authority in the American West, 1874–1939* (New York: Oxford University Press, 1990), 188; Estelle Freedman, *Their Sisters' Keepers: Women's Prison Reform in America, 1830–1930* (Ann Arbor: University of Michigan Press, 1981), 109–110; Rafter, *Partial Justice*, 64–65. Though race is not explicitly mentioned in many reformatory documents as a qualification for the job, social customs would have dictated that these super-

intendents were white. It is possible that some of the lower-level matrons were women of color, though it seems unlikely in institutions, like the KSIFW, that were racially integrated.

7. "Chapter 298," in Clippings: Kansas State Industrial Farm for Women, 1917, KSHS, 437; Allan M. Brandt, *No Magic Bullet: A Social History of Venereal Disease in the United States since 1880* (New York: Oxford University Press, 1985), 90; Freedman, *Their Sisters' Keepers*, 46, 58; Lekkerkerker, *Reformatories for Women*, 267.

8. "Thinking Women Must Provide the Solution," *Topeka Capital*, December 15, 1918.

9. Mary E. Odem, *Delinquent Daughters: Protecting and Policing Adolescent Female Sexuality in the United States, 1885–1920* (Chapel Hill: University of North Carolina Press, 1995), 95–96; Elizabeth Alice Clement, *Love for Sale: Courting, Treating, and Prostitution in New York City, 1900–1945* (Chapel Hill: University of North Carolina Press, 2006), 7; Noralee Frankel and Nancy Schrom Dye, *Gender, Class, Race, and Reform in the Progressive Era* (Lexington: University Press of Kentucky, 1991), 164; Freedman, *Their Sisters' Keepers*, 155.

10. Samuel J. Crumbine, *Frontier Doctor* (Philadelphia: Dorancy, 1948), 226–227.

11. Patrick G. O'Brien, "'I Want Everyone to Know the Shame of the State': Henry J. Allen Confronts the Ku Klux Klan, 1921–1923," *Kansas History* 19 (Summer 1996): 102.

12. K. Allen Greiner, "Samuel J. Crumbine: Individualizing the Standard for Twentieth-Century Public Health," in *John Brown to Bob Dole: Movers and Shakers in Kansas History*, ed. Virgil W. Dean (Lawrence: University Press of Kansas, 2006), 176; *Health 1924 Report*, 5; Untitled, *Topeka Capital*, June 2, 1923, in "Governors of Kansas, Clippings, vol. 1, 1923–1926," KSHS.

13. Julia Perry to Lucy Johnston, July 4, 1913, box 2, folder 12, Lucy B. Johnston Papers, KSHS, 2. Underline in original.

14. A. B. Carney to Lucy B. Johnston, December 7, 1931, box 27, folder 5, Harry Woodring Governor's Records, KSHS; Untitled, *Meade County News*, July 17, 1913, http://chroniclingamerica.loc.gov/lccn/sn85030287/1913-07-17/ed-1/seq-7/.

15. The superintendents were Daisy Sharp (1932–1933); Mrs. Pennington (only a few weeks, 1933); Ethel K. Pember (1934–1936); Sara Mae Cain (1936–1938); and Etta B. Beavers (1939–1942). *KSIFW 1932 Report*; *KSIFW 1934 Report*; *KSIFW 1936 Report*; *KSIFW 1938 Report*; *KSIFW 1940 Report*; *KSIFW 1942 Report*.

16. Kansas governors during these years were Harry Woodring, Democrat, 1931–1933; Alf Landon, Republican, 1933–1937; Walter Huxman, Democrat, 1937–1939; and Payne Ratner, Republican, 1939–1943. "Governors," Kansas State Library, https://kslib.info/388/Governors.

17. For examples of letters from superintendents of the KSIFW about their employment following a change in political party in the governor's office, see Daisy Sharp to Andrew Schoeppel, August 3, 1943, box 27, folder 4, Andrew Schoeppel Governor's Records, KSHS; Etta Beavers to Frank Carlson, January 14, 1947, box 27, folder 4, Frank Carlson Governor's Records, KSHS.

18. This woman's name was Mae Butcher at the time of her employment at the KSIFW; she worked under Superintendent Ethel Pember. Mae McBrian to Frank Carlson, January 15, 1948, box 27, folder 9, Frank Carlson Governor's Records, KSHS.

19. See Public Welfare Temporary Commission, *Report of the Public Welfare Temporary Commission to the State of Kansas* (1933), v, x, https://catalog.hathitrust.org/Record/001742592/Home.

20. Lekkerkerker, *Reformatories for Women*, 112.

21. Annie C. Porritt, "Trumpet Call to Action: From the Social Hygiene Committee of the National League of Women Voters," *Woman Citizen*, 1920, 1258.

22. *KSIFW 1924 Report*, 9.

23. *KSIFW 1924 Report*, 11.

24. Rowland, "Social Services in Kansas," 225.

25. Pascoe, *Relations of Rescue*; Freedman, *Their Sisters' Keepers*, 155.

26. *Report of the Public Welfare Temporary Commission*, 225.

27. *KSIFW 1938 Report*; *KSIFW 1940 Report*; Lekkerkerker, *Reformatories for Women*, 260.

28. Lekkerkerker, *Reformatories for Women*, 275–277.

29. *Report of the Public Welfare Temporary Commission*, 225; Freedman, *Their Sisters' Keepers*, 71, 77.

30. Lekkerkerker, *Reformatories for Women*, 280.

31. *KSIFW 1930 Report*, 6; Lekkerkerker, *Reformatories for Women*, 278–279.

32. Lekkerkerker, *Reformatories for Women*, 255.

33. Prison Industries Reorganization Administration (PIRA), *The Prison Labor Problem in Kansas* (1938), 9, https://kgi.contentdm.oclc.org/digital/collection/p16884coll8/id/737/.

34. Lekkerkerker, *Reformatories for Women*, 264.

35. Lekkerkerker, *Reformatories for Women*, 265.

36. *Report of the Public Welfare Temporary Commission*, 225.

37. *KSIFW 1924 Report*, 3.

38. *Report of the Public Welfare Temporary Commission*, 225.

39. Lekkerkerker, *Reformatories for Women*, 273.

40. See Julian B. Carter, *The Heart of Whiteness: Normal Sexuality and Race in America, 1880–1940* (Durham, NC: Duke University Press, 2007).

41. Evelyn E. Woodruff to Harry Woodring, March 18, 1931, box 27-11-01-03, folder 5, Harry Woodring Governor's Records, KSHS. Underline in original.

42. No author to Guy Helvering, May 30, 1931, box 27-11-01-03, folder 5, Harry Woodring Governor's Records, KSHS, 3.

43. No author to Helvering, May 30, 1931, 3.

44. Evelyn E. Woodruff to Emma Sells Marshall, January 9, 1932, box 27-11-01-03, folder 5, Harry Woodring Governor's Records, KSHS, 5.

45. No author to Helvering, May 30, 1931, 4.

46. H. C. Castor to Harry Woodring, October 14, 1931, box 2, folder 11, Lucy B. Johnston Papers, KSHS.

47. Harry Woodring to Jay C. Everett, October 20, 1931, box 27-11-01-03, folder 5, Harry Woodring Governor's Records, KSHS.

48. Harry Woodring to Lucy B. Johnston, October 26, 1931, box 2, folder 11, Lucy B. Johnston Papers, KSHS.

49. Emma Sells Marshall to Julia B. Perry, January 8, 1932, box 27-11-01-03, folder 5, Harry Woodring Governor's Records, KSHS.

50. Petition, box 27-11-01-03, folder 5, Harry Woodring Governor's Records, KSHS.

51. Woodruff to Woodring, March 18, 1931.

52. Petition.

53. Mrs. F. W. Boyd to Harry Woodring, February 3, 1932, box 27-11-01-03, folder 5, Harry Woodring Governor's Records, KSHS.

54. Petition.

55. Woodring to Everett, October 20, 1931.

56. Harry Woodring to Caleb W. Smick, November 2, 1931, box 27-11-01-03, folder 5, Harry Woodring Governor's Records, KSHS.

57. Paul W. Garrett and Austin H. MacCormick, *Handbook of American Prisons and Reformatories* (New York: National Society of Penal Information, 1929), xxxiii; Rafter, *Partial Justice*, 55; Kristin Luker, "Sex, Social Hygiene, and the State: The Double-Edged Sword of Social Reform," *Theory and Society* 27, no. 5 (1998): 616; Lekkerkerker, *Reformatories for Women*, 182.

58. Kansas Woman's Christian Temperance Union, October 1917, *KWCTU Report*, Kansas State Industrial Farm Clippings, KSHS, 1.

59. Lekkerkerker, *Reformatories for Women*, 181; Rafter, *Partial Justice*; Freedman, *Their Sisters' Keepers*. For a discussion of the idea of reform as part of the evolution of punishment, see Michel Foucault, *Discipline and Punish: The Birth of the Prison*, 2nd ed., trans. Alan Sheridan (New York: Vintage Books, 1995).

60. Wendy Kline, *Building a Better Race: Gender, Sexuality, and Eugenics from the Turn of the Century to the Baby Boom* (Berkeley: University of California Press, 2001), 21–27; Molly Ladd-Taylor, *Fixing the Poor: Eugenic Sterilization and Child Welfare in the Twentieth Century* (Baltimore: Johns Hopkins University Press, 2017); Scott W. Stern, *The Trials of Nina McCall: Sex, Surveillance, and the*

Decades-Long Government Plan to Imprison Promiscuous Women (Boston: Beacon Press, 2018), 88–89; Rafter, *Partial Justice*, 68. For a discussion of the place of observation and classification of bodies in the evolution of discipline and the penal system, see Foucault, *Discipline and Punish*.

61. Walter L. Treadway, L. O. Weldon, and Alice M. Hill, "Psychiatric Studies of Delinquents: Physical, Mental, and Social Conditions of Prostitutes Detained or Quarantined in Extra-Cantonment Zones of Kansas and Kentucky," *Public Health Reports* 35, no. 21 (1920): 1208.

62. Walter L. Treadway, "Psychiatric Studies of Delinquents. Part IV. Some Constitutional Factors in Prostitution," *Public Health Reports* 35, no. 27 (1920): 1592, 1582.

63. Kline, *Building a Better Race*, 25, 42.

64. *KSIFW 1922 Report*, 6; *KSIFW 1930 Report*, 3; *KSIFW 1924 Report*, 3.

65. *KSIFW 1920 Report*, 6.

66. Rafter, *Partial Justice*, 73; Lekkerkerker, *Reformatories for Women*, 222; Freedman, *Their Sisters' Keepers*, 153.

67. Rafter, *Partial Justice*, 33.

68. *KSIFW 1940 Report*, 5.

69. *KSIFW 1930 Report*, 3.

70. "Locate Detention Farm for Women," *Topeka Capital*, August 11, 1917; *Health 1920 Report*, 351. See also Lekkerkerker, *Reformatories for Women*, 288; Brandt, *No Magic Bullet*, 90.

71. *KSIFW 1940 Report*, 12.

72. *KSIFW 1924 Report*, 4.

73. Freedman, *Their Sisters' Keepers*, 52–57, 67–70.

74. Mildred Reed, "A Prison without Walls Is Women's Industrial Farm!" *Topeka State Journal*, August 21, 1920.

75. Dr. Florence Brown Sherbon, "State Womens' Farm Is Place for Rebuilding," *Topeka Capital*, March 29, 1931.

76. *KSIFW 1922 Report*, 22.

77. *KSIFW 1926 Report*, 24.

78. Lekkerkerker, *Reformatories for Women*, 294.

79. *KSIFW 1938 Report*, 6.

80. *KSIFW 1926 Report*, 13.

81. See, for example, *KSIFW 1924 Report*, 4.

82. *KSIFW 1920 Report*, 7.

83. *KSIFW 1920 Report*, 8.

84. *KSIFW 1926 Report*, 14.

85. Lekkerkerker, *Reformatories for Women*, 492.

86. *KSIFW 1938 Report*, 11.

87. Garrett and MacCormick, *Handbook of American Prisons and Reformatories*, 365.

88. Lekkerkerker, *Reformatories for Women*, 119.

89. Lekkerkerker, *Reformatories for Women*, 454.

90. *KSIFW 1930 Report*, 4.

91. *KSIFW 1932 Report*, 3.

92. *KSIFW 1922 Report*, 5.

93. Brandt, *No Magic Bullet*, 90; Freedman, *Their Sisters' Keepers*, 149; Lekkerkerker, *Reformatories for Women*, 460.

94. Rafter, *Partial Justice*, xxii; Christina Simmons, "Companionate Marriage and the Lesbian Threat," *Frontiers: A Journal of Women Studies* 4, no. 3 (1979): 57; Luker, "Sex, Social Hygiene, and the State."

95. Luker, "Sex, Social Hygiene, and the State."

96. *Administration 1918 Report*, 13.

97. *KSIFW 1918 Report*, 5; *Report of the Public Welfare Temporary Commission*, 225; *Health 1920 Report*, 362; Lekkerkerker, *Reformatories for Women*, 181. For a discussion of kinship networks among female prisoners themselves, see Regina G. Kunzel, *Criminal Intimacy: Prison and the Uneven History of Modern American Sexuality* (Chicago: University of Chicago Press, 2008), 117–121.

98. *KSIFW 1922 Report*, 5.

99. Odem, *Delinquent Daughters*, 142.

100. Alice M. Hill, "Psychiatric Studies of Delinquents: Part III. Social and Environmental Factors in the Moral Delinquency of Girls Committed to the Kansas State Industrial Farm," *Public Health Reports* 35, no. 26 (1920): 1520.

101. *KSIFW 1924 Report*, 9–10.

102. The 1918 biennial report is the only one that provides information about maternity; it reported that 35 percent of the inmates had given birth to children. See *KSIFW 1918 Report*, 14; Hill, "Psychiatric Studies of Delinquents," 1532–1534.

103. *KSIFW 1930 Report*, 9. See also *KSIFW 1932 Report*, 9.

104. *KSIFW 1934 Report*, 9.

105. *KSIFW 1938 Report*, 3.

106. *KSIFW 1942 Report*, 14.

107. *KSIFW 1922 Report*, 5.

108. *KSIFW 1922 Report*, 6.

109. Lekkerkerker, *Reformatories for Women*, 370.

110. *Health 1920 Report*, 341.

111. Garrett and MacCormick, *Handbook of American Prisons and Reformatories*, 366.

112. *Report of the Public Welfare Temporary Commission*, 223–224.

113. "Chapter 298," in Clippings: Kansas State Industrial Farm for Women, 1917, KSHS, 441; Rowland, "Social Services in Kansas," 219; Rafter, *Partial Justice*, 75.

114. Garrett and MacCormick, *Handbook of American Prisons and Reformatories*, xxxiv.

115. Rafter, *Partial Justice*, 77, 182.

116. Stern, *Trials of Nina McCall*, 70; L. Mara Dodge, *Whores and Thieves of the Worst Kind: A Study of Women, Crime, and Prisons, 1835–2000* (DeKalb: Northern Illinois University Press, 2002), 84; Lekkerkerker, *Reformatories for Women*, 195; Rafter, *Partial Justice*, 116–117. While the general trend in women's reformatories was to focus on minor sexuality-related offenses, this was not universally the case. For example, the Ohio reformatory studied by Nicole Rafter primarily imprisoned women convicted of childcare or alcohol-related offenses. Rafter, *Partial Justice*, 118–119.

117. *KSIFW 1920 Report*, 6.

118. Rafter, *Partial Justice*, 74–75, 81.

119. *KSIFW 1926 Report*, 3.

120. Rafter, *Partial Justice*, 62, 67; Lekkerkerker, *Reformatories for Women*, 123, 191, 382, 557. For a discussion of the parole missions at other American Plan institutions, see Stern, *Trials of Nina McCall*, 115.

121. Lekkerkerker, *Reformatories for Women*, 188, 389; Rafter, *Partial Justice*, 67.

122. Lekkerkerker, *Reformatories for Women*, 9.

123. *KSIFW 1922 Report*, 6; see also *KSIFW 1924 Report*, 5; *KSIFW 1938 Report*, 3.

124. *KSIFW 1924 Report*, 13.

125. Martha Falconer, "The Part of the Reformatory Institution in the Elimination of Prostitution," *Social Hygiene* 5, no. 1 (1919): 6.

126. *KSIFW 1932 Report*, 3.

127. Rafter, *Partial Justice*, 74.

128. *KSIFW 1918 Report*, 5.

129. *KSIFW 1920 Report*, 6; see also *KSIFW 1924 Report*, 4.

130. *KSIFW 1938 Report*, 3.

131. *KSIFW 1926 Report*, 14.

132. *KSIFW 1942 Report*, 5.

133. *KSIFW 1918 Report*, 3.

134. Garrett and MacCormick, *Handbook of American Prisons and Reformatories*, 367.

135. Crumbine, *Frontier Doctor*, 223–224. Though this quote speaks to Crumbine's perception of the state charges' attitudes toward interns, it should be read with caution as a direct representation of inmates' feelings. The autobiography was written some twenty years after this alleged interaction occurred, and the

language of the quote reads much like Crumbine's own writing rather than a direct quote of an inmate.

136. Sherbon, "State Womens' Farm."

137. Darlene Doubleday Newby, "A Study of the Causes of Delinquency of Women Quarantined for Disease at the State Industrial Farm for Women," *Bulletin of the Kansas State Board of Health*, February 1921, 20.

138. *Health 1920 Report*, 359.

139. *Health 1920 Report*, 356.

140. Ruth M. Alexander, *The Girl Problem: Female Sexual Delinquency in New York, 1900–1930* (Ithaca, NY: Cornell University Press, 1998); Karin L. Zipf, "In Defense of the Nation: Syphilis, North Carolina's 'Girl Problem,' and World WarI," *North Carolina Historical Review* 89, no. 3 (2012): 294.

141. *Health 1920 Report*, 357.

142. *KSIFW 1922 Report*, 7; *KSIFW 1918 Report*, 4. For other examples of KSIFW staff talking about the need for inmates to develop self-control, see *KSIFW 1922 Report*, 8; *KSIFW 1924 Report*, 3; *KSIFW 1928 Report*, 3; *KSIFW 1930 Report*, 3.

143. For a discussion of the relationship between the evolution of discipline and an emphasis on inmates regulating their own behaviors and bodies, see Foucault, *Discipline and Punish*.

144. Rafter, *Partial Justice*, 38.

145. *KSIFW 1924 Report*, 10.

146. Lekkerkerker, *Reformatories for Women*, 290, 302.

147. For a discussion of women escaping from American Plan institutions, see Stern, *Trials of Nina McCall*, 144–145.

148. *KSIFW 1922 Report*, 4.

149. *KSIFW 1942 Report*, 5.

150. See Foucault, *Discipline and Punish*.

151. *KSIFW 1924 Report*, 6.

152. Lekkerkerker, *Reformatories for Women*, 234; see also 399–401.

153. Sherbon, "State Womens' Farm."

154. No author to Helvering, May 30, 1931, 3.

155. Racial segregation in women's reformatories varied regionally, with institutions in the South being more likely to segregate than those in the North. Some states sent Black women to separate institutions entirely, usually to regular prisons that lacked the emphasis on reform. Lekkerkerker, *Reformatories for Women*, 234; Freedman, *Their Sisters' Keepers*; Stern, *Trials of Nina McCall*, 70, 98–99; John Parascandola, *Sex, Sin, and Science: A History of Syphilis in America* (Westport, CT: Praeger, 2008), 68; Kunzel, *Criminal Intimacy*, 28–29; Sherbon, "State Womens' Farm"; Michael A. Rembis, *Defining Deviance: Sex, Science, and Delinquent Girls, 1890–1960* (Urbana: University of Illinois Press, 2011), 103–105.

156. *KSIFW 1926 Report*, 7.

157. Julia Perry to State Board of Administration, March 2, 1932, box 27-11-01-03, folder 5, Harry Woodring Governor's Records, KSHS; *KSIFW 1930 Report*, 6.

158. Sherbon, "State Womens' Farm."

159. *Report of the Public Welfare Temporary Commission*, 223, 224.

160. *KSIFW 1940 Report*, 9.

161. *KSIFW 1920 Report*, 6; *KSIFW 1922 Report*, 4; *KSIFW 1934 Report*, 3; Rowland, "Social Services in Kansas," 212; Connelley, *History of Kansas*, 4:1957.

CHAPTER 5. PATHS TO THE KANSAS STATE INDUSTRIAL FARM FOR WOMEN

1. Inmate Interviews, 1923: 2045.

2. All grammar and spelling errors in the inmate interviews are from the original text. Pseudonyms are used for all inmates and people mentioned in their interviews to protect the identities of those involved.

3. For a discussion of social control in institutional contexts, see William G. Staples, *Castles of Our Conscience: Social Control and the American State, 1800–1985* (Cambridge: Polity Press, 1990); Pippa Holloway, *Sexuality, Politics, and Social Control in Virginia, 1920–1945* (Chapel Hill: University of North Carolina Press, 2006); Michel Foucault, *The Birth of the Clinic: An Archaeology of Medical Perception*, 1st American ed. (New York: Pantheon Books, 1973). For research at the intersection of health and social control, see Irving Kenneth Zola, "Medicine as an Institution of Social Control," *Sociological Review* 20, no. 4 (1972): 487–504; Trevor Hoppe, "Controlling Sex in the Name of 'Public Health': Social Control and Michigan HIV Law," *Social Problems* 60, no. 1 (2013): 27–49; Martin French and Gavin Smith, "'Health' Surveillance: New Modes of Monitoring Bodies, Populations, and Polities," *Critical Public Health* 23, no. 4 (2013): 383–392; Patrick O'Byrne and Dave Holmes, "Public Health STI/HIV Surveillance: Exploring the Society of Control," *Surveillance and Society* 7, no. 1 (2009): 58–70.

4. Dutch researcher Eugenia Lekkerkerker, who wrote a 1931 book about women's reformatories in the United States, described the intent of these interviews as not only to get basic demographic information but also to prompt inmates to reflect on their past and create a sense that the institution was invested in their future. Reflecting a medicalized approach to deviancy, reformatories saw intake interviews as a baseline for treatment and the first steps in getting buy-in from inmates for the goals of the institution. One difference between the Kansas interviews and national practices is that the Kansas interviews were relatively short and structured, with only a one-page form with prescribed spaces to fill in information. Lekkerkerker recommended that interviews be more open to allow inmates to freely tell their stories. For an example of a more open interview form

used in Massachusetts reformatories, see Eugenia C. Lekkerkerker, *Reformatories for Women in the United States* (Groningen: J. B. Wolters, 1931), 352–356.

5. Inmate Interviews, 1923: 2045. It is unclear whether these descriptions reflect women's self-reported racial/ethnic identity or the interviewer's inference based on their appearance. All racial categorizations used in this book reflect the language used on these interview forms. Given that widespread definitions of whiteness were being solidified during this period in history (see chapter 2 for further discussion), distinctions between women who were, for example, Irish and French may have had socially important meanings.

6. Scott W. Stern, *The Trials of Nina McCall: Sex, Surveillance, and the Decades-Long Government Plan to Imprison Promiscuous Women* (Boston: Beacon Press, 2018), 68–69.

7. Samuel J. Crumbine, *Frontier Doctor* (Philadelphia: Dorancy, 1948), 226.

8. Lekkerkerker, *Reformatories for Women*, 352–353.

9. "Mother Kills Her Two Children," *Topeka Daily Capital*, July 19, 1916; "Child Slayer in Jail," *Ottawa (KS) Herald*, July 24, 1916; "Convict a Woman," *Oskaloosa (KS) Independent*, October 6, 1916; "Effie Beverly Kills Her Children," *Caldwell (KS) News*, July 20, 1916; "Woman Convicted of Murder," *Topeka Daily Capital*, September 30, 1916.

10. Elizabeth Alice Clement, *Love for Sale: Courting, Treating, and Prostitution in New York City, 1900–1945* (Chapel Hill: University of North Carolina Press, 2006), 16. See also Nancy Cott, "Eighteenth Century Family and Social Life Revealed in Massachusetts Divorce Records," in *A Heritage of Our Own*, ed. Nancy Cott and Elizabeth Pleck (New York: Simon & Schuster, 1979); Julian B. Carter, "Introduction: Theory, Methods, Praxis: The History of Sexuality and the Question of Evidence," *Journal of the History of Sexuality* 14, no. 1 (2005): 1–9.

11. Stephen Robertson, "What's Law Got to Do with It? Legal Records and Sexual Histories," *Journal of the History of Sexuality* 14, no. 1 (2005): 178.

12. I occasionally looked at additional interviews in order to find sources that corroborated each other. For example, if an inmate mentioned that she was arrested with a friend, I was often able to locate the friend's interview because their prisoner numbers were close together.

13. Inmate Interviews, 1931: 4795.

14. Inmate Interviews, 1925. Interview numbers for inmates under age fourteen are not included in order to protect their privacy.

15. Inmate Interviews, 1927: 3293.

16. I grouped the racial categories recorded on the interview form as White/Northern European, White/Irish or Scotch, Black, Indian, and Other. The interview form did not note whether women were of Hispanic origin. See chapter 2 for a brief description of the racial makeup of the interview sample. For differences in

arrest patterns, White/Northern European women made up 49.4 percent of the overall arrest sample, yet they made up 60.4 percent of the women who reported being arrested through a targeted arrest. Other groups were underrepresented in this arrest category. These numbers compare to 24.7 percent overall versus 20.1 percent of targeted arrests for White/Irish or Scotch inmates, 15.6 percent overall versus 12.8 percent targeted arrests for Black inmates, 6 percent versus 5.8 percent for Indian inmates, and 4.1 percent versus 0 percent for the Other category.

17. For a discussion of how working-class parents utilized California laws in a similar way during this period, see Mary E. Odem, *Delinquent Daughters: Protecting and Policing Adolescent Female Sexuality in the United States, 1885–1920* (Chapel Hill: University of North Carolina Press, 1995). As Odem argues, the burgeoning set of laws regulating sexuality during this period were not simply used against the working class as a whole but were sometimes strategically used in intergenerational conflicts within the working class as a way to exercise parental authority.

18. Inmate Interviews, 1931: 4832.

19. Inmate Interviews, 1924: 2335.

20. Inmate Interviews, 1926: 2817.

21. Stephanie Coontz, *Marriage, a History: How Love Conquered Marriage* (New York: Penguin, 2006).

22. Inmate Interviews, 1927: 3152; Inmate Interviews, 1927: 3153.

23. Inmate Interviews, 1923: 2042.

24. Inmate Interviews, 1932: 5024.

25. Inmate Interviews, 1926: 2734.

26. Inmate Interviews, 1931: 4714.

27. Inmate Interviews, 1924: 2182.

28. Inmate Interviews, 1924: 2183.

29. Inmate Interviews, 1924: 2184.

30. Inmate Interviews, 1924: 2183.

31. Inmate Interviews, 1932: 5214.

32. Inmate Interviews, 1931: 4819.

33. Inmate Interviews, 1925: 2485.

34. Kansas, the home of hatchet-bearing Carrie Nation, was a stronghold of temperance activity and had some of the strictest prohibition laws in the country in the 1920s and 1930s. While the national prohibition law prevented the sale, transportation, and manufacture of alcohol, Kansas's "bone-dry" law went a step further and made it illegal to be in possession of liquor. Robert Smith Bader, *Prohibition in Kansas: A History* (Lawrence: University Press of Kansas, 1986), 186.

35. Inmate Interviews, 1926: 2913; Lansing Historical Museum, "KSIF Prisoners 2913 & 2914," https://lansingmuseum.omeka.net/items/show/50.

36. Inmate Interviews, 1932: 4972.

37. Inmate Interviews, 1932: 5170.

38. Inmate Interviews, 1924: 2249. The racial references in this quote were not common in the overall sample. With a few exceptions, the inmates did not specifically talk about race.

39. Inmate Interviews, 1926.

40. Inmate Interviews, 1926: 3030.

41. Inmate Interviews, 1927: 3400.

42. Inmate Interviews, 1932: 4978.

43. Inmate Interviews, 1927: 3351.

44. Inmate Interviews, 1932: 5226.

45. Inmate Interviews, 1925: 2547.

46. Inmate Interviews, 1931: 4864.

47. Inmate Interviews, 1925: 2586.

48. White/Northern European women were underrepresented in this arrest category, making up only 29.5 percent of the women arrested in raids (compared to being 49.4 percent of the overall arrest sample). White/Irish or Scotch made up 18.4 percent of the raid arrests (compared to 24.7 percent of sample); Indian women were 4.3 percent of raids (versus 6 percent of sample); and inmates in the "Other" category were 5.7 percent of raid arrests (versus 4.1 percent overall).

49. Inmate Interviews, 1926: 2917.

50. Inmate Interviews, 1926.

51. Inmate Interviews, 1929: 4134.

52. Inmate Interviews, 1929: 3893.

53. Inmate Interviews, 1931: 4944.

54. Inmate Interviews, 1931: 4945.

55. Inmate Interviews, 1928: 3543.

56. Inmate Interviews, 1926: 3471.

57. Inmate Interviews, 1926: 2898.

58. Inmate Interviews, 1926: 2620.

59. Inmate Interviews, 1926: 2964.

60. Inmate Interviews, 1928: 3536.

61. Inmate Interviews, 1932: 5209.

62. *KSIFW 1926 Report*, 12.

63. Inmate Interviews, 1926: 3014.

64. Inmate Interviews, 1927: 3115.

65. Inmate Interviews, 1928: 3528.

66. Inmate Interviews, 1932: 5030.

67. Inmate Interviews, 1932: 5047.

68. Inmate Interviews, 1932: 5137.

69. Inmate Interviews, 1925: 2599.

70. Inmate Interviews, 1932: 5199.

71. *Health 1920 Report*, 357–358.

72. Inmate Interviews, 1924: 2101.

73. Inmate Interviews, 1925: 2417.

74. Inmate Interviews, 1925: 2632. Hazel had a fourteen-month-old girl who was born out of wedlock. She then married another man, only to have that marriage annulled after she cheated on him with one of his friends. Hazel reported that she had lived in quite a few places: she was born in Rome, Italy, her family lived in Illinois, she was married in Oklahoma, and six months later she was living in Leavenworth, Kansas.

75. Inmate Interviews, 1925: 2576.

76. Inmate Interviews, 1932: 5231.

77. For examples of inmates who reported that their doctors proclaimed them cured, see Inmate Interviews, 1928: 3796, and 1932: 5084.

78. Inmate Interviews, 1924: 2231.

79. Inmate Interviews, 1924: 2375.

80. Inmate Interviews, 1924: 2259.

81. Allan M. Brandt, *No Magic Bullet: A Social History of Venereal Disease in the United States since 1880* (New York: Oxford University Press, 1985), 131.

82. Inmate Interviews, 1932: 5187.

83. Inmate Interviews, 1929: 4230.

84. Inmate Interviews, 1932: 5250.

85. Inmate Interviews, 1929: 3957.

86. Inmate Interviews, 1931: 4611.

87. Inmate Interviews, 1932: 5236. Beauty operators were one of a small group of professions that were required to be tested for venereal diseases for state licensing in Kansas. This was one of the few interviews in the sample that indicated that the inmate found out she had the disease through this mandatory testing. This particular inmate had graduated high school, and her apprenticeship with a beauty operator would have been one of few promising career options for Black women during this period.

88. Inmate Interviews, 1926: 3081.

89. Inmate Interviews, 1932: 5006.

90. Inmate Interviews, 1927: 3346.

91. Inmate Interviews, 1923: 2019.

92. Inmate Interviews, 1932: 5018.

93. For accounts of American Plan laws being used to detain "problematic" women in other states, see Stern, *Trials of Nina McCall*, 78.

94. *Health 1920 Report*, 357.

95. For a discussion of women's appreciation of the concrete services and benefits they received in homes for wayward women, see Peggy Pascoe, *Relations of Rescue: The Search for Female Moral Authority in the American West, 1874–1939* (New York: Oxford University Press, 1990), 75.

96. Inmate Interviews, 1926: 2852. This inmate also indicated that she married at the age of thirteen because she "got in bad with Mr. Stafford and had to get married." She complained that her "husband ran with negro women and everything," a rare mention of interracial sex in the interviews.

97. Inmate Interviews, 1931: 4902.

98. "Kansas State Board of Health 10th Biennial Report," 360.

CHAPTER 6. STAKING A CLAIM TO RESPECTABILITY

1. Inmate Interviews, 1926: 2904.

2. See chapter 5 for a discussion of the approach to these sources as articulations of community standards.

3. Alice M. Hill, "Psychiatric Studies of Delinquents: Part III. Social and Environmental Factors in the Moral Delinquency of Girls Committed to the Kansas State Industrial Farm," *Public Health Reports* 35, no. 26 (1920): 1508.

4. Elizabeth Alice Clement, *Love for Sale: Courting, Treating, and Prostitution in New York City, 1900–1945* (Chapel Hill: University of North Carolina Press, 2006), 47; Kathy Peiss, *Cheap Amusements: Working Women and Leisure in Turn-of-the-Century New York* (Philadelphia: Temple University Press, 1986).

5. Inmate Interviews, 1924: 2072.

6. *Health 1920 Report*, 359.

7. Inmate Interviews, 1924: 2272.

8. Inmate Interviews, 1924: 2269. This price seems consistent with other historical accounts. Clement reports that two dollars was the going rate in New York City before World War I. Clement, *Love for Sale*, 99.

9. Inmate Interviews, 1926: 2924.

10. For a discussion of the military's portrayal of prostitutes as vectors of disease during World War I, see Clement, *Love for Sale*, 115–117.

11. Of the inmates in the sample, 17 percent were married, 24 percent were separated, 11 percent were divorced, and 4 percent widowed. This leaves just 44 percent of the inmates in the sample who had never been married. These numbers for the interview sample are largely consistent with marriage rates for the overall population of the Farm from the KSIFW biennial reports, which reported an average of 32 percent of inmates as married, 14 percent as separated, 12 percent as divorced, and 5 percent as widowed, leaving 38 percent who reported having never been married. Data from the 1938 biennial report is not included in these averages because the reported numbers from this year appear to have an error (they do not add up). *KSIFW 1918 Report*, 12; *KSIFW 1920 Report*, 22; *KSIFW 1922 Report*, 13; *KSIFW 1924 Report*, 28; *KSIFW 1926 Report*, 18; *KSIFW 1928 Report*, 16; *KSIFW 1930 Report*, 18; *KSIFW 1932 Report*, 17; *KSIFW 1934 Report*, 15; *KSIFW 1936 Report*, 13; *KSIFW 1940 Report*, 29; *KSIFW 1942 Report*, 26.

12. Hill, "Psychiatric Studies of Delinquents," 1531.

13. Alexander A. Plateris, *100 Years of Marriage and Divorce Statistics, United States, 1867–1967* (Rockville, Md.: U.S. Department of Health, Education and Welfare, Public Health Service, 1973), 9.

14. For a discussion of trends in marriage and divorce, see Stephanie Coontz, *Marriage, a History: How Love Conquered Marriage* (New York: Penguin, 2006); Nancy F. Cott, *Public Vows: A History of Marriage and the Nation* (Cambridge, MA: Harvard University Press, 2000).

15. Percentages in the preceding paragraphs do not always add up to 100 due to rounding.

16. Inmate Interviews, 1924: 2309. Maude was arrested for a second time two years after her initial arrest. The second time, she reported that she was picked up when a matron came to get two other women who were staying at her mother's house and "they took [Maude] up too." This photograph was taken after her second arrest in 1926. Inmate Interviews, 1926: 2902.

17. Inmate Interviews, 1930: 4550.

18. Inmate Interviews, 1923: 2000. This inmate reported that she and her husband were arrested in a raid where she was apparently mistaken for a prostitute: "They raided the place where we were staying and found my husband and I in bed. They asked us for our license, but we didn't have them so they arrested us. We sent a telegram to our people and proved we were married but they interned us on our blood." This couple's race undoubtedly played a role in this assumption that they were unmarried; the mention that her husband was interned as well ("they interned us") is a rare mention of a man being interned under Chapter 205.

19. Inmate Interviews, 1931: 4744. This inmate, age twenty when interviewed, reported that she had married at age sixteen and then had two children. Her husband reportedly "ran around with other women and wouldn't work," causing their separation. She reported: "I have heard that he was bumming his way to California and got Killed."

20. *Kansas Board of Health Bulletin*, January 1922, 10.

21. Inmate Interviews, 1927: 3198; Clement, *Love for Sale*, 115–117; John D'Emilio and Estelle B. Freedman, *Intimate Matters: A History of Sexuality in America*, 2nd ed. (Chicago: University of Chicago Press, 1997), 204; Allan M. Brandt, *No Magic Bullet: A Social History of Venereal Disease in the United States since 1880* (New York: Oxford University Press, 1985), 9.

22. These numbers exclude those who claimed that they inherited the disease.

23. Inmate Interviews, 1924: 2234. This inmate also indicated that her husband had left her after a four-month marriage, while she was "sick with my baby girl." The daughter was living with the inmate's mother at the time of her quarantine.

24. Inmate Interviews, 1926.

25. Inmate Interviews, 1930: 4286.

26. Inmate Interviews, 1924: 2369.

27. Inmate Interviews, 1930: 4326.

28. *Kansas Board of Health Bulletin*, 10.

29. Brandt, *No Magic Bullet*, 20–22, 135–137.

30. *KSIFW 1924 Report*, 9.

31. Inmate Interviews, 1924.

32. For an example of the critique of having children at the Farm, see Public Welfare Temporary Commission, *Report of the Public Welfare Temporary Commission to the State of Kansas* (1933), 229–231, https://catalog.hathitrust.org/Record/001742592/Home.

33. Inmate Interviews, 1931: 4722.

34. For a discussion of feminist campaigns to outlaw marital rape in the 1970s, see Estelle B. Freedman, *Redefining Rape: Sexual Violence in the Era of Suffrage and Segregation* (Cambridge, MA: Harvard University Press, 2013), 281–282.

35. Inmate Interviews, 1927.

36. Inmate Interviews, 1927.

37. Inmate Interviews, 1925.

38. Inmate Interviews, 1927: 3411.

39. Beth L. Bailey, *From Front Porch to Back Seat: Courtship in Twentieth-Century America* (Baltimore: Johns Hopkins University Press, 1989); Brian Donovan, "Gender Inequality and Criminal Seduction: Prosecuting Sexual Coercion in the Early 20th Century," *Law and Social Inquiry* 30, no. 1 (2005).

40. Inmate Interviews, 1931: 4789.

41. Inmate Interviews, 1931: 4790.

42. Inmate Interviews, 1927: 3143.

43. Inmate Interviews, 1925: 2563.

44. Inmate Interviews, 1926: 2937.

45. For a discussion of historical changes in the definition of rape, see Freedman, *Redefining Rape.*

46. Of the interviews in the sample, 76 percent (364 women) had an answer recorded next to the prompt "Cause of downfall." Responses to this question on the form were usually one or two words. "Bad company" was the most frequently used phrase in response to this question (51 percent, 185 women). Next were women who reported a husband, fiancé, or boyfriend as being the cause of their downfall (21 percent, seventy-five women). Women who indicated that environmental influences were the cause of their downfall (5 percent, eighteen women) used phrases such as bad parents, wasn't taught morals, lack of education, etc. Other responses to this prompt were more internally focused, such as women who cited personal characteristics (12 percent, forty-five women), or were miscellaneous (8 percent, thirty women). Eleven inmates, or 3 percent of the women, simply had "Never had any" recorded next to this prompt.

47. Inmate Interviews, 1926: 2903.

48. Inmate Interviews, 1929: 4052.

49. Inmate Interviews, 1930: 4539.

50. Inmate Interviews, 1931: 4827.

51. Inmate Interviews, 1930: 4248.

52. Inmate Interviews, 1923: 2065. Betsy, who was arrested along with Josephine, confirmed this account in her interview: "Josephine & I went car riding & went out together a number of times to skating rinks and dance & nearly always had dates. It is a fact that I influenced Josephine to make her first wrong step. I called her 'piker' & such & told her the price for her first date. She didn't want to, but finally gave in." Inmate Interviews, 1923: 2064.

53. Inmate Interviews, 1928: 3603.

54. Inmate Interviews, 1925: 2530; 1930: 4539; 1925: 2472; 1926: 3063.

55. Alan Hunt, "Regulating Heterosocial Space: Sexual Politics in the Early Twentieth Century," *Journal of Historical Sociology* 15, no. 1 (2002): 1–34; Ann Louise Wagner, *Adversaries of Dance: From the Puritans to the Present* (Urbana: University of Illinois Press, 1997).

56. Inmate Interviews, 1924: 2091.

57. Inmate Interviews, 1931: 4744.

58. *Health 1920 Report* , 352–353.

59. Mildred Reed, "A Prison without Walls Is Women's Industrial Farm!" *Topeka State Journal*, August 21, 1920.

60. J. Farnham, *How to Meet Men and Marry* (New York: Simon Publications, 1943), quoted in Pamela S. Haag, "In Search of 'the Real Thing': Ideologies of Love, Modern Romance, and Women's Sexual Subjectivity in the United States, 1920–40," *Journal of the History of Sexuality* 2, no. 4 (1992): 547–577, quotation on 574.

61. Clement, *Love for Sale*, 19; D'Emilio and Freedman, *Intimate Matters*; Barry Reay, "Promiscuous Intimacies: Rethinking the History of American Casual Sex," *Journal of Historical Sociology* 27, no. 1 (2014): 3; Haag, "In Search of 'the Real Thing.'" For discussions of romantic love in modern discourses about gender and sexuality, see Mary Crawford and Danielle Popp, "Sexual Double Standards: A Review and Methodological Critique of Two Decades of Research," *Journal of Sex Research* 40, no. 1 (2003): 13–26; Dorothy C. Holland, *Educated in Romance: Women, Achievement, and College Culture* (Chicago: University of Chicago Press, 1990); Pepper Schwartz and Virginia Rutter, *The Gender of Sexuality* (Lanham, MD: Rowman & Littlefield, 1998).

62. Inmate Interviews, 1924: 2126; 1927: 3182. Interestingly, this second inmate appeared to be using the phrase "only man I have been with" only in reference to having sex outside of marriage, indicating her understanding that the interviewer was only asking about disreputable sexuality. At age forty-five, she had

been married twice before. The man with whom she was having a relationship had hidden liquor in her basement, which led to their arrest.

63. Inmate Interviews, 1924: 2295; 1931: 4766; 1930: 4334.

64. Inmate Interviews, 1932: 5156.

65. Due to the nature of how these interviews were conducted, it is also quite possible that the inmates did talk about their emotional connections with partners, but the interviewer only wrote down the facts of the situation.

66. Inmate Interviews, 1927: 3382.

67. Inmate Interviews, 1926: 2748.

68. Inmate Interviews, 1927: 3492.

69. Inmate Interviews, 1924: 2177. This inmate also indicated in the interview that she left home at age sixteen to work for the man that she would later marry. Her mother apparently knew that her daughter "was living with Mr. Baker as his wife" but did not say anything. They lived together five months before marrying. This was apparently an abusive relationship, as Emma reported that "Mr. Baker carries a long knife and has threatened me with it and also choked me."

70. Inmate Interviews, 1926: 2906.

71. Inmate Interviews, 1929: 4181.

72. Inmate Interviews, 1926: 2954.

73. Inmate Interviews, 1927: 3394. This inmate reported that she had two years of college education, indicating that she may have been from a higher social class than many other inmates.

74. Julian B. Carter, *The Heart of Whiteness: Normal Sexuality and Race in America, 1880–1940* (Durham, NC: Duke University Press, 2007); Haag, "In Search of 'the Real Thing'"; Reay, "Promiscuous Intimacies."

75. For examples of research exploring the connection between discourses of sexuality and respectability today, see Steph Lawler, "Mobs and Monsters: Independent Man Meets Paulsgrove Woman," *Feminist Theory* 3, no. 1 (2002): 103–113; Beverley Skeggs, *Formations of Class and Gender: Becoming Respectable* (London: Sage, 1997).

76. Haag, "In Search of 'the Real Thing,'" 569. For a discussion of the critical role of respectability in court cases related to sexuality, see Brian Donovan, *Respectability on Trial: Sex Crimes in New York City, 1900–1918* (Albany: State University of New York Press, 2016).

CONCLUSION

1. John Parascandola, *Sex, Sin, and Science: A History of Syphilis in America* (Westport, CT: Praeger, 2008), 116–131; Scott W. Stern, "The Long American Plan: The U.S. Government's Campaign against Venereal Disease and Its Carriers," *Harvard Journal of Law and Gender* 38 (2015): 413; Scott W. Stern, *The Trials of*

Nina McCall: Sex, Surveillance, and the Decades-Long Government Plan to Imprison Promiscuous Women (Boston: Beacon Press, 2018), 206–217.

2. Stern, *Trials of Nina McCall*, 220–225.

3. Allan M. Brandt, *No Magic Bullet: A Social History of Venereal Disease in the United States since 1880* (New York: Oxford University Press, 1985), 164–171; Elizabeth Alice Clement, *Love for Sale: Courting, Treating, and Prostitution in New York City, 1900–1945* (Chapel Hill: University of North Carolina Press, 2006), 243–249; John D'Emilio and Estelle B. Freedman, *Intimate Matters: A History of Sexuality in America*, 2nd ed. (Chicago: University of Chicago Press, 1997), 261; Parascandola, *Sex, Sin, and Science*, 99–108; Stern, *Trials of Nina McCall*, 226–240.

4. *Health 1940 Report*, 128.

5. *Health 1942 Report*, 135, 143; Brandt, *No Magic Bullet*, 169; "Extend a Health Plan," *Kansas City (MO) Star*, November 1, 1941, 64.

6. *KSIFW 1940 Report*, 26–28; *KSIFW 1942 Report*, 23–25.

7. Christopher Lovett, "Bad Girls: Sex, Shame, Public Health, and the Forgotten Legacy of Samuel J. Crumbine in Kansas, 1917–1955," *Kansas History* 41, no. 1 (Spring 2018): 19–41; Stern, "Long American Plan"; Kansas Historical Society, "Sinners and Saints, Part 6: Vice and Reform in Kansas," http://www.kshs.org/p/online-exhibits-sinners-and-saints-part-6/10723; Kansas Historical Society, "Records of the Kansas State Industrial Farm for Women," http://www.kshs.org/archives/214395. For the laws that are built off of the original 1917 Chapter 205 legislation, see Kansas Office of Revisor of Statutes, "65-128. Rules and Regulations of Secretary to Prevent Spread and Dissemination of Diseases; Testing and Quarantine; Protection of Providers and Recipients of Services," https://www.ksrevisor.org/statutes/chapters/ch65/065_001_0028.html; Kansas Office of Revisor of Statutes, "65-129. Penalties for Unlawful Acts," https://www.ksrevisor.org/statutes/chapters/ch65/065_001_0029.html. For the 2005 legislation that gives people the right to challenge their quarantine in court, see Kansas Office of Revisor of Statutes, "65-129c. Same; Orders for Isolation or Quarantine; Form and Content; Notice; Hearing in District Court; Application and Effect; Procedure; Orders for Relief; Emergency Rules of Procedure," https://www.ksrevisor.org/statutes/chapters/ch65/065_001_0029c.html.

8. Lovett, "Bad Girls," 41.

9. Darlene Doubleday Newby, "A Study of the Causes of Delinquency of Women Quarantined for Disease at the State Industrial Farm for Women," *Bulletin of the Kansas State Board of Health*, February 1921, 26–33.

10. Stern, "Long American Plan." For discussions of venereal disease control during World War I, see Nancy K. Bristow, *Making Men Moral: Social Engineering during the Great War* (New York: New York University Press, 1996); Brandt, *No Magic Bullet*.

11. Kristin Luker, "Sex, Social Hygiene, and the State: The Double-Edged Sword of Social Reform," *Theory and Society* 27, no. 5 (1998): 601–634; Peggy Pascoe, *Relations of Rescue: The Search for Female Moral Authority in the American West, 1874–1939* (New York: Oxford University Press, 1990); Michael A. Rembis, *Defining Deviance: Sex, Science, and Delinquent Girls, 1890–1960* (Urbana: University of Illinois Press, 2011).

12. Brandt, *No Magic Bullet*, 151–152; Parascandola, *Sex, Sin, and Science*, 96–97.

13. For discussions of ways in which sexuality has been used to draw racial boundaries in US history, see Patricia Hill Collins, *Black Sexual Politics: African Americans, Gender, and the New Racism* (London: Routledge, 2004); Brian Donovan, *White Slave Crusades: Race, Gender, and Anti-Vice Activism, 1887–1917* (Urbana: University of Illinois Press, 2005); Joane Nagel, *Race, Ethnicity, and Sexuality: Intimate Intersections, Forbidden Frontiers* (New York: Oxford University Press, 2003).

14. See Michel Foucault, *The History of Sexuality*, 3 vols. (New York: Pantheon Books, 1978). For examples of studies that discuss the importance of sexuality and morality in constructions of symbolic boundaries between groups, see Nicola Kay Beisel, *Imperiled Innocents: Anthony Comstock and Family Reproduction in Victorian America* (Princeton, NJ: Princeton University Press, 1997); Michèle Lamont, *Money, Morals, and Manners: The Culture of the French and the American Upper-Middle Class* (Chicago: University of Chicago Press, 1992).

15. John Pfaff, *Locked In: The True Causes of Mass Incarceration and How to Achieve Real Reform* (New York: Basic Books, 2017), 1.

16. See Brett Story, *Prison Land: Mapping Carceral Power across Neoliberal America* (Minneapolis: University of Minnesota Press, 2019); Pfaff, *Locked In*; Anne E. Parsons, *From Asylum to Prison: Deinstitutionalization and the Rise of Mass Incarceration after 1945* (Chapel Hill: University of North Carolina Press, 2018); Michelle Alexander, *The New Jim Crow: Mass Incarceration in the Age of Colorblindness* (New York: New Press, 2010); Dan Berger, *Captive Nation: Black Prison Organizing in the Civil Rights Era* (Chapel Hill: University of North Carolina Press, 2014); Max Felker-Kantor, *Policing Los Angeles: Race, Resistance, and the Rise of the LAPD* (Chapel Hill: University of North Carolina Press, 2018); Michel Foucault, *Discipline and Punish: The Birth of the Prison*, 2nd ed., trans. Alan Sheridan (New York: Vintage Books, 1995).

17. L. Mara Dodge, *Whores and Thieves of the Worst Kind: A Study of Women, Crime, and Prisons, 1835–2000* (DeKalb: Northern Illinois University Press, 2002), 259; Bureau of Justice Statistics, "Key Statistic: Total Correctional Population," http://www.bjs.gov/index.cfm?ty=kfdetail&iid=487; World Prison Brief, "More than 700,000 women and girls are in prison around the world, new report shows," September 22, 2015, http://www.prisonstudies.org/news/more-700000

-women-and-girls-are-prison-around-world-new-report-shows; Nomin Ujiyediin, "Rapid Rise in Inmate Population Strains Kansas' Lone Women's Prison," *Lawrence (KS) Journal World*, March 1, 2020, https://www2.ljworld.com/news/state-region/2020/mar/01/rapid-rise-in-inmate-population-strains-kansas-lone-womens-prison/.

18. Corey G. Johnson, "Female Inmates Sterilized in California Prisons without Approval," Reveal, Center for Investigative Reporting, July 7, 2013, https://www.revealnews.org/article/female-inmates-sterilized-in-california-prisons-without-approval/.

19. See Patricia Hill Collins, *Black Feminist Thought: Knowledge, Consciousness, and the Politics of Empowerment* (London: Routledge, 1999); Dorothy E. Roberts, *Killing the Black Body: Race, Reproduction, and the Meaning of Liberty* (New York: Vintage Books, 1999).

20. Ann Marie Bush, "Justice Department to Impose Reform at Topeka Women's Prison," *Topeka Capital-Journal*, January 9, 2015, http://cjonline.com/news/2015-01-09/justice-department-impose-reform-topeka-womens-prison; Caroline Sweeney, "Topeka Corrections Officer Faces Sex Charges after Inmate Comes Forward," *Topeka Capital-Journal*, August 26, 2014, http://cjonline.com/news/2014-08-26/topeka-corrections-officer-faces-sex-charges-after-inmate-comes-forward; Tim Carpenter, "DOJ: Topeka Correctional Facility Violates Inmates' Rights," *Topeka Capital-Journal*, September 6, 2012, http://cjonline.com/news/2012-09-06/doj-topeka-correctional-facility-violates-inmates-rights; Tim Carpenter, "A Guard's Drive for Sex," *Topeka Capital-Journal*, October 24, 2009, http://cjonline.com/news/state/2009-10-24/a_guards_drive_for_sex; Tim Carpenter, "Women's Prison: Sex Trade," *Topeka Capital-Journal*, October 3, 2009, https://www.cjonline.com/article/20091003/NEWS/310039798.

21. Luker, "Sex, Social Hygiene, and the State."

INDEX